Buying a Business

by Eric Tyson, MBA and Jim Schell

Buying a Business For Dummies®

Published by: **John Wiley & Sons, Inc.**, 111 River Street, Hoboken, NJ 07030-5774, www.wiley.com

For general information on our other products and services, please contact our Customer Care Department within the U.S. at 877-762-2974, outside the U.S. at 317-572-3993, or fax 317-572-4002. For technical support, please visit https://hub.wiley.com/community/support/dummies.

Wiley publishes in a variety of print and electronic formats and by print-on-demand. Some material included with standard print versions of this book may not be included in e-books or in print-on-demand. If this book refers to media such as a CD or DVD that is not included in the version you purchased, you may download this material at http://booksupport.wiley.com. For more information about Wiley products, visit www.wiley.com.

Library of Congress Control Number: 2024933513

ISBN 978-1-394-24575-8 (pbk); ISBN 978-1-394-24577-2 (ePDF); 978-1-394-24576-5 (epub)

SKY10070010_032024

Table of Contents

Introduction

Many folks dream of being their own boss and running their own business. Plenty of those dreamers envision starting their business from scratch. Fewer think about buying an existing business but that route may indeed be a better fit for your skill set and situation.

Buying a Business For Dummies can help you to understand what's involved in buying a small business rather than starting one from scratch. We walk you through all the important considerations to help you decide if buying a small business is right for you and how to find one in the best niche.

As with buying a home or other real estate, making an offer on and closing on a small business purchase involves plenty of research and due diligence. We detail what to do and what to avoid throughout the entire process. And, once you buy a business, we highlight how to improve your business and make the most of it.

About This Book

The following backgrounds and philosophies serve as a guide to the advice we provide — advice from the field that makes this small-business book stand out from the rest:

>> **We're small-business experienced, and we share the benefits of that experience with you.** Between us, we have seven-plus decades of experience in starting, buying, and running seven successful small businesses. In addition, we've worked with thousands of small-business owners. Jim has led numerous small-business peer-networking groups and has provided volunteer counseling services

to small-business owners. Eric has conducted financial counseling for small-business owners, taught financial-management courses, and worked as a management consultant.

Throughout this book, we share the experience we've gained, in the hopes that you'll use our advice to eliminate trial and error from your inventory of management tools. We also share an ample collection of straight-from-the-horse's-mouth anecdotes, each one based on a true story.

>> **We take an objective view of small-business ownership.** Although we firmly believe in the creative power of small business, we're not here to be its pitchmen.

Sadly, too many small-business books are written by folks with an agenda: a franchise to sell, a multilevel marketing scheme to promote, or a high-priced seminar to foist on the reader. Free of conflicts of interest, we're here to pass on the truth and let you decide. If you're the type of person who wants to get into this competitive career field, we'd like you to enter the race informed as well as inspired.

>> **We take a holistic approach.** Because small business can at times be both demanding and intoxicating, buying and running your own shop can threaten to consume your life. Although everyone knows that life is more than just business, striking a balance and staying in control can represent a colossal challenge. With that in mind, we take care to present the realities of buying and running a small business within the larger (and more important) framework of maintaining a happy personal and financial life.

>> **We look to the future.** As this book is published in 2024, the concept of Artificial Intelligence (AI) is going mainstream. Both AI and ChatGPT (just one of AI's many tools) increasingly should be considered by small business buyers and operators. However, just as with any other technology or innovation, we help you to weigh the costs against potential benefits in deciding which tools and strategies may make sense for your specific small business.

Foolish Assumptions

Too often, books about buying a small business assume that their readers are ready to make the leap into small business and are cognizant of the risks and pitfalls. We don't make that assumption here, and neither should you. That's why we include sections designed to help you decide whether buying and running a business is really for you. We spell out the business and finance terms, break down the tasks, and point out the dangers. We don't think that you're incapable of making the decision yourself; we just know that time is your most precious resource, and we think we can help you save it. You'll lose too many years of your career and commit valuable financial resources if you make the wrong choice.

Much of this book is targeted to buying a small business and running it intelligently. Even if you have a business in mind, buying and then operating a small business is much harder than it appears, so we show you the best ways to purchase, manage and grow your enterprise.

We've organized this book to satisfy different reading and personal styles. Some of you may read it from cover to cover, while others may refer to it to answer a specific question or address an immediate concern. For this reason, each chapter of the book is designed to stand on its own. We're flexible — read it as an all-in-one project or use it as a reference guide.

Icons Used in This Book

To help you find the information you need to assist you on your entrepreneurial path, we've placed icons throughout the text to highlight important points.

INVESTIGATE

This icon asks you to do some thinking and checking before you take the plunge. You have a lot of important choices to make when buying and running a business, so don't rush in.

REMEMBER

This icon points out stuff too good (and too important) to forget.

TECHNICAL STUFF

If you like to sweat the dull stuff, this icon points out the inner workings of the business world that you're likely to ignore as you get down to the real work.

TIP

This symbol indicates time-tested tips to make your small-business journey more profitable and easier. Often straight from the heart of experience, we clue you in on what works for us as we navigate the oft-troubled waters of small-business life.

TRUE STORY

We present tales from our own experiences to save you some trial and error. Enjoy the company of your fellow entrepreneurs and benefit from the lessons we've learned.

WARNING

The path of small-business ownership can be fraught with peril. Some deals may be too good to be true, and some people may have their own interests at heart, not yours. This icon points out the dangers and helps you steer clear of them.

Beyond the Book

To access this book's Cheat Sheet, go to www.dummies.com and enter "Buying a Business For Dummies Cheat Sheet" in the Search box. There you will find the key themes that we emphasize throughout this book.

Where to Go from Here

Where you go from here is up to you, but if you're just beginning to think about buying small business, we recommend that you read straight through, cover to cover, to maximize your knowledge regarding buying and operating a small business. But the A-to-Z approach isn't necessary. If you feel confident in your knowledge of certain areas, pick the topics that you're most interested in by skimming the table of contents or by relying on the well-crafted index at the back of the book.

1

Deciding to Buy a Business

Get to know the acquisition process and the professionals you can hire to help.

Assess whether you have the knowledge, time, and financial resources to purchase and be successful with an existing business.

Chapter **1**

Preparing to Buy a Business

Thinking or dreaming about owning your own business is easy and tempting to do. All it may take is knowing someone who is making decent money setting their own hours and perhaps even doing something they enjoy.

Starting a business from scratch of course is daunting and increases the obstacles and possibility for failure. Buying an existing business, possibly including a franchise, could be your ticket to small business ownership.

This chapter gives you the big picture of the acquisition process, what's involved, the pros you should consider having on your team, and how to budget for all this. But first, we help you assess — and if necessary, create a plan to improve — your financial fitness.

Figuring Your Financial Fitness

So you think you may want to buy a small business? We'd like to help you determine if that path makes sense for you; and if you can afford that, we'd like to help you turn that dream into reality.

You can't play if you can't pay. Buying a business requires solid financial fitness. Think of it as similar to buying a home if you've ever done that or considered that. You're going to need down-payment money and likely a loan to finance the bulk of the purchase price. And, in the early years of owning your business, you should be sure to have a decent financial cushion in place in case the business isn't performing at the level you expect it to.

If you're struggling to regularly save money, lack sufficient savings for a down payment, and are otherwise financially stressed, you may need to postpone setting the wheels in motion to buy a business.

REMEMBER

Having your personal finances in order is one of the most under-recognized keys to achieving success in your small business. Just one significant money oversight or mistake can derail your entrepreneurial dreams or venture.

The following sections describe the important financial tasks you need to undertake before buying a business.

Assess your financial position and goals

Where do you stand in terms of retirement planning? How much do you want to have saved to pay for your children's educational costs? What kind of a home do you want to buy?

These and other important questions can help shape your personal financial plans. Sound financial planning isn't about faithfully balancing your checkbook or investing in stocks based on a friend's tip. Rather, smart financial management is about taking a hard look at where you are, figuring out where you want to go, and making sure that you're prepared for occasional adverse conditions along the way — a process, incidentally, that isn't unlike what you'll be doing when you run your own business.

Measuring your net worth

The first step in assessing your financial position is giving yourself a financial physical. Start with measuring your *net worth*, a term that defines the difference between your financial assets and your financial liabilities.

Begin by totaling up your financial assets (all your various bank accounts, stocks, mutual funds, and so on) and subtracting from that the sum total of all your liabilities (credit card debt, auto loans, student loans, and so on). *Note:* Because most people don't view their home as a retirement asset, we've left your home's value and mortgage out of your net worth calculations. (Personal property — furniture, cars, and so on — doesn't count as a financial asset.) However, you may include your home if you want, especially if you're willing to tap your home's equity to accomplish goals such as retiring.

Now, don't jump to conclusions based on the size of the resulting number. If you're young and still breaking into your working years, your net worth is bound to be relatively low — perhaps even negative. Relax. Sure, you have work to do, but you have plenty of time ahead of you.

REMEMBER

Ideally, as you approach the age of 40, your net worth should be greater than a year's worth of gross income; if your net worth equals more than a few years of income, you're well on the road toward meeting larger financial goals, such as retirement.

Of course, the key to increasing your net worth is making sure that more money comes in than goes out. To achieve typical financial goals such as retirement, you need to save about 10 percent of your gross (pretax) income. If you have big dreams or you're behind in the game, you may need to save 15 percent or more.

If you know you're already saving enough, or if you know it won't be that hard to start saving enough, then don't bother tracking your spending. On the other hand, if you have no idea how you'll start saving that much, you need to determine where you're spending your money. (See the later section "Shrink your spending" for insight on how to start saving.)

Telling good debt from bad debt

After you calculate your net worth, categorize your liabilities as either good debt or bad debt:

» *Good debt* refers to money borrowed for a long-term investment that appreciates over time, such as a home, an education that bolsters your career prospects, investment real estate, or a small business.

» *Bad debt* (also called *consumer debt*) is money borrowed for a consumer purchase, such as a car, a designer suit, or a vacation to Cancun.

Why is bad debt bad? Because it's costly to carry, and if you carry too much, it becomes like a financial cancer. If the outstanding balance of all your credit cards and auto loans divided by your annual gross income exceeds 25 percent of your income, you've entered a danger zone, where your debt can start to snowball out of control.

WARNING

Don't even consider buying a small business until you've paid off all your consumer debt. Not only are the interest rates on consumer debt relatively high, but the things you buy with consumer debt also lose their value over time. A financially healthy amount of bad debt — like a healthy amount of cigarette smoking — is none.

Reducing debt

If you have outstanding consumer debt, pay it off sooner rather than later. If you must tap into savings to pay down your consumer debts, then do it. Many people resist digging into savings, feeling as if they're losing hard-earned money. Remember that your net worth — the difference between your assets and liabilities — determines the growth of your money. Paying off an outstanding credit card balance with an interest rate of

18 percent is like finding an investment with a guaranteed return of 18 percent — tax-free. (*Note:* We recognize that some small-business owners finance their small businesses via credit cards, and in some cases, because this debt would be investment debt and investment debt is "good debt," we feel this situation may be acceptable. We discuss business financing options in Chapter 7.)

If you don't have any available savings with which to pay off your high-interest-rate debts, you'll have to climb out of debt gradually over time. The fact that you're in hock and without savings is likely a sign that you've been living beyond your means. Devote 10 to 15 percent of your income toward paying down your consumer loans. If you have no idea where you'll get this money, detail your spending by expense category, such as rent, eating out, clothing, and so on. You'll probably find that your spending doesn't reflect what's important to you, and you'll see fat to trim. (This process is similar to budgeting and expense management in business; not being able to manage your personal expenses may be a telltale sign of your inability to manage a business.)

While paying down your debt, always look for ways to lower your interest rate. Apply for low-interest-rate cards to which you can transfer balances from your highest-interest-rate cards. Haggling with your current credit card company for a lower interest rate sometimes works. Also, think about borrowing against the equity in your home, against your employer-sponsored retirement account, or from family — all options that should lower your interest rate significantly.

TIP

If you're having a hard time kicking the credit card habit, get out your scissors and cut up your cards. You can still enjoy the convenience of purchasing with plastic by using a Visa or MasterCard debit card, which is linked directly to your checking account. The major benefit of using a debit card rather than a credit card is that you can't spend beyond your means. Merchants who take Visa or MasterCard credit cards also accept these companies' debit cards.

Buying insurance

Before you address your longer-term financial goals, you need to make sure that you're properly covered by insurance. Without proper insurance coverage, an illness or an accident can quickly turn into a devastating financial storm.

Buy long-term disability insurance if you lack it. This most overlooked form of insurance protects against a disability that curtails your greatest income-generating asset: your ability to earn money. If anyone depends on your employment income, buy term life insurance, which, in the event of your death, leaves money to those financially dependent on you. Make sure that your health insurance policy is a comprehensive one. Ideally, your lifetime benefits should be unlimited; if the policy has a maximum, it should be at least a few million dollars. (We provide more details on these important coverages later in this chapter in the section "Assessing and Replacing Benefits.")

Also check your auto and home policies' liability coverage, which protects you in the event of a lawsuit; you should have at least enough to cover twice your assets.

TIP

For all your insurance policies, take the highest deductible you can afford to pay out of pocket should you have a claim. Of course, if you have a claim, you'll have to pay more of the initial expense out of your own pocket, but you'll save significantly on premiums. Buy insurance to cover the potentially catastrophic losses, not the small stuff.

Planning for the long term

In coauthor Eric's experience as a financial counselor, he has seen many examples prove that earning a high income doesn't guarantee a high rate of savings. The best savers he knows tend to be goal oriented; in other words, they earmark their savings for specific purposes.

If you know that you're an undisciplined saver, you may consider adopting the technique of designating certain savings or investment accounts toward specific goals. After all, if you're feeling tempted to buy a luxury car, it's a lot harder to take money out of an account earmarked for Timmy's college education or your retirement than from a general savings account.

Perhaps because it's the farthest away, retirement is the most difficult long-term goal to bring into focus. Retirement is also much tougher to plan for than most goals because of all the difficult-to-make assumptions — inflation, life expectancy, Social Security benefits, taxes, rate of return, and so on — that go into the calculations.

TIP

Use a good retirement planning program. Check out the resources online from T. Rowe Price (www.troweprice.com) or Vanguard (investor.vanguard.com). These retirement planners can help you transform a fuzzy dream into a concrete action plan, forcing you to get specific about retirement issues you may not have thought about and opening your eyes to the power of compounding interest and the importance of saving now.

Goal-specific saving is challenging for most people given their many competing goals. Even a respectable 10 to 15 percent of your income may not be enough to accomplish such goals as saving for retirement, accumulating a down payment for a home, saving for children's college expenses, and tucking away some money for starting or buying a small business.

So you have to make some tough choices and prioritize your goals. Only you know what's important to you, which means that you're the most qualified person to make these decisions. But we want to stress the importance of contributing to retirement accounts, whether you use a 401(k), SEP-IRA, or IRA. Not only do retirement accounts shelter your investment earnings from taxation, but contributions to these accounts are also generally tax deductible.

As for the money you're socking away, be sure to invest it wisely. Doing so isn't as difficult as most financial advisors and investment publications make it out to be. (Some make it sound complicated in order to gain your confidence, business, and fees.)

REMEMBER

What's your reward for whipping your finances into shape and staying the course? Although it's true that money can't buy happiness, managing your personal finances efficiently can open up your future life options, such as switching into a lower-paying but more fulfilling career, starting your own business, or perhaps working part time at a home-based business when your kids are young so that you can be an involved parent. Work at achieving financial success and then be sure to make the most of it.

Shrink your spending

Do all you can to reduce your expenses and lifestyle to a level that fits with the entrepreneurial life you want to lead. Now is the time to make your budget lean and entrepreneurially friendly.

INVESTIGATE

Determine what you spend each month on rent, mortgage, groceries, eating out, insurance, and so on. Your banking records, your credit card transactions, and your memory of cash purchases should help you piece together what you spend on various things in a typical month. The best way to track your expenses is to pay either by credit card, debit card, or check. Cash doesn't provide you a paper trail to reconcile your expenses at the end of the month.

Beyond the bare essentials of food, shelter, healthcare, and clothing, most of what you spend money on is discretionary — in other words, luxuries. Even the dollars you spend on the so-called necessities, such as food and shelter, are usually only part necessity, with the balance being luxury.

If you refuse to question your current spending or if you view all your current spending as necessary, you'll probably have no option but to continue your career as an employee. You'll never be able to pursue your dream! Overspending won't make you happy; you'll be miserable over the years if your excess spending makes you feel chained to a job you don't like. Life is too short to work at a full-time job that doesn't make you happy.

Build up your cash reserves

Shrinking your spending is a means to an end — that end being the ability to save for a rainy day. In the world of small business, you're going to see your fair share of rainy days; you may even experience years predominated by rain. Ask someone who bought a restaurant in 2019 only to be smacked in the face in 2020 (and beyond) by pandemic-related shutdowns and restrictions.

Your wherewithal to stick with an entrepreneurial endeavor depends, in part, on your current war chest of cash. At a minimum, you should have three to six months of living expenses invested in an accessible account, such as a money market fund with low operating expenses. If you have consumer debt, after you finish paying off your debt, your top financial priority should be building this account. The bigger the stash, the better; if you can accumulate a year's worth of living expenses, great!

Stabilize income with part time work

One way to pursue your entrepreneurial dreams — and not starve while doing so — is to continue working part time in a regular job at the same time you're working part time in your own business. If you have a job that allows you to work part time, seize the opportunity. Some employers even allow you to maintain your benefits.

When coauthor Eric was planning to start his financial counseling business, he was able to cut back his full-time job to half-time for four months, using his time away from his regular job to start his financial counseling, teaching, and writing business. Similarly, in the first year of coauthor Jim's initial entrepreneurial venture, he continued his full-time job working for a wood-products business.

In addition to the monetary security you get from a regular job, splitting your time allows you to adjust gradually to a completely new way of making a living. Some people have a difficult time if they quit their regular full-time job outright and start working full time as an entrepreneur.

If you're not interested in keeping your current job, you can completely leave that job and line up a different form of work that will provide a decent income for at least some of your weekly work hours. Consulting for your former employer is a time-tested first "entrepreneurial" option with low risk — just one of many reasons why you should endeavor to leave your current job without burning bridges in the process.

Another option to working part time is to depend on your spouse's income while you work on building up your own. Obviously, this option involves sacrifice from the love of your life, so be sure to talk things through with your partner to minimize misunderstandings and resentments. Perhaps someday you'll be in a position to return the favor — that's what Eric did. His wife, Judy, was working in education when Eric started an entrepreneurial venture after business school. They lived a Spartan lifestyle on her income. Several years later, when Eric's business was on solid footing, Judy left her job to start her own business.

Assessing and Replacing Benefits

For some aspiring entrepreneurs, the thought of losing their employee benefits is even scarier than cutting off their paychecks. Insurance coverages in particular — especially health insurance — seem daunting to replicate outside of the friendly umbrella of a corporation or nonprofit institution.

You may be surprised at how quickly and cost effectively you can replicate your employer's benefits in your own business. As a small-business owner, you may have access to some valuable benefits that your employer doesn't or can't offer you. So if you're dreaming of starting your own business, don't view your employer's benefits package as a ball and chain tying you to your current job.

Retirement savings plans and pensions

If your employer offers retirement savings programs, such as a 401(k) plan or a pension plan, don't despair about not having these benefits in the future if you should start your own business. Of course, what you've already earned and accumulated (or *vested*) as an employee is yours.

Some of the best benefits of self-employment are the available retirement savings plans — specifically and most notably SEP-IRAs (Simplified Employee Pension Individual Retirement Accounts). SEP-IRAs allow you to shelter far more money than most corporate retirement plans do. With SEP-IRA plans, you can plow away up to 20 percent of your net income on a tax-deductible basis. Those with more employees may want to consider a 401(k) or SIMPLE plan, both of which allow employees to contribute money from their own paychecks.

Retirement plans are a terrific way for you, as a business owner, and your employees to shelter a healthy portion of earnings from taxes. Especially if you don't have employees, making regular contributions to one of these plans is usually a no-brainer. If you do have employees, the decision is a bit more complicated but still often a great idea.

Health insurance

If you're in good health and you've decided to start your own business, start investigating what will happen to your health insurance coverage when you leave your job. The first option to explore is whether you can convert your existing coverage through your employer's group plan into individual coverage. If you can, great; just don't act on this option until you've explored other health plans, which may offer similar benefits at a lower cost.

Also get proposals for individual coverage from major health plans in your area. Be sure to select a high deductible, if available, to keep costs down. The Affordable Care Act (also known as Obamacare), which was passed in 2010, is still the law of the land and has greatly affected health insurance options and pricing throughout the country.

Also, health savings accounts (HSAs) have become far more attractive and increasingly available. Like the best retirement accounts, HSAs offer an upfront tax deduction on contributions as well as tax-free compounding of investment earnings over time. HSAs also offer tax-free withdrawals so long as the money is used for eligible expenses. So, unlike any retirement account, HSAs are so-called triple-tax-free accounts. For all the details on these terrific tax-saving vehicles for small-business owners and their employees, turn to Chapter 12.

Disability insurance

Well in advance of leaving your job, be sure that you secure long-term disability insurance. *Long-term disability insurance* protects your income in the event of a disability. If you're like most people, your greatest financial asset is your ability to earn employment income. If you suffer a disability and are unable to work, how will you and your family manage financially? Most people, of course, couldn't come close to maintaining their current lifestyle if their employment income disappeared.

WARNING

Don't wait until you leave your job to shop for disability coverage. After you quit your job and no longer have steady employment income, you won't be able to qualify for a long-term disability policy. Most insurers will then want to see at least six months of self-employment income before they're willing to write a policy for you. The risk is that, if you become disabled during this time, you'll be completely without insurance.

Proven sources for securing long-term disability insurance include:

>> **Professional associations:** Thanks to the purchasing power of the group, associations that you may be a member of — or can become a member of — often offer less costly disability coverage than what you can buy on your own.

>> **Insurance agents:** Consider shopping for an individual disability policy through agents who specialize in such coverage.

Life insurance

If you have life-insurance coverage through your employer, odds are you can replicate it on your own. If you have dependents (children, a spouse, or others) who rely on your income, you need life insurance.

The amount of life insurance you carry depends on how much annual income you're trying to protect and over how many years. For example, to replace your income over the next decade, multiply your annual after-tax income by 8.5. So if you annually make $60,000 after taxes, you should buy about $500,000 of life insurance. You only need to replace your after-tax income because the death benefits on a life-insurance policy are free of income tax.

REMEMBER

Term life insurance, which is pure life-insurance protection, offers the best way to buy needed coverage at the lowest cost. Other policies, such as universal, whole, and variable life, which are collectively referred to as *cash-value policies*, combine life-insurance coverage with an investment account. For an equivalent amount of coverage, a cash-value policy typically costs about eight times what a term policy costs. Furthermore, in the early years of a cash-value policy, the bulk of that cost difference builds little in the way of cash value and instead goes mostly to pay insurance agent commissions and administrative costs.

TIP

In the long run, you would do best to separate your life insurance from your investments. Buy term insurance and invest your savings through your employer's retirement savings plan or your self-employed plan like an SEP-IRA. Contributions to 401(k) plans and the like typically offer an upfront tax deduction at the federal and state levels. Money put into a cash-value life-insurance plan offers no such deduction.

The good news is that if you need life insurance, you can probably purchase an individual life-insurance policy at a lower cost than you can purchase such coverage through your employer.

Insurance agency quotation services send you a handful of relatively user-friendly proposals from the highest-rated, lowest-cost companies available. Like other agencies, the services receive a commission if you buy a policy from them, which you're under no obligation to do. They'll ask you for your date of birth, whether you smoke, and how much coverage you'd like. Reputable firms in this line of work include AccuQuote (www.accuquote.com), ReliaQuote (www.reliaquote.com), and Term4Sale (www.term4sale.com).

Dental, vision, and other insurance

You may have other insurance programs besides the traditional health, life, and disability. Some employers offer insurance plans for dental and vision care, and occasionally some other unusual benefits, such as prepaid legal plans.

REMEMBER

As an aspiring or new entrepreneur, you can't afford to waste money. Insurance programs such as these that cover small potential out-of-pocket losses aren't worth purchasing. Don't waste your money buying such policies. Remember that insurance companies are in business to make money. On average, insurers pay out no more than about 60 cents in claims per dollar paid to them in policyholder premiums. The other 40-plus percent goes to administration and profits.

Social Security taxes

Another "benefit" of working for an employer is that the employer pays for half (7.65 percent of your income) of your Social Security and Medicare taxes. Don't despair of the extra cost of having to pay both halves of this tax when operating your own business. Although you do have to pay the entire tax (15.3 percent of your income up to a certain threshold amount) when you're self-employed, the IRS allows you to take half of this amount as a tax deduction on your Form 1040.

The value of your Social Security tax deduction as a self-employed person depends on your marginal tax rate; if you're in, say, the 24 percent federal income tax bracket, then the actual cost of your self-employment tax is 5.97 percent: $7.65 - (7.65 \times 0.24) = 5.81$. Thus, the tax isn't as painful as you think. (State tax deductions decrease the effective costs of self-employment taxes even further.)

TIP

When pricing your products or services, you can build the cost of this tax, as well as other benefits you'll pay for out of pocket, into your calculations. (After all, this is what your current employer does.) We explain pricing strategies in Chapter 13.

Time off

All work and no play make Mary and John dull and probably overstressed entrepreneurs. When you work for a company, we trust that it provides you with certain holidays and at least a couple of weeks of vacation each year. You may never have considered that your paycheck covers the cost of these normal workdays when you're allowed time off.

Again, when you price your products and services, you need to factor in that, given holidays and 2 to 3 weeks of annual vacation, you probably won't be working about 5 weeks out of the 52 weeks in a year. Although some new entrepreneurs don't take much vacation time or many holidays off, we certainly don't want you to plan for that; if you do, you might burn yourself out and not be much fun to be around!

Understanding Your Time and Financial Commitments to Buy

Successfully buying a business is a process that is best done over a number of months, not days or weeks. There's plenty of research, due diligence and soul searching to be done so please don't try to rush into this.

We would argue that this is an even bigger commitment and purchase than a home, which is more easily salable. Yes, you live in your home but buying a small business is a major financial commitment and will involve your full-time, year-round engagement, especially in the earliest years. And your acquired small business may well come with the responsibility of managing employees.

While research and due diligence can be worthwhile to perform, you can get too much of a good thing. You can easily spend 6 to 12 months or more trying to locate the right business to buy and then completing the steps necessary to complete the purchase.

But we've seen some folks search for years and be unable to consummate a deal. Sometimes the lack of action can be for the best but in other cases, analysis-paralysis sets in and prevents a purchase. You can always do more research and investigation — the goal should be to strike a balance between being reasonably well informed and moving forward with a decision and purchase.

REMEMBER

There's no such thing as the perfect business to buy and all deals have risks and pros and cons. Accept and embrace those facts and gray areas. Some folks get further into the process of looking at businesses to possibly buy and then decide that buying a business isn't for them. That can be a good and smart decision. But, if you spend years debating and worrying about making the ideal purchase, you may need some help making a decision and moving forward.

Stepping Toward Buying a Business

It's time to get organized! To help in your quest to buy a business, walk through these steps involved in making a wise purchase:

1. **Pick a business.** The types of businesses you could buy are quite varied and some will be more appealing and a better fit for you than others. Check out Chapters 3 and 4 for details.

2. **Inspect the business and run the numbers.** When you've found a potentially appealing business you might buy, you should conduct due diligence and do some number crunching to evaluate and value the business. We walk you through doing just that in Chapters 5 and 6.

3. **Negotiate and seal the deal.** As with buying a house, once you've found a business you'd like to buy, you'll assemble an offer and negotiate the price and terms of the deal. Chapters 7 and 8 explain what contingencies and strategies to use to close the deal at a favorable price.

4. **Transition into your business.** Once your purchase is complete you face the big task of taking over the reins of the business, getting up to speed on all facets of the

business, and beginning to make your mark and improvements. Peruse Chapters 9 to 11.

5. **Plan a growth trajectory.** If you expect to grow your business, you're going to need to hire and retain top-notch employees and know how to attract and satisfy customers. Chapters 12 and 13 covers those vital details.

Enlisting Help from Top-Notch Professionals

Running your own business can be a lonely endeavor. But that doesn't mean you have to go it alone — doing so can be foolish and undermine your chances for long-term success. You should tap into the expertise and knowledge of those who can assist you with important decisions leading up to your potential purchase.

Some of these pros or veterans cost decent money to hire, but there are also plenty of free or low-cost resources that you can learn a great deal from.

Start with free/low-cost industry resources

Consider this example. Suppose you're interested in buying a restaurant — could either be an existing restaurant with ongoing operations or perhaps a new franchise location.

Start by checking in with the industry association(s) which for the restaurant industry includes the National Restaurant Association and state-based restaurant associations. Look for magazines (for example, Restaurant Business Magazine, Nation's Restaurant News), websites/blogs (for example, Eater, Grub Street), and business news coverage of the industry that may further your knowledge and understanding.

Of course, you should be skeptical regarding the accuracy and objectivity of what you're reading and listening to, especially when it's coming from a source with a reasonably obvious bias.

But realize there's tremendous value in immersing yourself in learning about an industry and small business overall when you're considering committing serious money toward buying and operating a small business in that sector. Count this book among the numerous highly affordable resources that can assist you in making great small business purchase decisions!

Finding and interviewing reputable professionals

As you get further into the process of potentially buying a business, selectively hiring particular advisors and professionals to provide specific counsel and insights can be money well spent. But you've got to do your homework to ensure that you engage professionals who provide a return on the money you spend on them.

Here are the pros you might consider hiring to assist and advise you on your small business purchase:

» **Appraiser:** Once you're interested in making an offer on a business that appeals to you, an appraiser with small-business experience and expertise can assist you with valuing the business.

» **Attorney:** Legal advisors can help you with crafting a purchase contract including contingency terms and conditions to protect your interests. Contingencies might include things such as being able to inspect the business and its financial records and the ability to obtain a loan for a particular portion of the purchase price and for a competitive interest rate.

» **Business broker:** Some folks looking for an existing small business to buy look at businesses for sale through business brokers. Like real estate agents, a business broker is a salesperson who gets paid on commission (from the seller's proceeds) when they sell a listed business, so keep that conflict of interest in mind when working with them.

» **Small business consultant or advisor:** There are a modest number of consultants that specialize in working as advisors to small businesses.

>> **Tax advisor:** CPAs and other tax advisors can help you with analyzing and understanding a company's financial statements and potentially valuing a business. Often, small business owners' claims of profitability may not be corroborated by their tax returns where the business owner seeks to minimize their reported net income and hence their income taxes.

Estimating the Cost of Your Search and Business Acquisition

The simplest way for most people to understand what's involved financially in buying a business is comparing it to buying a home or investing in real estate you intend to rent out. Unless you have enough cash to buy the property outright without a loan, you typically have two things to consider — the purchase price of the property itself and the amount you need to make a down payment so that you can finance the rest of the purchase price (unless you have enough cash to buy the property outright without a loan).

When buying real estate, some of the due diligence such as having the property professionally inspected costs money and leads to contingencies in the purchase contract. Applying for a loan generally involves some upfront fees and qualifying for affordable financing is another typical contract contingency.

Calculating a down payment amount

Generally speaking, you should seek to make a down payment of at least 20 to 25 percent of the expected purchase price of a business in order to obtain decent financing terms. Lenders and business sellers will typically balk at low down payment, amounts such as 10 percent, and be concerned that you don't have enough skin in the game in the event that the business fails and you default on your loan(s).

Historically, borrowers who make lower down payments are far more likely to walk away from and default on their loans compared with borrowers who make more substantial down payments. That's why lenders will charge much higher interest rates and upfront loan fees with small down payment amounts (under 20 percent).

Suppose you're examining some businesses that you estimate would sell for around $300,000. Thus, a 20 to 25 percent down payment would require about $60,000 to $75,000 for your down payment. As you save and accumulate money you'd like to use toward a down payment, the 20 to 25 percent down payment amount can help you fine-tune the approximate target amount for the purchase price of a business.

Tallying search expenses

By far, the biggest expense in your search will be your time, which doesn't have an explicit out-of-pocket price tag attached to it. Of course, if you have other ways of selling your time and your business search impinges on your ability to work for pay, you could quantify the value of your time spent on the business search process as part of the cost of your search.

We explain earlier in the chapter in the section, "Enlisting Help from Top-Notch Professionals," that you may wish to engage several pros you during the search process to assist with evaluating prospective small businesses for sale. These may include experts such as an appraiser, attorney, small business consultant, and tax advisor among others. Such professionals typically charge around $250 to $300 per hour for their time. Hourly billing rates may be lower outside of metropolitan areas that have a higher cost of living.

Most often you are likely to hire such a person for an hour or so of their time to review and opine regarding a specific business you're considering buying, problem, or financial situation. Appraisals typically take several hours of time and hence cost more.

If you're going to involve a consultant, attorney, or some other expert for more intensive and extended input, they may have a contract for you to review. Be sure to thoroughly read it and question anything you don't understand or agree with. Contracts can of course be modified to address your concerns.

Finding funding

One of the obstacles standing in the way of turning your dreams of small business ownership into reality is being able to finance or pay the purchase price of a small business you wish to buy. Most buyers have to finance the majority of the purchase price.

So, after making a down payment toward the purchase, where is your financing likely to come from to pay the full sales price you've negotiated with the small business seller? You'll probably obtain a loan from a bank, the Small Business Administration, or the seller of the business.

Lending terms vary greatly among different sources, so it's imperative to shop around to find the best deal. See Chapter 7 for more on financing.

Chapter **2**

Is Buying a Business for You?

After a business has been created, it can have a life of its own. The umbilical cord to its creator can be cut, and the business can pass onto various owners. In some cases, a great small business can outlive its original owners — assuming, of course, that subsequent owners have the necessary entrepreneurial and management skills.

In this chapter, we discuss the reasons why you might buy a business, but we also steer you clear when your personality and resources don't make purchasing a good match.

Understanding Why to Buy a Business

Every year, hundreds of thousands of small businesses change hands. Why? For the same reasons that many people purchase an already-built home instead of building one from scratch — because building a home or business takes a lot of time and work and has lots of potential for problems.

We don't mean for you to take this building analogy too far. After all, you can start most small businesses without drawing on your carpentry skills. However, as with buying an existing home, you may find that the advantages of buying an existing business outweigh the advantages of building one yourself.

As if the issue of saving time and energy in the building process isn't enough, another reason for buying a business is that, historically, the failure rate is twice as high for starting a business as compared to buying one. So why doesn't everyone buy a business rather than start one? Because not that many good businesses make it to the auction block. Many of the good ones never hit the market; instead, they're passed on within the family or are sold in private transactions without ever being listed for sale.

In the following sections, we discuss reasons why you may want to buy an existing business rather than build one from scratch. (In Part 2, we discuss how to find the best businesses to buy.)

DISSATISFACTION: A CATALYST FOR CHANGE

TRUE STORY

As sometimes happens in life, people who end up buying a business often end up doing so as a result of some outside force or circumstance that propels them in that direction.

Consider the case of David, a veterinarian who worked for an owner who agreed to offer David 10 percent of the practice after David had worked there for a number of years. Over time, however, the owner engaged in various legal maneuverings that allowed him to wiggle out of the offer. David became dejected and upset; he'd been a loyal and highly competent employee over the years. His customers enjoyed working with him and requested his services when scheduling future appointments. David couldn't understand how the owner could treat him so poorly despite his years of excellent service to the business. David couldn't see that the owner was greedy and unethical because David was neither.

The silver lining to this story is that this horrible experience was the catalyst David needed to go into business for himself. Instead of building a practice from scratch, however, David bought an existing practice — and he's glad that he did. David hit the ground running with the established practice and used his energies and talents to make the practice significantly bigger and better. After many years of building the business and enjoying the challenges, David sold it and is enjoying his semiretirement as a highly financially secure multimillionaire.

To reduce start-up hassles and headaches

Running a business is always a juggling act, but you often have more balls in the air during those start-up years than at any other time in the life of the business. Beyond formulating a business plan, you have to develop a marketing plan, find customers, hire employees, locate space, and possibly incorporate. Although you still need a game plan when buying an existing business, many of these start-up tasks have already been done.

REMEMBER

Consider the learning curve for the type of business you're thinking of purchasing. Buying an existing business makes sense if the business is complicated. For example, purchasing a business that manufactures an intricate product makes more sense than purchasing a house-painting business, which doesn't require much more than the necessary tools and equipment and painting know-how. Also, unless you have already built the product the company manufactures and you understand the intricacies of the production process, starting such a complicated business from scratch is quite risky and perhaps even foolhardy.

To lessen your risk

In situations where a business has an operating history and offers a product or service with a demonstrated market, you remove some of the risk when you buy an existing company (compared with starting from scratch). Although no investment is a sure thing, the risk involved in an already-established business should be significantly lower than the risk involved in a start-up. Because an existing business has an operating history, you can use past financial statements to help you make more accurate financial forecasts than you can with a start-up venture that has no history.

WARNING

As we explain in Chapter 5, before you buy a business, you must do your homework, which means carefully inspecting the business you're considering buying and its financial statements (this careful inspection is known as *due diligence*). You can't take at face value how the business appears on paper or in site visits because more than a few business sellers have been known to dress up the books and the business to hide problems and flaws.

To increase profits by adding value

Some business owners who decide to sell their company don't see the potential for growth or don't want to grow their business. They may be burned out, content with their current earnings, lacking in needed business-management skills, or simply ready to retire. Finding a business that has the potential to improve operating efficiency and expand into new markets is difficult but not impossible — if you have the time and patience to wait for the right one to come along. In fact, finding small companies that are undervalued relative to the potential they have to offer is probably easier to do than finding undervalued stocks or real estate when investing in those markets.

REMEMBER

Just because you think you see the potential to improve a business, never, ever pay a high acquisition price based on your expectations of being able to add that value. Even if you're correct about the potential, why should you pay the current owner for the hard work and ingenuity you plan to bring to the business? If you're wrong, you can grossly overpay for the business.

If you're right, you can miss out on capturing the value that you will create and some potentially big profits. On the other hand, if you offer a fair price based on the value of the business at the time you purchase it, you can realize the rewards of your improvements after you make them. (We explain how to value a business in Chapter 6.)

WARNING

A smart seller will try to convince you that they have under-achieved with the business and that all it needs is your energy, enthusiasm, and fantastic business acumen. Don't fall for the compliments; remember that sellers sell the future while buyers buy the past. What this saying means is that the person who's buying the business shouldn't listen to the seller talk about the grandiose things that can be done with the business but should instead focus on what the business has already done (recognizing, of course, that the business may actually be worsening in the short-term and may not even be capable of generating what it did in the recent past). In other words, the buyer isn't buying the seller's vision; they're buying what's in place today.

To establish cash flow

One of the biggest unknowns involved in starting a business from scratch is estimating the new business's cash flow, otherwise known for sale or acquisition purposes as EBITDA (Earnings Before Interest, Taxes, Depreciation and Amortization). Will the business generate cash quickly, or will it take a long time? How long will collecting monies due from customers (receivables) take? How long will selling inventory take? How much will you have to invest in fixed assets? How quickly will your sales be established?

With start-up businesses, estimating these figures is fraught with the potential for wide margins of error. Fortunately, that's not the case when you buy an existing business. The track record of the previous owners has already answered most of these questions. Assuming that you don't walk in and make immediate, glaring changes to the business's products or operations, the cash flow pattern should continue somewhat as it has done in the past. Take it from us: As a small-business owner, you'll feel reassured by having a reasonably predictable cash flow. You and your family, your banker, and other investors will deeply appreciate it. Conversely, unpredictable cash flow is trouble-some at best and will keep you from sleeping at night. (Just remember that your cash flow needs may be higher than the current owner's because you may have to repay a loan you used to buy the business.)

As a bonus, borrowing money from banks and raising money from investors is often easier to do when you buy a business instead of doing a traditional start-up. Lenders and investors rightfully see more risk with a start-up than with an established enterprise with a good track record. Plus, they have the business's existing assets with which to collateralize their loans. For the amount they invest, investors usually demand a smaller percentage of ownership in an existing business than in a new business.

To capitalize on someone else's good idea

We've said it before: You don't need an original idea to go into business for yourself. Plenty of successful small-business people enjoy running a business; whether they repair cars or trim trees doesn't matter.

If you know you want to own a business but you lack an idea for a product or service to sell, chalk up another good reason to buy an existing business. Just make sure that you have some passion and expertise for the industry you're thinking about joining.

To open locked doors

In certain businesses, you can enter geographic territories only as a result of buying an existing business. For example, suppose that you want to own a Lexus dealership within an hour of where you currently live. If Lexus isn't granting any more new dealer-ships, your only ticket into the automobile industry may be to buy an existing Lexus dealership in your area.

To inherit an established customer base

If you're not good at selling (maybe because you dislike it), buying a business may be the best way for you to enter the world of business ownership. After all, buying an existing business gives you a ready-built stable of customers, which means you don't have to recruit them yourself. Then, if you can provide quality products or services and meet customers' needs, you can see your business grow through word-of-mouth referrals.

WARNING

In the long term, your lack of sales ability can negatively impact even an established business. All businesses, even those that don't want to grow, need to add new customers if only to replace those who inevitably leave. If you can't sell (or figure out how to sell) to new customers, your business eventually may flounder. Be sure your new business has employees on staff with sales skills or be ready to hire people with the necessary selling skills. (See Chapter 12 for details on hiring good employees, and check out Chapter 13 for more on retaining loyal customers.)

Knowing When You Shouldn't Buy

Of course, you can find more than a few downsides to buying an existing business. Similar to the advantages, the relative weight of these disadvantages depends largely on your personality and available resources.

You dislike inherited baggage

When you buy an existing business, you get the bad along with the good. All businesses have their share of problems and issues. A business may have problem employees, for example, or it may have a less-than-stellar reputation in the marketplace. Even if the employees are competent, they and the culture of the company may not mesh with your desired direction for the company in the future.

Do you have the disposition and ability to motivate your employees to change or to fire employees who don't want to change? Do you have the patience to work at improving the company's products and reputation? Do you have the cash to upgrade the technology or remodel the dated offices? All these issues are barriers to running and adding value to a company. Some people enjoy and thrive on such challenges; others toss and turn in their sleep with such pressures. Think back on your other work experiences for clues about what challenges you've tackled and how you felt about them. (Take the quiz in the section "Do You Have the Right Stuff," later in this chapter, to assess your workplace likes and dislikes.)

You're going to skimp on inspections

If you think buying a company is easy, think again. Before you sign on the dotted line, you should know exactly what you're buying, so you need to do a comprehensive inspection (also known as due diligence) of the company you're buying (see Chapter 5 for details on how to do so). For example, you (or a competent financial/tax person) need to analyze the existing business's financial statements to ascertain whether the company really is as profitable as it appears and to determine its current financial health.

REMEMBER

After you close the deal and transfer the money or duly record the IOUs, you can't turn back. Unless a seller commits fraud or lies (which is difficult and costly for a buyer to legally prove), it's "buyer beware" with the quality of the business you're buying. In Chapter 5, we cover all the homework you should do before you decide to buy.

THE WRONG REASONS FOR BUYING A BUSINESS

Jeff was a successful electronics wholesaler. As Jeff approached the age of 50, he and his wife began to think more and more about where they may spend their retirement. As is typical of many Midwesterners fed up with long and dreary winters, Florida jumped to mind.

During a winter vacation in Naples, Florida, Jeff was idly perusing the classified ads when he noticed a business for sale in the wholesale electronics industry. His curiosity got the better of him, so he visited the company and talked at length with the owner. Before you can mutter the words *spring break,* Jeff had purchased the company with one-third of the purchase price in cash and the balance borrowed as a long-term loan.

Jeff's primary reason for buying the business? To give himself and his family a chance to travel to Naples on the company expense account, mixing golf with business during those cold Midwestern winters. "A great way to ease into retirement," he told his friends.

Fast-forward two years. The Naples business was floundering badly. Apparently, many of the company's customers had been *relationship customers* (people who mainly did business with the company because of their friendship/relationship with the owner), and now that the previous owner was gone, so were they. (It didn't help that Jeff was only around three months out of the year, and the company's efficiency suffered accordingly.) Additionally, Jeff discovered that managing his new Deep South employees had little in common with managing his old Midwest employees. Meanwhile, the business was hemorrhaging money.

Six months later, Jeff reluctantly closed the company's doors by transferring the remaining inventory to Minneapolis, taking a $250,000 hit to his bottom line in the process. A hefty price to pay, he admitted, for a few rounds of wintertime golf and some tax deductions.

(continued)

(continued)

In the end, Jeff's business failed because he purchased it for the wrong reasons. He purchased the business to get away from Minnesota winters and to earn some meager tax deductions, which, Jeff can tell you in retrospect, weren't nearly enough. He didn't purchase it because he had a passion for his customers, or because he had an urge to make a difference for his employees, or because he had a driving need to create something meaningful, or for any other strategic business reason.

The lesson here? You should have compelling and achievable reasons to buy a business. As Jeff learned the hard way, golf in Florida and tax deductions just aren't enough.

You lack capital

Why do a lot of people start a business instead of buying one? Because they simply don't have enough cash — or credit potential — to buy one. Existing businesses have value over and above the value of their hard assets, which is why you generally need more upfront money and credit to buy a business than to start one. Although you may feel like you're more the business-buying type than the business-starting type, if you don't have the necessary dough, and if you can't find investors or lenders to provide it, then your avenue to business ownership may be decided for you, regardless of the avenue you'd prefer.

You think you'll miss out on the satisfaction of creating a business

Whether it nourishes their souls or simply gratifies their egos, entrepreneurs who build their own businesses get a different rush than those who buy existing companies. Certainly you can make your mark on a business you buy, but doing so takes a number of years. Even then, the business is never completely your own creation.

Recognizing Prepurchase Prerequisites

Not everyone is cut out to buy an existing business, and we're not just referring to those who don't have enough cash or credit. In fact, you can purchase a good small business with little or, in rare cases, no money down.

The process of buying a business requires a lot of work. However, successfully running the business day in and day out is much harder for most people than finding and buying it. Some succeed wildly at running the business they buy; others fail miserably. So what, then, are the traits common to people who successfully buy and operate an existing small business? We cover them in the following sections.

REMEMBER

Above all else, being persistent, patient, and willing to spend time on things that don't lead to immediate results pays off. You need to be willing to sort through the rubbish to find the keepers. If you're a person who needs immediate gratification in terms of completing a deal, you may become miserable as you search, or you may end up rushing into a bad deal. Try breaking the process into steps to provide more success points and give yourself time for clear thinking.

Business experience and training

You need to have the necessary business experience and background if you want to buy a business. If you were an economics or business major in college and you took accounting and other quantitatively oriented courses, you're off to a good start.

If you've worked on business-management issues within a variety of industries (as consultants who work as generalists do), you also may have the proper background. However, one danger in having done only consulting is that you're usually not on the front lines where you confront most of the serious day-to-day operational issues. We've seen plenty of sophisticated consultants who didn't have the foggiest idea how to meet payroll or decipher an accounts receivable aging report.

If neither of these backgrounds applies to you, you won't necessarily fail if you decide to buy a business, but the odds against you increase. If you don't have a business background and work experience, you may still succeed. However, you'll probably simply survive (and just surviving probably isn't what you're after). Plus, your prospects for outright failure are relatively high, as compared to your experienced competitors.

TIP

We strongly encourage you to get some hands-on, small-business management experience, which is more valuable than any degree or credential you earn through course work. You'll find no substitute for real-life experiences in marketing to and interacting with customers, grappling with financial statements, dealing with competitive threats, and doing the business of everyday business.

If you want to own a computer repair service, go work in a good one. If you want to run a jet-ski rental business, go work in a successful one. Try to wear as many hats in the business as the boss allows. Consider the experience as paid, on-the-job training for running your own business. You're getting your unofficial MBA, and someone is even paying you for it!

We're not saying that you should avoid academia in learning how to run a business. You may, in fact, have to attain a certain credential to do the work that you want to do. If you don't need a specific credential, taking selected courses like accounting or marketing, as well as reading relevant business books (like this one), can boost your knowledge.

WARNING

For those of you with a large company or government background, be advised that there's a huge difference between working for a large company or a government entity and owning a small business. Most of the skills required simply aren't transferable, plus you must wear a plethora of business hats (sales, marketing, shipping and receiving, customer service, and so on) when you own a small business. Too many corporate or government employees have bit the proverbial dust when buying a small business because they made the erroneous assumption that running a small business requires the same skills as working in a large organization.

Down payment money

When purchasing a business, as in purchasing real estate, you generally must make a significant down payment on the negotiated purchase price. In most cases, you need to put down at least 25 to 30 percent of the total purchase price. Bankers and business sellers who make loans to business buyers normally require down payments to protect their loans. They've learned from past experience that small-business buyers who make small down payments are more likely to walk away from a loan obligation if the business gets into financial trouble.

TRUE STORY

For example, consider what happened with coauthor Jim's fourth business, which he sold for 33 percent of the sales price in cash and the balance (67 percent) in a ten-year loan. Two years after the sale, the buyers declared bankruptcy, leaving Jim holding the bag on the remainder of the loan, which was still more than 60 percent of the purchase price. Had Jim not required a down payment, he would have received no cash from the deal, only a long-term note that he would eventually eat; on the other hand, had he required 50 percent down, he would've received another 17 percent of the purchase price in cash, thereby reducing the amount of the note he would eventually write off.

TIP

If you lack a sufficient down payment, try asking family or friends to invest or lend you the cash. You can also set your sights on a less-expensive business or seek out business sellers willing to accept a smaller down payment.

If you find a business for sale in which the owner wants less than 20 percent down, you may be on to something good. Be careful, though; owners willing to accept such small down payments may be having a difficult time selling because of problems inherent in the business or simply because they've overpriced the business. Smart sellers generally seek to maximize the amount of the down payment. Your intent as a buyer should be to keep the down payment to a minimum (subject, of course, to obtaining favorable loan terms), thereby retaining as much cash as possible to use in operating the business.

WARNING

Beware of the all-cash deal, even if you can afford it. If the business turns out to be something less than what was presented, you, the buyer, will lose all your leverage to negotiate. He who has the cash has the power — and you don't if you've paid 100 percent cash up front for the business purchase.

You can purchase many existing small businesses with a loan from the seller. Also, check with banks that specialize in small-business loans, especially those that offer SBA (Small Business Administration) guarantees. For more financing options, see Chapter 7.

Do You Have the Right Stuff?

To discover whether you have the right stuff to run your own small business, take the test we offer in this section. Please don't close this book just because we said the word *test!* Tests don't have to be a pain in the posterior. In fact, they can be relatively painless (and useful) when you don't have to study for them, there are no right or wrong answers, and you're the only one who will find out the outcome.

REMEMBER

Some words of caution here: This Small-Business Owner's Aptitude Test isn't scientific, but we think it's potentially useful because it's based on our combined seven decades of experience working *as* entrepreneurs, as well as *alongside* them. The purpose of this test is to provide a guideline, not to cast in concrete your choice to start or buy a business. The results will be most meaningful when it comes time to make your decision if you're in the highest- or lowest-scoring groups. If you fall somewhere in the middle, we recommend more serious soul searching, consultation with friends and other small-business owners, and a large grain of salt.

Getting started with the instructions

Score each of the following 20 questions with a number from 1 to 5. We explain the scoring with each question and will explain after you complete all the questions what your score means. Determine the appropriate numerical score for each question by assessing the relative difference between the two options presented and by how fervently you feel about the answer.

For example, one question asks, "Do you daydream about business opportunities while commuting to work, flying on an airplane, or waiting in the doctor's office, or during other quiet times?" Give yourself a 5 if you find yourself doing this a lot, a 1 if you never do this, or a 2, 3, or 4, depending on the degree of work-related daydreaming you do. A business, especially one that you own yourself, can be downright fun and all-consuming. For most successful entrepreneurs, their minds are rarely far away from their businesses; they're often thinking of new products, new marketing plans, and new ways to find customers.

TIP

To make the test even more meaningful, have someone who doesn't have a vested interest in or a strong opinion about your decision — such as a good friend — also independently take the test with you as the subject. We seldom have unbiased opinions of ourselves, and having an unrelated third party take the test on your behalf can give you a more accurate view. Then compare the two scores — the score you arrived at when you took the test compared to the score your friend or peer compiled for you. Our guess is that your true entrepreneurial aptitude, at least according to our experience, lies somewhere between the two scores.

Answering the questions

After reading each question, write your response from 1 to 5 on a separate sheet of paper.

1. In the games that you play, do you play harder when you fall behind, or do you tend to fold your cards and cut your losses? (5 if you play harder, 1 if you wilt under pressure)

2. When you go to a sports event or concert, do you try to figure out the promoter's or the owner's gross revenues? (5 if you often do, 1 if you never do)

3. When things take a serious turn for the worse, is your first impulse to look for someone to blame, or is it to look for alternatives and solutions? (5 if you look for alternatives and solutions, 1 if you look for someone to blame)

4. Using your friends and/or coworkers as a barometer, how would you rate your energy level? (5 if it is high, 1 if it is low)

5. Do you daydream about business opportunities while commuting to work, flying on an airplane, waiting in the doctor's office, or during other quiet times? (5 if you often do, 1 if you never do)

6. Look back on the significant changes you've made in your life — schools, jobs, relocations, relationships: Have you fretted and worried about those changes and not acted, or have you looked forward to them with excitement and been able to make those tough decisions after doing some research? (5 if you've looked forward to the decisions and tackled them after doing your homework, 1 if you've been overwhelmed with worry about the change and paralyzed from action for too long)

7. Is your first consideration of any opportunity always the upside or is it always the downside? (5 if you always see the upside and recognize the risks, 1 if you dwell on the downside to the exclusion of considering the benefits)

8. Are you happiest when you're busy or when you have nothing to do? (5 if you're always happiest when busy, 1 if you're always happiest when you have nothing to do)

9. As an older child or young adult, did you often have a job or a scheme or an idea to make money? (5 if always, 1 if never)

10. Did you work part time or summer jobs as a youth, or did you not work and primarily recreate/enjoy a total break over the summer? (5 if you often worked, 1 if you never did)

11. Did your parents own a small business? (5 if they worked many years owning small businesses, 1 if they never did)

12. Have you worked for a small business for more than one year? (5 if you have, 1 if you haven't)

13. Do you like being in charge and in control? (5 if you really crave those two situations, 1 if you detest them)

14. How comfortable are you with borrowing money to finance an investment, such as buying a home or an automobile? (5 if owing money is not a problem, 1 if it's a huge problem)

15. How creative are you? (5 if extremely creative, 1 if not creative at all)

16. Do you have to balance your checkbook to the penny or is "close" good enough? (5 if "close" is good enough, 1 if to the penny)

17. When you fail at a project or task, does it scar you forever or does it inspire you to do it better the next time? (5 if it inspires you for the next time, 1 if it scars you forever)

18. When you truly believe in something, whether it's an idea, a product, or a service, are you able to sell it to someone? (5 if almost always, 1 if never)

19. In your current social and business environment, are you most often a follower or a leader? (5 if almost always a leader, 1 if always a follower)

20. How good are you at achieving/keeping your New Year's resolutions? (5 if you almost always achieve/keep them, 1 if you never do)

Scoring the test

Now total your score. Here's how to assess your total:

80 to 100: Go for it. If you read this book and continue to show a willingness to be a sponge, you should succeed!

60 to 79: You probably have what it takes to successfully run your own business but take some time to look back over the questions you scored the lowest on and see whether you can discern any trends.

40 to 59: Too close to call. Review the questions on which you scored low and don't scrimp on learning more to tilt the scales in your favor.

20 to 39: We could be wrong, but you're probably better off working for someone else or pursuing one of the other alternatives to starting your own business.

Analyzing your results

The truth about a subjective test such as this one is that it can serve as a helpful indicator, but it won't provide you with a definitive answer. We issue this disclaimer because the Small-Business Owner's Aptitude Test is, in effect, a measure of the way you have acted in the past and not necessarily how you will perform in the future.

Your future as a small-business owner will hold many surprises. (Don't panic! By the time you finish this book, you'll be prepared for many of them.) The skills and traits that you need to cope with those surprises will ultimately determine whether your choice to start or buy a small business is the right one. What exactly are those skills?

>> **Numbers skills:** These skills include those related to borrowing money, accounting for it, and reporting on the financial performance of your company.

>> **Sales skills:** As a small-business owner, you're always trying to sell your products to someone — be it your customers, employees, or vendors.

>> **Marketing skills:** All small-business owners must market their products or services — no one is exempt.

>> **Leadership skills:** The small-business owner is the Grand Poobah of his venture. Grand Poobahs are only as good as the manner in which the business's employees are led.

Does this mean that if you don't have these skills, you should remain on the receiving end of a paycheck? Thankfully, it does not.

REMEMBER

Many successful entrepreneurs who have come before you made it without being able to personally perform all the skills necessary to run a business. What we're saying is that, over the course of your career, you'll have to either develop these skills or involve someone in the business who already has them (a partner, a key employee, or a hired advisor or consultant, for example). In addition to immersing yourself in this book, you may also wish to check out the latest edition of our *Small Business For Dummies* (Wiley).

Skills aside, successful entrepreneurs also need to have or adopt several required traits:

>> **Confidence:** Small-business owners have to be able to coexist with risk and possibly debt. Capitalism offers its participants no guarantees; thus, the small business and consequently its owner are almost always at risk and sometimes in debt. Yet, the owner still has to sleep at night.

>> **Intuition:** Call it intuition or call it gut instinct, small-business owners have to call things right more often than wrong, or they'll soon be calling it quits.

>> **Optimism:** Successful small-business owners often see good fortune, not misfortune; upsides, not downsides; and opportunities, not problems. The small-business owner can always hire a devil's advocate (that's what lawyers and accountants are for), but the enthusiasm and optimism necessary to drive the vision must come from the entrepreneur.

>> **Drive:** Successful small-business owners are driven to create a product, service a customer, and build a successful business. Like the craving for chocolate, this drive doesn't go away.

>> **Passion:** An entrepreneur's passion can be infectious. Your employees, your vendors, and your customers — everyone you encounter — should feel your passion and feed off it.

If you don't have all five of these traits, should you resign yourself to always being an employee? In answering this question, you first need to recognize that being a good employee today also requires some of these traits, so owning a business isn't your only option. Then you need to come to terms with the fact that if you don't have most of these traits in healthy supply, you're probably better off as an employee rather than a small-business owner.

2

Picking the Business that Fits Your Situation

IN THIS PART . . .

Determine which business niche is right for you.

Research thoroughly to find the business that best fits your situation.

Conduct a comprehensive evaluation of the business before you buy.

Chapter 3

Determining Your Niche

lthough your business niche and the original idea behind the business you buy are important, neither makes the primary difference when it comes to the survival of the business once you're in charge. Rather, the primary difference maker is *you!* The niche and the idea are only small parts of the puzzle that is success. In this chapter, we discuss a few of the most important puzzle pieces, including the cornerstone piece (that being you), and then we explain why you need to put them all together to ensure your newly acquired business's success.

Why You Don't Need a New Idea to Be Successful

Many small-business owners (the vast majority, in fact) don't break new ground. Plenty of tax preparers, dry cleaners, and restaurant owners happily make a comfortable-or-better living by doing what many others before them have already done. All of these types of businesses can be bought from an existing owner or in the form of a franchise.

Having a groundbreaking idea, extensive product knowledge, or unbridled enthusiasm has little real influence on your long-term business success. Even if you make the best chocolate chip cookies this side of Mrs. Fields, your business can still crash and burn. Maybe you don't sell enough cookies, or you have a hard time accounting for the ones you do sell. Maybe you sell ocean tankers filled with cookies, but your prices are too low to make a profit, or maybe your customers won't pay their bills.

Having a good product and knowing the product well are only the beginning of building a successful business; you must also perform a long list of sometimes arduous day-to-day chores to be a successful small-business owner. Those chores may include the following:

>> Find good customers and convince them to buy (see Chapter 13).

>> Deal with difficult, hard-to-please customers.

>> Provide cost-effective customer service that retains customer loyalty (see Chapter 13).

>> Understand financial statements, including balance sheets, profit and loss statements, and cash flow statements (see Chapter 5, or *Small Business For Dummies*, by Eric Tyson and Jim Schell, for this information and more).

- » Grant credit to customers and know how (and to whom) to grant it.

- » Collect *receivables* (the money you're owed).

- » Juggle and prioritize the payment of *payables* (the money you owe to others).

- » Understand the mystifying concept of cash flow and then figure out how to manage it.

- » Compute inventory turn, days-in-receivables, current ratios, and return on sales.

- » Use such management tools as organization charts, job descriptions, and performance reviews (see Chapter 12).

- » Purchase the right computer and software and then figure out how to use it.

- » Collect and disburse sales tax, income tax, and Federal Insurance Contributions Act (FICA) tax, and perform all those other services the government requires of small businesses (we explain government requirements in Chapter 11 and taxes in Chapter 15).

- » Protect yourself from lawsuits — both from your employees and your customers — including sexual harassment suits and product liability suits.

- » Avoid (and deal with when you can't) such headaches as Occupational Safety and Health Administration (OSHA), workers' compensation, and unemployment problems.

- » Deal with drug- and alcohol-related problems, pacify smokers and nonsmokers, and recognize and deal with malingerers, embezzlers, and shoplifters.

- » Know how and when to use small claims court.

- » Know how to hire, fire, train, motivate, and hold employees accountable; control expenses; manage crises; balance cultures; deal with bankers; budget; forecast — the list goes on and on.

Of course, not all businesses have to deal with all the items in the preceding list. If your business doesn't have inventory, for example, you won't have to deal with the myriad issues relating to it.

REMEMBER

Our point here is that the niche or idea won't ultimately make or break your business; the day-to-day execution of the business itself is what ultimately determines success — or failure. Or stated another way, you show us a crackerjack businessperson, and we'll show you someone who can get rich in the cookie business whether or not they personally have the foggiest idea about how to bake the darned things.

Choosing Your Business

Finding the right business to buy or start can be a bit stressful, but don't worry. We offer plenty of help in the following sections. We assist you in matching your skills, interests, and job history with a suitable business, and we help you select the niche that works best for you, given who you are, what you like to do, and what you're capable of doing.

Consider your category

Before you decide which business venture would be best for you, you need to understand the four major business categories that you can consider: retailing, service, manufacturing, and wholesaling. Here are some important characteristics you need to know about these four categories:

>> **Retailing:** Retailing is the general category that most people are familiar with because the typical American deals with at least one retailer every day. Since most people are familiar with the retail business, the learning curve is usually much easier in retailing than in the other three categories (although this benefit is true for your retailing

competitors as well). Also, because most retail businesses deal primarily with cash or near-cash equivalents (credit cards), funding requirements for accounts receivable are relatively low compared with some of the other business categories, which means, in turn, that the capital requirements for entry can be comparatively low, depending on how much inventory is required. (See Chapters 1 and 2 to determine your initial cash needs.)

E-commerce (retailing over the Internet) is changing the parameters of the retailing category. The barrier to entry in retail-oriented entrepreneurial endeavors is becoming smaller as some successful retailing entrepreneurs choose web pages over storefronts. However, success online isn't as easy or as lucrative as some would have you believe.

» **Service:** The service industry is the fastest growing of the four categories, in part due to the low cost of entry (that is, you typically need no significant inventory outlays and minimal capital-intensive equipment). Additionally, if you're among the increasing number of service providers who choose to work out of their homes, occupancy expenses are relatively low and tax advantages are a potential perk.

» **Manufacturing:** Save up your hard-earned cash if you're thinking of becoming a manufacturer; this category is a veritable cash-guzzling machine. Inventory, accounts receivable, equipment, physical plant, employees — you name the cash-draining asset, and most manufacturers have gotta have it.

Although manufacturing is typically the most expensive of the four categories in terms of entry-level capital requirements, it offers great potential for rewards. Look at the high-tech industry for examples of wealth being created (not just for the founders but for key employees as well) in short periods of time; companies such as Microsoft, Intel, and Apple were start-up manufacturers earlier in their lifespan.

>> **Wholesaling:** The middleman in capitalism's distribution channel, *wholesalers* act as intermediaries between manufacturers and retailers or consumers. The wholesaler's role is to buy large quantities of products at discounted prices (discounted from retail prices that is) from manufacturers, break them down into smaller quantities, and sell them at a markup to retailers or consumers. Like manufacturers, wholesalers require significant cash outlays for inventory, receivables, physical plant, and employees; thus, the start-up capital requirements for wholesalers are correspondingly high.

Take advantage of accidental opportunities

Many small-business owners are "accidental" entrepreneurs — that is, they stumble on a good business to start or buy; Jim was one of these. Maybe a favorite retail store suddenly comes up for sale (this is exactly what jump-started coauthor Jim's entrepreneurial career), or a friend informs them of a can't-miss opportunity, or a customer of the business they're working for now invites them to do some freelance consulting — an invitation that turns into a business opportunity. In these cases, the lucky entrepreneur doesn't set out to own a business. Instead, they stumble on the right opportunity. As with so many other directions people take in life, the time and the place just happen to be right.

REMEMBER

When considering your accidental opportunity, if you don't enjoy what you're about to do, your chances for success will decrease. Make sure that your accidental opportunity is in a niche that you like.

Inventory your skills, interests, and job history

Most people aren't lucky or fortunate enough to stumble upon the right business. And the kinds of people who discover the right business are often those who are willing to go to a lot of trouble to find good opportunities.

If the perfect business opportunity doesn't just fall into your lap (and, actually, even if it does), you need to do some introspection to determine what type of business is right for you. The following questions can help you take an inventory of your business expertise and interests. (You can get a piece of paper and treat these questions like a quiz if you want to.) The answers you get will help you select the best possible business opportunity for you.

>> **What top-three business skills have you displayed over your business career?** Examples include sales, accounting, marketing, administration, writing, communications, quantitative analysis, hiring, training, employee motivation, product development, customer service, focus, delegation, accountability, attention to detail, and so on.

>> **In which business skills are you the weakest?** Refer to the examples in the preceding bullet for ideas.

>> **Over your working history (including part-time and full-time jobs), what three jobs have you enjoyed the most and why?** After listing three jobs, consider (and list) the reasons why you liked those particular jobs.

>> **During your working history, what three jobs have you enjoyed the least and why?** Similar to the preceding question, consider and then list the reasons why you disliked those particular jobs.

>> **What are your top-three overall personal skills?** Examples include leadership, communication, intelligence, creativity, vision, cheerleading, invention and/or innovation, listening, problem-solving, counseling, and so on.

>> **If this were a perfect world and you could select the industry in which you'd like to spend the rest of your life, what would be your top-three choices?** Examples include sports, music, movies, art, finance, education, telecommunications, electronics, computers, medicine, architecture, agriculture, transportation, insurance, real estate, financial services, food and beverage services, apparel design and manufacture, furniture and home

products, outdoor products, printing, photography, chemistry, plastics, and so on.

>> **What three favorite hobbies or special interests of yours may be conducive to creating a business?** Many people turn a hobby or special interest (such as photography, golf, or coin collecting) into a business.

>> **Given what you know about the retailing, service, manufacturing, and wholesale career choices, rank these four in order of desirability.** Refer to the earlier section "Consider your category" for details on each of these categories.

TIP

When you can't think of an answer to one or more of these questions, ask your partner or a couple of good friends for advice. Oftentimes, they know things about you that you overlook.

REMEMBER

Don't expect to answer these questions and determine that — eureka! — you should immediately open a retail clothing store, start a financial consulting business, or import rare ostrich eggs. Instead, use these questions to help you inventory your skills, interests, and job history. The results should help stimulate the thought processes that will assist you in developing a list of businesses that may work for you.

If, for example, your strengths (and interests) are in sales, you may want to consider a business where sales is the primary function of the business (manufacturer's representative, for instance). If you indicate that you have weaknesses in such areas as attention to detail, delegation, and administration, you may want to consider operating a business solo as opposed to one that requires employees. If you determine that over your job history, you didn't like those jobs where you dealt directly with customers, the retail business would probably not work for you.

These questions are intended to help you take an introspective look at yourself and lead you to where you would logically fit in the broad spectrum of business opportunities. That's why we say you'll find no quick answers here, but rather an opportunity to jump-start the narrowing-down process. Come back to these questions several times over a period of weeks; few people arrive at a solution the first time through.

Narrow your choices

When considering a business opportunity, you need to answer the following questions to assure yourself that the business you're considering is the right one for you:

>> Is it a business that suits your personality?

- Consider a bricks-and-mortar retail business if you like dealing directly with people, don't mind keeping regular hours, and can handle being tied to one spot for long periods of time. The converse, of course, also applies. If you don't like dealing directly with people, keeping regular hours, or being tied to one spot for long periods of time, don't consider the retail business.

- Consider a service business if you like dealing with people, solving problems, and working in spurts and flurries.

- Consider a wholesaling business if you're a detail-oriented person, if you enjoy supervising employees, and if you don't mind risking the significant amount of capital that carrying and distributing inventory requires.

- Consider the manufacturing business if you're a quality-conscious and detail-oriented person who enjoys searching for solutions to such engineering-oriented issues as process and flow and quality control. You should also enjoy supervising employees. You'll also need access to significant financing.

Within each of the four major business categories, you can get more specific and narrow down your choices to specific industries. For example:

- Consider the financial services or accounting/tax-preparation business if you like working with numbers.

- Consider the restaurant or entertainment business if you don't mind working unusual hours.

- Consider a banking, telephone sales, or consulting business if you don't mind spending long periods of time sitting at a desk.

» **Is it a business or product in which you have experience?** Experience is the world's best teacher. If you don't have it, your competitors who do have it are bound to have a sizable competitive edge over you. Sixty percent of successful business owners have gravitated to products or services in industries with which they were previously familiar.

» **Is it a business with too much risk?** Can you live with the risk inherent in this business? Generally, the bigger the capital requirement, the larger the risk. Are you sure you're prepared to live with the risk of starting a manufacturing company? If not, consider becoming a service provider instead — it's more suited to the average pocketbook. (If you have an idea for a new widget but don't have the resources to manufacture it, you can always outsource the manufacturing of it and then sell, service, and maintain it yourself.) You'll still need plenty of cash to carry inventory.

» **Is it a business in which you have a competitive advantage?** Can you make, service, or sell your product better? If not, you need to ask yourself what will motivate your customers to work with you. (If your answer is price, you're in trouble already, unless you've figured out a clear and high-quality way to create and deliver a product or service cheaper and better than the industry leaders.)

» **Is it a business in which you can become a specialist?** There's power in being a specialist, and there's danger in being a generalist. Today's movers and shakers have learned a valuable lesson from past experience: Focus on doing those things you can do better than anyone else.

Go in search of fast growth

Every year *Inc.* magazine publishes its list of "The 500 Fastest-Growing Companies in America" (*Inc.* also publishes the top 5,000; the top 500 are just the top companies from that list). This list includes tomorrow's potential goliaths of the business world. Such companies as Microsoft, Timberland, Oracle, and Cablevision have graced and then graduated from the list since its inception.

REMEMBER

As you look at the most recent *Inc.* list, pay attention to the niches that are currently enjoying the fastest growth. A number of past *Inc.* 500 fastest-growing companies are no longer in business. Risk and growth are common bedfellows, and one entrepreneur's riches may lead to another entrepreneur's rags. Thankfully for most people, other, less glamorous industries offer plenty of room for success. Because the industry you choose can greatly affect your success, consider the following industry-specific questions:

>> **Do you believe in the industry you plan to do business in?** Industries such as the tobacco industry or debt-collection industry aren't for everyone. Be sure to select an industry that will allow you to sleep at night and feel good about what you're doing.

>> **Is it an industry that isn't overcrowded or dominated by a few well-marketed companies?** You say you're thinking about a coffeehouse or a bagel shop? Good luck. You'd better know something or be prepared to offer a different product or service than Starbucks, Bruegger's, or Noah's Bagels. Jim works with a small business owner who has a falafel shop; she's killin' it.

Every industry has a saturation point; you want to make sure that your chosen industry isn't one of them. (You can usually determine the saturation point by observing how successful the existing businesses are. You can usually measure such success by observation — the condition of the business's premises, the quality and professionalism of the employees, and the prices charged; for example, is there room in the prices to make a profit?)

>> **Is your potential business in an industry that's moving at a pace that you can be comfortable with?** Some industries move faster than others; for example, the biotech industry moves faster than the gift-shop industry. Make sure that you have a comfort level with the pace of your chosen industry. Some industries will leave you breathless (and moneyless) if you can't keep up with the

pace. The gift-shop industry will leave you bleary eyed and passionless if you thrive on the rush you get from constant activity and change.

>> **Is it an industry that you can get passionate about?** Can you love the product and the customers? Passion helps sell products to customers and vision to employees.

Take advantage of government resources

Everyone likes to poke fun at the government (hey, what else are governments for, anyway?). But now and then, when you least expect it, your government surprises you and does something useful. The small–business arena is one of those areas where the government has made strides in doing something helpful. We cite the following examples:

>> **The Small Business Administration (SBA):** The SBA offers a wide variety of educational materials and seminars for both current and aspiring small-business owners. They also provide financial assistance through loans and loan-guarantee programs. In recent years, these programs have become significantly more user-friendly, and today the SBA is, in most cities anyway, an excellent resource for the capital-seeking small-business owner who has trouble finding funding through the conventional private-sector sources. For more information on SBA loans, see Chapter 5; for more information on how the SBA can be of assistance locally, go to www.sba.gov to find the field office near you.

>> **Service Corps of Retired Executives (SCORE):** A federally funded nonprofit, SCORE consists of more than 10,000 volunteers in hundreds of cities across the United States who provide free counseling and advice to prospective or existing small businesses.

SCORE, an excellent concept to be sure, can be a tad on the hit-or-miss side due to the fact that the majority of SCORE's volunteers are former employees of large companies. Thus, not all of them have known what it's like to own a small business. If you happen to be assigned to the right volunteer, however, SCORE can be the best deal in town — occasionally even providing you with a much-needed mentor. SCORE is definitely a service worth trying, especially given its cost to you, which is absolutely nothing — it's free! Visit its website at www.score.org to pose online questions to counselors or to contact the office nearest you (or call 800-634-0245).

>> **Small Business Development Centers (SBDCs):** There are hundreds of SBDCs in the United States, most of which are located on college and university campuses. The SBDC program is sponsored by the SBA in partnership with state and local governments and the educational community. Its mission is to provide business counseling, training, and various other educational resources to help both start-ups and existing small businesses.

Unlike SCORE, SBDC services are provided on a fee basis, and SBDC employees are usually educators (rather than volunteers like SCORE). Most have not owned a small business of their own. As a result, similar to SCORE, the services they offer can be hit or miss. For the SBDC center nearest you, visit www.sba.gov/sbdc.

>> **The SBA Answer Desk:** This free service of the SBA allows you to call 800-827-5722 to speak with a living, breathing SBA employee who will provide you with a thorough list of governmental resources and referrals, along with a smattering of advice. Your questions can be specific or general; ultimately, you'll be referred to a website, a SCORE or SBDC chapter, or an SBA publication.

>> **Your state's Department of Commerce and/or Economic Development Department:** Most Commerce or Economic Development Departments have small-business assistance centers, most of which are replicated on the web. These centers contain information on licensing and permit regulations and provide information packets on starting and running a business. Check your state government pages, use an Internet search engine, or call your state's Department of Commerce or Economic Development Department. (Some states include commerce under the Office of the Secretary of State.)

Chapter **4**

Finding the Right Business to Buy

After you make the decision to purchase a business, be realistic as you start your search for a worthy business to buy. Give yourself plenty of time to research potential candidates. After all, haste makes for lost money if you purchase a business without thinking through what you want and taking the proper steps to buy a quality business for a fair price.

Finding a good business can easily take a year or two. Even if you can afford to search full time, you can still expect to spend several months on the prowl. This chapter offers our suggestions for uncovering the best business to buy.

Defining Your Business-Buying Appetite

Many businesses are for sale (in other words, everything has its price). To conduct an efficient search, you need to set some preliminary criteria. Although you don't have to define every detail of the business you want to purchase, setting a few well-chosen parameters can help focus your search and keep you from spinning your wheels.

Although everyone has a different set of business-shopping criteria, you probably want to specify the following general issues:

>> **Type of business:** Businesses to buy come in four major categories:

- Retail (includes restaurants)
- Manufacturing
- Service
- Wholesale

Usually a good manufacturing business is the hardest to find, followed by service and wholesale businesses. Most communities have an adequate quantity of retail and restaurant businesses available to buy.

>> **Industry:** We highly recommend that you focus on specific niches in industries that interest you or that you know something about. Focusing helps you conduct a more thorough search and find high-quality companies. In addition to the industry knowledge you bring to the table, the knowledge you accumulate in your search can pay big dividends during your years of ownership.

TIP

If you have a hard time brainstorming about specific industries, here's a suggestion to jump-start your cerebral synapses. Take a walk through your local Yellow Pages. If you're older, you likely know that these used to be printed and distributed to people's homes. Now online Yellow Pages can be found through sites like https://www.therealyellowpages.com. Listed alphabetically are all the businesses known to exist in your area (many of the online sites allow you to download directories or browse and search them). Remember that a separate Yellow Pages directory exists for businesses that sell mainly to consumers, while a "business-to-business" phone directory lists businesses whose customers are primarily other businesses. Look at either or both, depending on the types of businesses in which you're interested.

You also may want to buy a business in a sector that's experiencing fast growth so that you, too, can ride the wave. Check out *Inc.* magazine's annual *Inc.* 500 list of the fastest growing smaller companies in America and their *Inc.* 5000 list of fast-growing private companies.

>> **Lifestyle:** The type of lifestyle you want your small business to provide can narrow your search significantly. If you're going into small business because you'd like to work from home, for example, then you obviously don't want to buy a business that depends on a nonresidential, bricks-and-mortar location. Also, consider how large an income you hope to generate, how many employees you want to manage, and whether or not you want to travel.

>> **Size/purchase price:** Unless you can cleverly craft a deal with a low down payment, the money you have to invest in a business constrains the size of business you can afford. As a rule, figure that you can afford to pay a purchase price of about three times the down payment amount you have earmarked for the business. For example, if you have $30,000 saved for the down payment, you should look at buying a business for $100,000 or less. Because many business sellers overprice their businesses, you can probably look at businesses listed at a price above $100,000 — perhaps even as high as $150,000 — because you can probably negotiate to buy such businesses for less.

>> **Location:** If you're rooted to a location already and don't want to move or have a long commute, the business's location further narrows the field. Although you may be willing to consider broader territory — maybe even nationally if you're willing to relocate — evaluating businesses long distance is difficult and expensive. Unless you're in the market for a highly specialized type of company, try to keep your search reasonably local.

>> **Opportunity to add value:** For most people, managing an ongoing business is enough of a challenge. As with real estate, most people are happier leaving the fixer-uppers to the contractors with experience in rehab, otherwise known as turnaround experts in the business world. However, some buyers want to purchase a business with problems that need fixing or with untapped opportunities. In fact, some businesses with correctable problems (weak or unproductive employees, inadequate systems and controls, or a shortage of cash, for instance) offer significant untapped potential and usually can be purchased at bargain prices.

After you define your shopping criteria, you're ready to go to the marketplace of businesses for sale. We recommend that you type your criteria on a single page so that you can email or hand it to others who can put you in touch with businesses for sale. (For ideas on whom to give it to, see the next section.)

Generating Leads

Break out your Sherlock Holmes cap and magnifying glass because finding a good business to buy is a lot more like doing detective work than shopping at the mall. Be prepared to turn over a lot of stones and follow a lot of tracks, many of which will lead to dead ends. But perseverance pays off, and the following sections cover some proven resources for generating leads in your search for the right business to buy.

Perusing publications

If you focus on specific industry sectors, you may be surprised to discover how many specialty newsletters and magazines are out there. Just think of the fun you can have reading publications like *Piano Technicians Journal* and *Diaper Delivery Service Business Guide!* Specialty publications and associated websites get you into the thick of an industry and also contain ads for businesses for sale or business brokers who work in the industry.

A useful reference publication that you can find in public libraries is the *Small Business Sourcebook* (Gale). This enormous reference contains listings of publications, trade associations, and other information sources by industry. Also peruse the classified ads in leading business publications, such as *The Wall Street Journal*, where owners wanting to sell small businesses can buy ads in the full-run or regional editions of the newspaper.

Conducting literature searches of general-interest business publications helps you identify articles that can keep you up-to-date on your industry of interest. You can use online computer searches to find the most useful articles.

Networking with advisors

Speak with accountants, attorneys, bankers, financial advisors, Chamber of Commerce employees, and business consultants who specialize in working with small businesses. These advisors sometimes are the first to find out about a small-business owner's desire to sell. Advisors can also suggest good businesses that aren't for sale but whose owners may consider selling in the future.

TIP

Make the effort to get to know and interact with these people personally. Set up a time for a phone call and/or an in-person meeting. Relationships and trust are built through live interactions, not texting and emails.

Knocking on doors

If you were a homeowner and someone came to your door and said they were interested in buying your home, you'd probably say that you're not interested in selling. If the interested buyer said they really liked the type of property you had and was willing to pay what you consider to be a good price, the person may get a little more of your attention, but you'd still likely turn them away. But if you, as the homeowner, were considering selling anyway, you'd be all ears — especially if you think you can sell directly and save paying a broker's selling commission.

Some business owners who haven't listed their businesses for sale are right now thinking about selling. So if you approach enough businesses that interest you, you may find some of these not-yet-on-the-market businesses. (Who knows, the business owner you approach may not be interested but may know another business owner who is.) The reason to go to this trouble is that you increase the possibility of finding the right business. You may also get a good deal on such a business. You can negotiate with the seller from the beneficial position of not having to compete with other potential buyers.

TIP

Instead of calling on the phone or knocking on the business's door, start by sending a concise letter of introduction that explains what kind of business you're seeking and what buyer qualifications you possess. This step demonstrates that you're investing some time in the endeavor. Follow up by phone a week or so after you send the letter.

Enlisting business brokers

Some sellers list their businesses for sale with business brokers (also known as *intermediaries*). Just as a real estate agent makes a living by selling real estate, business brokers earn their livelihood by selling businesses. Business brokers provide a number of services:

>> Establish a confidential selling process

>> Maintain an inventory of businesses for sale

>> Assist in determining a fair market value of a business

>> Work with potential buyers

>> Help clients negotiate and structure their offers

>> Assist through the close of the transaction

You'd hire a business broker for similar reasons that you'd hire a real estate broker:

>> **Technical expertise:** Business brokers understand the process. They also understand the pros and cons of most businesses because they've seen a number of similar

businesses throughout their career. The trick here is to find an experienced broker you can trust. When you've done that, the broker can take a lot of mystery out of the process and a lot of risk out of the purchase.

>> **Emotional noninvolvement:** The broker serves as a middleman between the buyer and seller. As everyone who has ever bought or sold a business knows, the process can get quite emotional.

>> **An ability to see the deal from both sides:** You can bet you and the seller will have differing points of view!

Of course, working with business brokers isn't problem-free. Here are some of the main issues you may face if you decide to go the broker route:

>> **Commission conflicts:** Brokers aren't business advisors; they're commissioned salespeople. That fact doesn't make them corrupt or dishonest, but it does mean that their interests aren't always in line with yours. Their incentive is to do a deal and do the deal soon — and the more you pay, the more they make. Business brokers typically get paid 8 to 10 percent of the sales price of the business. Technically, the seller pays this fee, but as with real estate brokers, the buyer effectively pays, too, because the seller builds the commission into the price.

If a broker isn't involved, the seller can sell for a lower price and still clear more money, which makes the buyer better off, too.

>> **Undesirable businesses:** Problem and marginal businesses are everywhere, but a fair number of them end up with brokers. The reason: The owners had trouble selling them on their own.

>> **Deceiving packaging:** This problem relates to the previous two potential pitfalls. Brokers help not-so-hot businesses look better than they really are. This typically involves stretching the truth — that is, omitting the negatives and hyping the positives. (Yes, owners selling their business themselves may do these things as well, but not as "effectively.")

WARNING

You (and your advisors) need to exercise due diligence on the business you're thinking of buying. Never, ever trust or use the selling package a broker (or an owner) prepares for a business as your sole source of information. Unscrupulous brokers, as well as unscrupulous sellers, can stretch the truth, lie, and commit fraud. (See Chapter 5 for more on how to evaluate a business.)

>> **Access to limited inventory:** Unlike a real estate broker who typically has access, through a shared listing service, to almost all the homes currently for sale in a particular area, a business broker can generally tell you only about his office's listings. Confidentiality is an issue because a shared listing service increases the number of people who can find out that a business is for sale and the particulars of the sale, which may hurt future business or cause a key employee exodus.

TIP

If you plan to work with a business broker, use more than one. Working with a larger business brokerage firm or one that specializes in listing the type of businesses you're looking for can maximize the number of possible prospects you see. In some areas, brokerages pool listings to allow access.

>> **Few licensing requirements:** Unlike real estate agents in most states, the federal government doesn't regulate the business brokerage field or require any official licensing. The majority of states don't have any requirements, either, so anyone can hang out a shingle and work as a business broker. Some states require real estate licenses of business brokers who operate in their states. After all, real estate transactions or leases are part of many business deals. Some states allow those with securities brokerage licenses to operate as business brokers.

REMEMBER

Business brokers generally sell smaller small businesses — those with less than $1 million in sales annually. These businesses tend to be family owned or sole proprietorships and include restaurants, dry cleaners, other retailers, service firms, and small manufacturers and wholesalers. Approximately half of such small businesses are sold through brokers.

Most business brokerage firms sell different types of businesses. Some firms, however, specialize in only one industry or a few industries. If you don't have your heart set on buying a particular type of business — a computer repair business, for example — one advantage of working with brokers is that they can expose you to other businesses you may not have considered. Brokers can also share their knowledge about some of your ideas — like the fact that, if you buy a computer repair business, you'll need to work on the weekends to fix your best customers' computers so that they're ready for Monday. Still want to buy one?

So how do you find potential business brokers? Ask tax, legal, and business consultants for good brokers they know. Also check out ads for businesses for sale; they may lead you to a broker. If you've found a broker you think you'd like to work with, check that the broker works full time in his profession and has solid experience. Some business brokers only dabble in the broker business part time and make their living other ways. These brokers may lack focus and experience.

TIP

When evaluating a potential broker, ask for the names of several buyers whom the broker has worked with in the past six months. Ask for buyers of businesses in your field of interest so that the broker can't simply refer you to the three best deals of his career. Then contact those buyers to see what they thought of the broker. Also, check with the local Better Business Bureau and any state regulatory department (for example, real estate, attorney general, or department of corporations) that oversees business brokers to see whether any complaints have been filed against the broker in question.

Considering a Franchise

Among the types of businesses that you can purchase are franchises. Some companies increase the number of their locations by selling replicas, or *franchises*, of their business. When you purchase a franchise, you buy the local rights within a specified geographic area to sell the company's products or services under the company's name and to use the company's system of operation. In addition to an upfront franchisee fee, franchisers typically charge an ongoing *royalty* (percentage of sales).

As a consumer, you've likely done business with franchises. Franchising is a huge part of the business world. Companies that franchise — such as Chick-fil-A, McDonald's, H&R Block, Subway, Hertz, and Supercuts — abound in many business categories. Purchasing a good franchise can be more expensive in upfront dollars but can also be a relatively safer ticket into the world of small-business ownership. In the next sections, we cover the pros and cons of buying a franchise.

Franchise advantages

Unlike when you buy other businesses, you don't buy an existing enterprise when you purchase a franchise. Although the parent company should have a track record and multiple locations with customers, you start from scratch when you purchase a new franchise (unless you purchase an existing franchise directly from its owners). As the proud owner of a new franchise, you don't have customers. Just as you'd have to do with any new business, you must recruit your customers.

So why would you want to pay a chunk of money to buy a business without getting any customers in the deal? Actually, you should consider purchasing a good franchise for the same reasons that you'd purchase any other solid, established business. A company that has been in business for a number of years and has successful franchisees proves that there's a demand for the company's products and services and that its system for providing those products and services works. The company has worked out the bugs, developed marketing programs that work, established a brand, and (you hope) solved common problems. As a franchise owner, you benefit from and share in the experience that the parent company has gained over the years.

Franchises offer two additional advantages that most other small businesses don't:

>> **A larger and successful franchise company has brand-name recognition.** In other words, consumers recognize the company name and may be more inclined to purchase

its products and services. Or stated another way, the franchiser has already done the marketing and public relations. When you purchase the franchise, you're buying into the fruits of those efforts.

>> **A franchise offers centralized purchasing advantages.** As you'd hope and expect from a corporation made up of so many locations, the franchisor can buy supplies and accessories at low prices. Such volume-purchasing generally leads to bigger discounts to customers and bigger profit margins to franchise holders. In addition to possibly saving franchisees money on supplies, the parent company can take the hassle out of figuring out where and how to purchase supplies.

Franchise disadvantages

Franchises aren't for everyone. As with purchasing any other small business, pitfalls abound in buying franchises. Some common problems that you need to watch for include the following:

>> **You may not be the franchise type.** When you buy a franchise, you buy into a system that the franchiser has created for you. People who like structure and established rules and systems more easily adapt to the franchise life. But if you're the creative and free-wheeling sort (that is, the typical entrepreneur) who likes to experiment and change things to keep life interesting, you'd probably be an unhappy franchisee.

Unlike starting your own business in which you may get into the game without investing a lot of time and money, buying a franchise business that ends up not being what you want can be a more expensive learning experience. For example, you may discover that you don't like being responsible for hiring, training, and evaluating entry-level employees running a restaurant franchise.

>> **You're required to buy overpriced supplies.** Centralized, bulk purchasing through the corporate headquarters is supposed to save franchisees time and money on supplies and other expenditures. Some franchisers, however,

attempt to make big profit margins by putting large markups on the proprietary items that they contractually obligate franchisees to buy from them.

>> **The franchise may be unproven.** One of the problems with buying a franchise is that you may not be buying an ongoing, established business complete with customers. If the concept has not stood the test of time and survived the experiences of other franchisees, you don't want to be a guinea pig as an early franchisee. Plus, some franchisers are more interested in simply selling franchises to collect the upfront franchise money. Reputable franchisers want to help their franchisees succeed so that they can collect an ongoing royalty from the franchisees' sales.

>> **The franchise may be a pyramid scheme.** Unscrupulous, short-term-focused business owners sometimes attempt to franchise their business and sell as many franchises as quickly as possible. Some even have their franchisees sell franchises and share the loot with them. Everything becomes focused on selling franchises rather than operating a business that sells a product or service intended to satisfy customers. In rare cases, franchisers engage in fraud and sell next to nothing, except the false hope of getting rich quick. (See the next section for more on these schemes.)

Evaluating Multilevel Marketing (MLM) Firms

A twist, and in many cases a bad one, to the franchising idea (see the preceding section) is a *multilevel marketing* (MLM) company. Multilevel marketing was designed to replace the retail store as a conduit for selling certain products. Advocates of the MLM business model maintain that, when given identical products, the one sold face to face (without the cost of maintaining a storefront and hiring employees and paying insurance) is less expensive than the same product sold in a store. Additionally, MLM advocates believe that buying a product from someone you know and trust makes more sense than buying from a clerk behind a retail counter or from a website.

Sometimes known as *network companies*, MLM companies can be thought of as a poor person's franchise. For those weary of traditional jobs, the appeal is obvious: Work part time from home, with no employees and no experience necessary and make big bucks. We've heard claims that you can make tens of thousands of dollars per month for just a few hours per week.

As a representative for an MLM company, you're treated as an independent contractor, and your job is to solicit new customers as well as to recruit new representatives. These new reps are known in the industry as your *down line.* The big selling point is that you make money not only off your own customers but also off the business that your down-line recruits bring in.

Being wary of pyramid schemes

The number one trait of MLM that leads to its all-too-frequent excesses is that everyone can get in for little money upfront; thus, everyone does get in. And we do mean everyone — hence, MLM's often shaky reputation.

WARNING

The problem is that the worst of the MLM companies are the equivalent of *pyramid schemes.* They fail to offer a proven service or product and exist solely to "sign up" as many reps as they can before someone realizes that the castle has been built on a cloud — at which point they take the money and run.

MLMs have been known to offer the pitch that you can make tens of thousands of dollars monthly while sitting on your duff and letting someone else do the work. All you have to do is sign up a few friends and relatives to sell the company's widgets. Then, before you can shout the words *easy money*, the big bucks come rolling in. We know many people who have been taken for thousands of dollars in MLM schemes; all they found was a quick way to lose money and to alienate friends and relatives.

REMEMBER

Anyone considering becoming an MLM investor needs to keep in mind that any network marketing arrangement is really just another form of a job. No company, MLM or otherwise, can offer to pay you money while you're busy watching Netflix. As with any other worthwhile venture, time — three to five years, in most cases — and a lot of hard work are required to create a business that will provide you with a decent living. If the MLM business were as simple as some in the business lead you to believe, everyone would dive in and get rich.

For sure, some legitimate, successful companies are MLMs — Mary Kay and Tupperware, for example. However, they're the exception rather than the rule, particularly among the types of MLMs that you're likely to have aggressively pitched to you by others.

Finding the better MLMs

Quality MLM companies make sense for people who really believe in and want to sell a particular product or service and don't want to or can't tie up a lot of money by buying a franchise or other business. Just remember to check out the MLM company and realize that you won't get rich in a hurry, or possibly ever. Capitalism has taught us over the years that whatever looks too good to be true usually is. Be sure to check the references of the MLM company that you're considering.

INVESTIGATE

Remember that due diligence requires digging for facts and talking to people who don't have a bias or reason to sell to you. Do the same homework that we recommend in Chapter 5 when you're thinking about buying into an MLM firm. Assume that an MLM company isn't worth pursuing until your due diligence proves otherwise.

Legitimate MLMs put as much emphasis, if not more, on the products or services they offer as they do on recruiting new reps, and they don't claim that you'll make a killing without working hard to find new customers. Although not shy about advertising the big earnings its successful salespeople make, Mary Kay doesn't hype the income potential. Local sales directors typically earn $50,000 to $100,000 per year, but this income comes after years, not weeks or months, of hard work. Mary Kay rewards its top sellers with gifts, such as the coveted pink Cadillac.

The ingredients for Mary Kay's success include competitive pricing, personal attention, and social interaction, which many stores don't or can't offer their customers. "We make shopping and life fun . . . we make people look and feel good," says one of

Mary Kay's sales directors. Mary Kay encourages prospective reps to try the products first and host a group before they sign up and spend approximately $100 to purchase a showcase of items to sell. To maximize sales, Mary Kay representatives are encouraged to keep a ready inventory because customers tend to buy more when products are immediately available. If reps want out of the business, they can sell the inventory back to the company at 90 cents on the dollar originally paid, a good sign that the company stands behind its product.

WARNING

If you do decide to buy into an MLM company that seems reputable, think twice before signing up relatives, friends, and coworkers in your MLM venture — at least until you're satisfied that the concept is a viable one. The particular danger in doing business with people you care about, and who care about you, is that, in addition to your reputation and integrity, your friendships and family relations are at risk.

Checking Out Work-from-Home Opportunities

Ads that promote ways to make piles of cash while working out of your home are easy to find these days, especially in the magazines that cater to small-business owners and wannabes and through email spam solicitations. They read something like this:

> "Earn $10,000 monthly! We'll even help you hire agents to do the work for you . . . FREE! Thirty days is all it takes!"

> "FIRE YOUR BOSS AND DOUBLE YOUR INCOME! Earn $2,000 to $5,000 weekly — starting within 3 to 6 weeks. Own your own business. Control your destiny! Work from home! No overhead; no employees; no commute! 55 to 70 percent ± profit margins."

> "Work out of your home. Company needs help. Earn $500 to $900 per week. Anyone can do this — will train. Full time or part time. Only for the serious — please!"

And so the refrain goes. In many cases, these ads are just another form of overhyped multilevel marketing scams and should be avoided. In these and other similar ads, no legitimate company may exist, but rather, you'll find a person or two with a post office or email box somewhere who wants to sell you a package of "confidential information" explaining the business opportunity du jour. This package of confidential information may cost you several hundred dollars or more. More often than not, this information ends up being worthless marketing propaganda and is rarely useful.

Our advice? Read this book and tap the other helpful resources we list in it to understand more about legitimate small-business opportunities. You'll find more and better information, and the price will be far lower.

WARNING

Remember one more thing about such money-making, can't-miss "opportunities": Never buy into one that's pitched over the telephone or that requires a nonrefundable cash outlay — unless, that is, you want to lighten your pocketbook and feel like a loser.

Myriad opportunities are available in today's fast-paced entrepreneurial economy. The best ones come from your studies into the local economic environment, from your discovery of a niche within your current job, or from your exhaustive research of the business community as a whole. Beware of those "opportunities" that promise overnight success. And beware of those "opportunities" that promise you something for nothing.

IN THIS CHAPTER

» Conducting a comprehensive
pre-offer evaluation of the company,
its owners, and its employees

» Investigating the company's
financial statements and lease
contract terms

» Considering the unique issues in
franchises

Chapter **5**

Evaluating a Business to Buy

Before you make an offer to buy a small business, do some digging into the company to minimize your chances of mistakenly buying a problematic business or overpaying for a good business. This investigative process is known as *due diligence*, and it's every bit as important as hiring an attorney or signing the purchase agreement.

Smart buyers build plenty of contingencies into a purchase offer for a small business, just as they do when buying a home or other real estate. If your financing doesn't come through or you find some dirty laundry in the business (and you're not buying a laundromat), contingencies allow you to legally back out of the deal. However, knowing that all your purchase offers will include plenty of contingencies shouldn't encourage you to make any purchase offer casually.

Making an offer and doing the necessary research are costly, in both time and money, but you'll be glad you did both after the deal is done and you can rest easy, knowing that you've purchased a good business. So before making an offer for any business, make sure that you investigate all the important issues that we discuss in the upcoming sections.

Examining Owners' and Key Employees' Backgrounds

A business is usually only as good or bad as the owners and key employees who run it. Ethical, business-savvy owners and key employees generally operate successful businesses worthy of buying. Unscrupulous, marginally competent, or incompetent business owners and key employees are indicative of businesses that you should avoid.

INVESTIGATE

Just as you wouldn't (we hope) hire employees without reviewing their resumes, interviewing them, and checking employment references, you shouldn't make an offer to buy a business until you do similar homework on the owners and key employees of the business for sale. Include in that homework the credibility of the CPA who signed off on the financial statements. Here's a short list of what to look for and how to find it:

>> **Business background:** Request and review the owners' and key employees' resumes. Are the backgrounds impressive and filled with relevant business experience? Just as you should do when hiring an employee, check resumes and LinkedIn profiles to make sure that the information they provide is accurate. Glaring omissions or inaccuracies send a strong negative message as to the kind of people you're dealing with.

>> **Personal reputations in the business community:** The geographic and professional communities to which most business owners and employees belong are quite small. Any business that has been up and running for a number of years has had interactions with many people and other companies.

Take the time to talk to others who may have had experience dealing with the business for sale (including vendors, the Chamber of Commerce, the Better Business Bureau, and so on) and ask them their thoughts on the company's owners and key employees. Of course, we shouldn't need to remind you that you can't always accept the statements of others at face value. You have to consider the merits, or lack thereof, of the source.

>> **Credit history:** If you were a banker, you certainly wouldn't lend money to people without first assessing their credit risk. At a minimum, you would review their credit history to see how successful they've been at paying off their loans on time. Even though you won't be lending money to the business seller you're dealing with, we recommend that you check their credit records. A problematic credit record may help you uncover business problems that the owner has had that they may be less than forthcoming in revealing. The major agencies that compile and sell personal credit histories and small-business information are Experian (www.experian.com), Equifax (www.equifax.com), TransUnion (www.transunion.com), and Dun & Bradstreet (www.dnb.com).

>> **Key customers:** In most cases, the people who can give you the best indication of the value of a business for sale are its current customers. Through your own research on the business or from the current owner, get a list of the company's top five to ten customers and ask them the following questions:

- In general, how is the company perceived by its customers?

- Does it deliver on time?

- How do its products or services compare to its competitors' offerings?

- Does it have a culture of integrity?

- What does the company do best?

- What does it need to improve?

>> **Key employees:** If the employees of the business for sale are aware of the prospects of the impending sale, be sure to interview them and get their insider's take on the condition of the business. Also try to find out whether they intend to remain as employees under the new ownership.

>> **Accounting firm:** Investigate the credibility and background of the accounting firm that generated the financial statements of the company you're considering buying. Interview the tax advisor who signed off on the financials, ask them specific questions about the balance sheet and profit and loss statement (P&L) to make sure it was that person who prepared them. Also ask them specific questions on line items on the financials that are key to you as a buyer. Additionally, if they're good and the synergy is right between the two of you, you might decide to continue the relationship.

Finding Out Why the Owner Is Selling

As part of your due diligence of a potentially attractive business, investigate why the owner is selling. Small-business owners may be selling for reasons that shouldn't matter to you (such as they've reached the age and financial status where they simply want to retire), or they may be selling for reasons that you need to think twice about (such as the business is a never-ending headache to run, it isn't very profitable, or competition is changing the competitive landscape).

Just because an owner wants to sell for some negative reason doesn't necessarily mean you shouldn't buy the business. If the business has a low level of profitability, it isn't necessarily a lemon; quite possibly the current owner hasn't taken the proper steps (such as cost management, effective marketing, and so on) to boost its profitability. You may well be able to overcome hurdles that the current owner can't. But before you make a purchase offer and then follow through on that offer, you absolutely, positively must scrutinize many aspects of the business, including, first and foremost, why the current owner wants out.

INVESTIGATE

Here's how to discover why the current owner is selling (where appropriate, get the current owner's permission to speak to certain people):

>> **Chat with the owner.** Okay, so this isn't a terribly creative, Sherlock Holmes–type method, and, yes, we know that many sellers aren't going to be completely candid about why they're selling, but you need to ask. You can verify the answer you get from the owner against what other sources (like the business's listing broker) tell you about the owner's motivations to sell.

>> **Talk to the business owner's advisors.** As we explain throughout this chapter, while evaluating the worth of a business, you should speak to various advisors, including those you hire yourself. Don't overlook, however, the wealth of information and background that the current owner's advisors have. These advisors may include lawyers, accountants, bankers, and/or the business's own board of advisors or directors. Sure, they may not be completely candid, but your job is to read between the lines of what they have to say.

>> **Confer with industry sources.** Most industries are closely knit groups of companies, each one knowing, in general, what's going on with the other businesses in the same industry. Most importantly, the vendor salespeople or manufacturers' representatives who sell products or services to the industry can be a useful source for information. Just remember to take what anyone says with a grain or two of salt.

>> **Seek out customers.** The business's current customers usually have a good idea of why a business is for sale. They can provide you with the information you need to determine whether the current owner is selling from strength or from weakness.

>> **Discuss with employees.** Some employees probably know the real answer as to why the business is for sale. Your job: Find out what they know.

REMEMBER

In your discussions with and investigations about the current owner, also reflect upon these final, critical questions: How important is the current owner to the success of the business? What will happen when they are no longer around? Will the business under new management lose key employees, key customers, and so on?

KNOWING HOW TO TELL WHETHER A SELLER IS MOTIVATED

Imagine that you're in the market to buy a home. While touring houses for sale in a neighborhood you'd like to live in, you discover two houses — one on Elm Street and the other on Oak Street — that meet your want list of criteria. Both houses have the right amount of space and good-sized yards and are located on quiet streets. In all other respects, the two houses are similar, and your analysis of comparable house sales in the neighborhood indicates that each house is worth about $240,000.

The Elm Street house is priced at $299,000, and the Oak Street house is priced at $249,000. The owner of the Oak Street house has already had the house inspected, has provided a copy of the inspection report, and has offered to correct the problematic items in the report at their cost. You also notice that the Oak Street house has been cleaned up both inside and out and looks ready to move into.

Now, assuming that you like both houses equally well, which house would you be more interested in making an offer on? It should be no contest. Clearly, the Oak Street house owner is more motivated and serious about selling. You can tell this not only from the more realistic asking price but also from all the time, effort, and money the owner has put into getting the house ready to sell.

So when you're shopping for a small business to buy, look for similar ways to identify a motivated seller. Just as with real estate, a significant portion of small-business sellers aren't serious or motivated about selling. And just as with some house sellers who don't need to sell, some small-business owners stick a high price on their business and are willing to sell only if some salivating pushover comes along and is willing to (over)pay.

Other small-business owners aren't emotionally ready to part with their "babies." If you follow our advice in this chapter and in Chapter 6, you won't be anyone's fool because you'll know how to value a business for sale and how to identify whether the owner is motivated to sell.

Surveying the Company Culture

Buying a small business is similar to adopting someone else's child. Depending on the strength of its already-formed personality and the degree to which it meshes with yours, you may or may not be successful in molding that business into your image.

Thus, another important element of your due diligence is to find out what kind of culture the business has. How, for example, are employees viewed and treated in the company? In meetings, are subordinates allowed (or even encouraged) to challenge the thinking of their supervisors?

TRUE STORY

Larry was an MBA from one of the nation's top business schools. He thought he could make a bundle of money by buying a small manufacturing company and running it better than its current owners. Given his blue-chip credentials, he thought running the company would be a snap. So Larry purchased the company with a 35 percent down payment of the purchase price, with the seller carrying a note for the balance.

Larry's first task was to clean house of the "deadwood," terminating key employees so that he could replace them with people who would better measure up to his high standards. Larry made his downsizing decisions after just a couple of weeks on the job. He didn't seem to know (or perhaps didn't care) that the company had a history and culture of respect for its employees. Even during slow economic times, previous management hadn't let people go but instead had scaled back hours of operation.

Not surprisingly, after nearly 20 percent of the staff was gone, Larry had earned himself the reputation as the "grim reaper" because many of Larry's new hires couldn't do the jobs as well as the previous job holders who had been fired. The original staff that remained, not surprisingly, feared for their jobs; thought Larry was callous, incompetent, and uncaring; and worried about the future of the company. Many of the best remaining employees had updated their resumes and were actively seeking employment elsewhere to escape Larry's new negative culture. Gradually, most of the good employees who had survived Larry's initial firings quit as the company went into a financial tailspin. Eventually, Larry himself had to move on.

What's the point of this story? What should Larry have done differently?

>> **Before buying the company, Larry should've taken the time to understand the company's culture.** Changing employees may not be impossible in the company you buy, but attempting to change the culture, especially in such a short period of time, is a too-often-perilous endeavor. Cultures are a sensitive business asset and should be treated accordingly. Larry should've spent more time assessing and considering the company's culture both before he bought the business and after he completed the purchase.

>> **Larry should've known that preconceived notions rarely withstand the scrutiny of day-to-day operations.** Buying and running a company isn't as easy as people like Larry may think. An MBA from a top business school and specific work experience don't come close to guaranteeing success when buying and managing a business. Larry should have maintained the company as it had been run until he studied and learned its real strengths and weaknesses, knew the business well enough to recognize the skills of the employees, and could formulate an informed plan to move the company forward.

Deciding on Terms

There's a saying in the business brokerage world that goes "you name the price, I'll name the terms." Which means . . . there's a lot more to buying a business than the purchase price. Included in this list are the following negotiable items:

>> **Cash:** Most sellers want an all-cash deal so they have certainty of getting all their money from the sale of their business. Most buyers don't want to pay all cash, often because they can't afford to do so or want some security in the event that they uncover hidden problems in the business.

- **Promissory note:** Most buyers would like the seller to extend them a loan for a portion of the purchase price of the business. This is negotiable, as well as the duration of the note and the interest rate.

- **Purchase price allocation:** Buyers would like one accounting allocation, sellers another. The decision they reach is important; it impacts the taxes the seller and buyer will pay. You'll need the help of a small business experienced tax advisor to make sure you're getting the allocation that works best for you.

- **Earnout:** Earnout is a provision whereby part of the purchase price is held back based on the future performance of the business. Buyers prefer an earnout clause, sellers don't.

Here's an example of why "terms" are so important. Suppose you pay $450,000 for a business that you think is only worth $400,000, a $50,000 difference. However, you negotiate a 15-year loan from the seller at 1 percent interest. Assuming even a modest rate of future annual inflation, your terms have made up for that $50,000, and possibly more.

Inspecting the Financial Statements

Reviewing the financial statements — including the balance sheet and the profit and loss statement — of the business for sale is a hugely important part of your due diligence.

The following sections explain what to look for and what to watch out for in the profit and loss statement and balance sheet. If you're unfamiliar with those statements, you're at a huge disadvantage in evaluating businesses for sale.

Interpreting the profit and loss statement

A company's *profit and loss statement*, or *P&L* (also known as the *income statement*), details its profits (or lack thereof), which are simply revenues minus expenses. Revenues are the money that the company receives from its customers as payment for its products or services. Expenses are the company's costs of doing business. Just as much of your personal income or revenue goes toward income taxes, housing, food, and clothing, company expenses exhaust much and sometimes all of a company's revenue.

In Figure 5-1, we offer a sample P&L to help you understand how they are constructed and used to manage a business effectively.

Big Spenders Corp.
Profit and Loss Statement
For the year ending December 31, 2011

	Prior Year	Budget	Current Year	Percent Change Compared to Prior Year
Sales (revenues)	$450,000	$475,000	$500,000	11%
– Cost of goods sold	$200,000	$210,000	$225,000	12.5%
= Gross margin	$250,000	$265,000	$275,000	10%
Expenses				
Wages and salaries	$75,000	$77,000	$97,000	29%
Rent	$50,000	$52,000	$54,000	8%
Selling expenses	$55,000	$58,000	$61,000	11%
Telephone	$10,000	$11,000	$11,000	10%
Utilities	$10,000	$11,000	$11,000	10%
Total expenses	$200,000	$209,000	$234,000	17%
Net income (pretax)	$50,000	$56,000	$41,000	(18%)

FIGURE 5-1: A sample four-column profit and loss statement.

Deciphering important information from a P&L (formatted like the one in Figure 5-1) is easy:

>> Go to the net income figure under the Current Year column — the P&L number that every small-business

owner is most interested in. Using the percentage in the next column, you can quickly determine how profitable Big Spenders Corporation has been this year compared to the previous year. (Profits are down by 18 percent.)

>> A quick glance at the top row of the statement reveals that the profitability decrease isn't due to falling sales, which are up by 11 percent, nor is it due to a declining gross margin, which is up by 10 percent. Because sales and gross margin are both positive, you can assume that the problem must be related to expenses.

>> Moving down the expense items, you see that wages and salaries are up by 29 percent. This means that, although sales have increased by 11 percent and the gross margin is up by 10 percent, the whopping increase in wages and salaries has caused the problem. A quick comparison to the wages and salaries budget reveals that the 29 percent increase wasn't budgeted; therefore, whatever has happened wasn't planned for. You can then delve into your wages and salaries account to determine what caused the problem.

TECHNICAL STUFF

Some companies may include an additional three columns on the P&L. These three columns represent the percentage of the total for the Prior Year, Budget, and Current Year categories. For example, using the sales total as 100 percent, every figure in each column would represent a percentage of that total. Thus, continuing with the Big Spenders Corporation example from Figure 5-1, the percentage of the total for the Current Year column would reveal a gross margin to sales of 55 percent ($275,000 divided by $500,000), wages and salaries to sales of 19 percent ($97,000 divided by $500,000), and net income to sales of 8.2 percent ($41,000 divided by $500,000). The only disadvantage of adding these three columns is that it clutters up the P&L and makes it more difficult to read.

When considering buying a business, take the time to examine the following issues on the company's profit and loss statement:

>> **The owner's salary and bonuses:** Of utmost importance when computing the profitability of any business is the determination of how much money the current owner is (or has been) taking out of it. The profitability of the

business may look large at first glance, but the owner may be getting paid little in order to fatten the bottom line. Or the owner may be getting paid an excessive salary and bonuses, minimizing the business's apparent profitability in the process. (In most cases, the owner will be quick to tell you about their penchant to take excessive salary and bonuses and reluctant to reveal if they have been underpaid.)

>> **Change in revenues over time:** Examine at least the last three years of profit and loss statements. Do you see a steady or increasing rate of growth in a company's revenues? If a company's revenues are growing slowly or shrinking, you have to ask the important question, "Why?" Is it because of poor service or product performance, better competitor offerings, ineffective marketing, or an owner who is financially set and unmotivated to grow the business? Before you buy is the time to find out the answer to this question.

>> **Revenues by product line:** For companies with multiple divisions or product lines, ask for the revenue details of each product line. Find out what's spurring, or holding back, the company's overall growth. One red flag is if the business has acquired other businesses that don't really fit with the company's other business units. Some larger small companies that are struggling to build revenues sometimes try to "enter" new businesses through acquisition but then don't manage them well because they don't understand the keys to success in those businesses.

>> **Revenues by individual stores:** With retail stores, such as a picture-framing enterprise that has multiple locations, examine the revenues on a store-by-store basis. If the business has been opening new sites, also determine the change in revenues from opening new locations versus the change at existing locations. A company can show overall revenue growth by simply adding new stores while the existing locations may actually be experiencing declining revenues.

>> **Expense details:** To help you identify which expense categories are growing and which ones are shrinking over time, take a look at the expense categories for the past three years and calculate what percentage of the

company's revenue each category makes up. As a well-managed and financially healthy company grows, expenses as a percentage of revenues should decrease. Not all expense categories necessarily decrease. Research and development, for example, may be expanding in a company awash in revenues and seeking to create and offer new products and services.

» **Assets:** Go down the asset list on the balance sheet, making sure that those that you're buying are what the balance sheet says they are. Key assets include accounts receivable (if you're buying them), inventory (is what you're buying salable?), and condition of the equipment (make sure the equipment is in good working condition). For more on this subject, see the upcoming section, "Reviewing the balance sheet."

» **The bottom line:** The net result of revenues that increase faster than expenses is a fatter *bottom line* (the last line of the profit and loss statement that indicates net profits or losses after taxes). When you examine how a company's profits change relative to total revenue received, focus on *operating income*, which is the net income from operations before one-time write-ups or write-downs. (Sometimes companies experience one-time, revenue-enhancing or revenue-reducing events that can change profits temporarily.)

Even healthy, growing businesses can get into trouble if their expenses balloon faster than their revenues. Well-managed companies stay on top of their expenses during good and bad times. Don't be fooled into thinking that all is well financially just because a company's revenues have been increasing. It's easier for companies to get sloppy during good times.

» **Other expenses:** Thoroughly examine other expense items — such as automobile expenses and travel and entertainment — for insight as to how the business has spent its money in the past. You may unearth some excessive, unnecessary expenses that, if you're successful in cutting, can immediately improve your bottom line.

A term you may come across when you're dealing with attorneys, accountants, business brokers, or sophisticated buyers is *EBITDA*. EBITDA is an acronym that stands for Earnings Before Interest, Taxes, Depreciation, and Amortization. Many business sales are made based on a multiple of EBITDA earnings rather than net income. Be aware of which of the two methods you'll be using in determining the value of the business.

AUDITED AND UNAUDITED FINANCIAL STATEMENTS

In your initial evaluation of a potential business to purchase, you'll receive (at your request) the company's financial statements. Some business owners will be reluctant to release too much financial data, usually due to concerns about confidentiality or because they may not be convinced that you're a serious buyer.

You may be asked to sign what's called a *nondisclosure agreement* (NDA), which legally binds you to keep confidential any information that the company shares. NDAs are fine as long as signing one doesn't tie your hands from evaluating similar businesses for sale, including those that compete with the one under consideration. Don't sign an NDA without your attorney's consent.

If the financial statements you receive haven't been independently audited by a reputable accounting firm, be extremely cautious in assuming accuracy and honesty in the statements. On the other hand, don't take financial statements at face value simply because they've been audited. The accountant who did the audit could be incompetent or unethical (too friendly with the seller).

A surefire way to uncover inflated profitability as reported on the financial statements that the current business owner shares with you is to ask the seller for a copy of the business's income tax returns. Owners are more likely to try to minimize reported revenue and maximize expenses on their tax return to keep from paying more tax. (***Warning:*** If you discover that the business owner has overtly tried to cheat the government, chances are they may try the same thing on you.)

For those businesses that are sold as a multiple of EBITDA, this is where the major negotiations take place. Most small businesses sell for a multiple of somewhere between 2 and 5. The higher the multiple, the better such factors are as trend, quality of assets, quality of customers, and quality of key employees. The seller obviously wants a higher multiple, the buyer a small one.

Reviewing the balance sheet

A *balance sheet* is a snapshot-in-time summary of a company's assets and liabilities. This financial report is typically prepared as of the last day of the company's fiscal year-end, which for most companies is December 31. (Some companies have a fiscal year that ends at a different time of the year.)

REMEMBER

The P&L is designed to analyze profitability issues: sales, margins, and expenses. The purpose of the balance sheet, on the other hand, is to analyze an entirely different issue: resource (dollar) allocation. Did you decide to allocate your dollars to increasing inventory, or to paying off loans, or to accumulating cash? The small-business owner makes many asset-allocation decisions over the course of their career; the balance sheet provides a year-end snapshot that summarizes the history of those decisions.

In Figure 5-2, we provide a sample balance sheet to help you understand how this important financial statement works.

TIP

We've prepared the balance sheet in Figure 5-2 in the same four-column format that we use in the P&L (refer to Figure 5-1). This format is designed to simplify the comparison of the prior year, budget, and current year figures. Although we suggest that you consider this format when preparing your own balance sheet, we should note that most businesses don't budget their balance sheets but still operate successfully.

In the example in Figure 5-2, Big Spenders Corporation completed the current year with an increase in net worth of $34,000 ($125,000 to $159,000) over the prior year. By comparing the Current Year column on the balance sheet with the Prior Year column, you can readily determine what has happened to the mixture of assets and liabilities over the year — in other words, how Big Spenders Corporation's management decided to allocate the company's resources, especially cash.

Big Spenders Corp.
Balance Sheet
For the year ending December 31, 2011

Assets	Prior Year	Budget	Current Year	Percent Change Compared to Prior Year
Current assets				
Cash	$25,000	$35,000	$5,000	(80%)
Accounts receivable	$50,000	$55,000	$55,000	10%
Inventory	$50,000	$55,000	$85,000	70%
Total current assets	$125,000	$145,000	$145,000	16%
Fixed assets				
Land, buildings	$100,000	$95,000	$95,000	(5%)
Furniture, fixtures	$50,000	$47,000	$47,000	(6%)
Equipment	$50,000	$47,000	$47,000	(6%)
Total fixed assets	$200,000	$189,000	$189,000	(5.5%)
Total assets	$325,000	$334,000	$334,000	4.9%
Liabilities				
Current liabilities				
Accounts payable	$75,000	$69,000	$80,000	6.7%
Short-term notes payable	$10,000	$10,000	$10,000	-
Total current liabilities	$85,000	$79,000	$90,000	6%
Long-term liabilities				
Mortgages payable	$70,000	$65,000	$65,000	(7%)
Long-term notes payable	$45,000	$0	$20,000	(55%)
Total long-term liabilities	$115,000	$65,000	$85,000	(26%)
Total liabilities	$200,000	$144,000	$175,000	(12.5%)
Owners' equity (net worth)	$125,000	$190,000	$159,000	27%
Total liabilities & net worth	$325,000	$334,000	$334,000	4.9%

FIGURE 5-2:
A sample balance sheet.

To give you another example of how easy it is to glean information from this four-column balance sheet format, look at the Percent Change Compared to Prior Year column. Note that although the total current assets didn't change appreciably, two of the categories within the Current Assets category — cash and inventory — did. The cash account, as of December 31, is only $5,000, while inventory has ballooned to $85,000. Sometime during the current year, a larger inventory has built up, depleting the company's cash reserves in the process.

An examination of the Budget column confirms the fact that this inventory accumulation was unplanned and unbudgeted. (Incidentally, this is a perfect example of how a company can be profitable and still get into financial trouble.) As evidenced by the balance sheet, Big Spenders Corporation currently has $90,000 in short-term liabilities but only $5,000 available in cash. As a result, despite being profitable, Big Spenders is in a classic cash crunch.

The only other percentage on this sample balance sheet that should attract immediate attention is the 55 percent decrease in long-term notes payable. Sometime during the year, management decided to pay off a portion of its long-term debt — a decision that, in light of the company's present cash shortage, they would now probably like to reverse.

REMEMBER

The *assets* section of the balance sheet summarizes what the company holds or owns that is of significant value. The *liabilities* section details what the company owes to others. Here are several key line items to look for when reviewing a company's balance sheet:

>> **Accounts receivable:** Also known as *receivables,* this line item is money that's owed to a company for products or services already sold but not yet paid for. As companies grow, so, too, do their receivables (unless the business deals only in cash, in which case the business shouldn't have any receivables at all). Be on the lookout, however, for accounts receivable that are growing at a faster rate than the company's revenues (in other words, receivables that are becoming a larger portion or percentage of the company's revenues). Bloated receivables may indicate that the company is having problems with the quality of its product or pricing. Dissatisfied customers pay more slowly and/or haggle for bigger discounts. Out-of-proportion receivables may also indicate that the company's customers are having financial problems of their own. Be sure to ask for the business's *accounts receivable aging* — a listing of the monies owed to the company accompanied by the length of time the bills have gone uncollected.

WARNING

Throw a red flag if the business doesn't maintain an aging of receivables — unless all its customers are paid to date.

>> **Property and equipment:** All companies require equipment, such as office furniture, computers, and so on, otherwise known as *fixed assets*. Manufacturing companies also own machinery for making their products. Equipment becomes less valuable as it becomes more obsolete over time. This depreciation of fixed assets is charged against profits by the company as a cost of doing business each year. Thus, even if a company ceases buying new equipment, its balance sheet will continue to show fixed asset charges — not for purchases but for depreciation of the value of property and equipment. As depreciation is subtracted from the value of the equipment, the amount shown for fixed assets on the balance sheet will gradually decrease.

TIP

If a company hasn't been periodically upgrading its equipment, you can get stuck buying a company that needs a lot of costly new equipment. When a company's balance sheet indicates a continual decline in the bookkeeping value of the company's equipment, beware that the company may simply be deferring new equipment purchases. Inspect the company's equipment and talk with others who are familiar with the type of business so that you can understand how outdated the equipment really is and how much you're likely to have to expend on replacement equipment if you buy the business.

>> **Inventory:** The balance sheets of manufacturing and retail companies should detail *inventory*, which is simply the cost of the products that have not yet been sold. As a business expands over time, inventory should follow suit. However, beware if you see inventory increasing faster than revenues because it may signal several problems, including customers who are scaling back on purchases, poor management, or an obsolete or inferior collection of goods. Inventory is the most dangerous asset of all because a swollen inventory often represents cash that can't be redeemed.

>> **Accounts payable:** When companies purchase supplies, equipment, or products for resale for their business, they generally have a period of time (typically 30 days) to pay the bills. Similar to inventory and accounts receivable, *accounts payable* (which appear on the liability side of a

company's balance sheet) usually increase with a company's increasing revenues. Accounts payable that are growing faster than revenues may or may not indicate financial trouble. The increase may simply be good financial management (the slower a company is with paying bills, the longer the funds can be drawing interest in corporate accounts). On the other hand, if the company is struggling to make ends meet, an accumulation of accounts payable can occur and can be an early warning sign of financial trouble.

>> **Debt:** *Debt,* both short term and long term, is money that the company has borrowed and must someday pay back. Footnotes to the financial statements (assuming they're audited) generally detail the terms of the debt, such as when the debt is to be paid back. In the next section, we explain important ratios and calculations you can use to help you size up the amount and type of debt a company is carrying. If the financials you're working with haven't been audited, be sure to either ask for a thorough explanation of the debt or, better yet, leave the debt out of the purchase. The vast majority of buyers don't want to assume the seller's debt; unless there are extenuating circumstances, you shouldn't want the debt either.

>> **Other assets:** This catchall category is for the other assets of the company and can include stuff that will make your eyes glaze over. For example, companies keep a different set of books for tax purposes (yes, doing so is legal). Not surprisingly, companies do this because the IRS allows, in some cases, more deductions than what the company is required to show from an accounting standpoint on its financial statements. (If you were a company, wouldn't you want your shareholders, but not the IRS, to see more profits?) The benefit of deferring taxes is treated as an asset until the IRS gets more of its share down the road.

Even if you're competent in reading financial statements, never purchase a business without involving a good tax advisor to help you evaluate the value of the business and the financial terms of the transaction. Buying a business isn't the time to rely on your own trial and error; be sure to involve someone in the buying process who can bring their financial/tax expertise to the table.

WHAT ARE THE "OFF-BALANCE-SHEET" ASSETS WORTH?

The value of a company's assets includes not only tangible items, such as inventory, accounts receivable, furniture, fixtures, and equipment, but also soft assets, such as the firm's name and reputation with customers and suppliers, customer lists, patents, and so on. These soft assets are also known, in accounting jargon, as *goodwill.* In many cases, the value of this goodwill is greater than the value of the hard assets.

If you're seriously interested in making an offer to buy a particular business, take time to investigate the worth of the company's good-will. As part of your investigation, be sure to assess whether the current customers of the business will continue buying from the business after you take it over and to evaluate the quality of the key employees. And don't forget to look into the business's relationships with suppliers — are they good or bad? In addition, check out the competition — does it seem formidable?

Ask key employees these questions:

- What do you like the most about your company? What do you like the least?

- How do you see the future of the company?

- Can the products or services be improved?

- What would be the first improvement you'd make if you owned the business?

Ask suppliers these questions:

- Does the company pay its bills on time?

- Do you get an inordinate amount of returns from them?

- Compared to other companies in the industry, how does the company treat its suppliers — as partners or as a necessary evil?

- If you could change one thing about the company, what would it be?

Some final points about goodwill: Companies work hard to attract and retain customers through advertising, product development, and service. Companies can't put an exact value on the goodwill they've generated, but when they purchase (acquire) another firm, some of the purchase price is considered goodwill. Specifically, if a company is acquired for $100 million yet has a net worth (assets minus liabilities) of just $50 million, the extra $50 million is considered to be goodwill. This goodwill then becomes an asset on the balance sheet, which, similar to equipment, is amortized (depreciated) over the years ahead. (Goodwill is amortized over ten years.)

Understanding key ratios and percentages

Before you can take the numbers generated by the P&L and balance sheet and turn them into meaningful management tools, you need to consider two overall points about the numbers, ratios, and percentages that come from those financial statements:

>> **Comparisons work best.** Your company may have what appears to be a respectable percentage of net profit on its sales, but if that percentage is less than it was during the same period the preceding year, trouble may lie ahead. Numbers are most effective when you can use them to identify trends — and identifying trends always requires a comparison of numbers over time.

>> **The industry matters.** Acceptable numbers in one industry may not be acceptable in another. Industries vary widely in the numbers they generate. For example, if you're in the software business, you may be disappointed with a 15 percent profit return on your sales dollar (we explain what that means in the next section). If you're in the grocery store business, however, you'd probably be ecstatic with a 5 percent profit return on sales.

If you don't know the acceptable ratios and percentages in your industry, contact your appropriate trade association. Most trade associations can give you the benchmark ratios and percentages that you need to know to compare your own business to industry averages. Check out the *Small Business Sourcebook* (www.gale.com) to find a list of the trade associations applicable to your profession or search for them online.

TIP

We strongly suggest that you learn how to extract the key ratios and percentages from your financial statements by yourself instead of depending on your bookkeeper or tax advisor to do so. The process itself gives you a better idea of where the numbers come from and how you can use the financial statements for other ratios and percentages that may be meaningful to your individual business. Although any ratio or percentage alone won't give you all the information you need to become a sophisticated financial manager, the knowledge of how they all work together will make you much more effective as an owner/manager.

In the following sections, we explain the most common percentages and ratios that a small-business owner should understand.

Return on sales (ROS)

Return on sales (ROS) is a percentage determined by dividing net pretax income (from the P&L) by total sales (also from the P&L). The resulting figure measures your company's overall efficiency in converting a sales dollar into a profit dollar. ROS very much depends on what type of business you operate.

REMEMBER

ROS is an excellent figure on which you and your employees can focus. It's relatively easy to track, understand, and explain. Some businesses use this percentage as a company-wide scorecard to help their employees understand how the businesses make money, thus motivating them to do their part in assuring and improving profitability. (Most employees think their businesses make much, much more money than they really do.)

Return on equity (ROE)

Return on equity (ROE) is a percentage determined by dividing pretax profits (from the P&L) by equity/net worth (from the balance sheet). The resulting figure represents the return you've made on the equity dollars that are effectively invested in your business.

Over several years, if your return on equity isn't higher than 5 percent or thereabouts (which is the average return on money invested in such secure investments as short-term, high-quality bonds), you may want to consider selling your business and investing the proceeds in bonds. Your return would be similar, but your risk, the work involved, and the stress would be much less.

This assumes, of course, that you're in business to make money. If, however, you're motivated by something else — creativity, growth, independence — or if you simply like owning your own business, you may be content with miniscule earnings, even though you can make a similar or better financial return elsewhere.

Note: Both ROS and ROE are impacted heavily by the amount of money the owner decides to take out of the business in the form of salaries, bonuses, and benefits. Obviously, the more taken out, the lower the ROS and ROE percentages will be.

Gross margin

Gross margin is a percentage determined by subtracting your cost of goods sold (from the P&L) from total sales (also from the P&L). This figure represents your business's effective overall markup on products sold before deducting your manufacturing and/or service-providing expenses.

How high or low your gross margin is depends on your industry, your business, your pricing strategy, and the products or services you're selling. The trade association for your industry can give you industry-wide benchmark numbers for gross margin.

REMEMBER

Trend is especially important with gross margin. Over time, you want to see an increasing rather than decreasing gross margin.

Current ratio

Current ratio is a ratio determined by dividing current assets (from the balance sheet) by current liabilities (also from the balance sheet). The resulting figure measures your business's *liquidity* (in other words the ability to raise immediate cash from the sale of your assets); thus, this ratio is of great interest, especially to your lenders and/or outside investors.

The higher the current ratio, the more liquid your business. Generally, current ratios in excess of 2 to 1 are considered very healthy; anything less than 1 to 1 is in the danger zone. Again, trend is especially important here. Over time, you want to see an increasing rather than decreasing current ratio.

Debt-to-equity ratio

The *debt-to-equity ratio* is a ratio determined by dividing equity/net worth (from the balance sheet) by debt/total liabilities (also from the balance sheet). The resulting ratio indicates, in effect, how much of the business is owned by the owners (represented by equity/net worth) and how much is owned by its creditors (represented by debt/total liabilities).

Generally, a 1-to-1 ratio is considered healthy; anything less is questionable. To further illustrate this point, refer to the Big Spenders Corporation balance sheet in Figure 14-2. Note that Big Spenders owes its creditors and debtors $175,000 (its total liabilities), while the company's net worth is $159,000 (the owners' equity). This means that as of the date that this balance sheet was assembled, Big Spenders Corporation's creditors and debtors had $16,000 more working for the company than the owners did (the difference between $175,000 and $159,000); therefore, its debt-to-equity ratio exceeds 1.0 or 100 percent. If the owners needed another loan to make ends meet, they'd have a hard time showing that their financial stake in the company justified another loan.

REMEMBER

Keeping the debt-to-equity ratio within the healthy 1-to-1 parameter is of paramount importance. For example, when the debt-to-equity ratio exceeds 1.0 or 100 percent, such cash-draining options as adding inventory, hiring new employees, and buying new equipment should be put on hold until the ratio becomes more lender friendly.

Inventory turn

Inventory turn is the number of times your inventory turns over in a year. You determine the number by dividing your total cost of goods sold for the year (from the P&L) by your average inventory (beginning inventory ± ending inventory ÷ 2). For example, if your beginning inventory (on January 1) was $100,000 and your ending inventory (on December 31) was $150,000, your average inventory would be $125,000. Your inventory turn measures how well you're managing your inventory. The higher the number, the more times your inventory has turned, which is always preferable.

The number of times your inventory turns is highly dependent on your industry (manufacturer, wholesaler, or retailer) and your role in it. Typical inventory turns can range anywhere from 5 to 20 times a year (see the next section "Managing Your Inventory" for details). Consult your trade association for inventory turn ratios that apply to your industry.

Number of days in receivables

You determine the *number of days in receivables* — that is, the average length of time between selling a product or service and getting paid for it — by first computing your average sales day. Divide your total sales for the period (from the P&L) by the number of days in that period (for a year, use 365). Then divide your average sales day into your current accounts receivable balance (from the balance sheet). The resulting figure gives you the number of days in your receivables.

Generally speaking, fewer than 30 days in receivables is considered excellent, between 30 and 45 days is acceptable, and more than 45 is cause for concern. (See the later section "Collecting Your Accounts Receivable" for more advice on this topic.)

EBITDA

EBITDA is an acronym that stands for Earnings Before Interest, Taxes, Depreciation, and Amortization. EBITDA is computed by deducting interest, taxes, depreciation, and amortization from net income. Those four expenses are non-operating expenses, so after removing them from net income you have a number that represents the pure operating results of your business. The EBITDA number is usually used in transactions that relate to buying and selling a business — in other words, valuing a business.

Uncovering Lease Contract Terms

A soon-to-expire lease at a low rate can ruin a business's future profit margins. With a retail location, the ability to maintain a good location is critical as well.

INVESTIGATE

Check comparables — that is, what similar locations lease for — to see whether the current lease rate is fair and talk to the building owner to discover his plans. Ask for and review (possibly with the help of a legal advisor) the current owner's lease contract. Pay extra-careful attention to the provisions of lease contracts that discuss what happens if the business is sold or its ownership changes.

Evaluating Special Franchise Issues

As we discuss in Chapter 4, buying a reputable franchise can be the right ticket into the small-business world. However, no matter what type of franchise you're buying, you need to do plenty of homework before you agree to buy. The following sections describe the unique steps you need to take when evaluating a franchise.

WARNING

You may be tempted to cut corners when reviewing a franchise from a long-established company. Don't. You may not be a good fit for the specific franchise, or perhaps the "successful" company has been good at keeping its franchisee problems under wraps.

Thoroughly review regulatory filings

INVESTIGATE

The Federal Trade Commission (FTC) requires all franchisers to issue what's called the *Uniform Franchise Offering Circular* (UFOC) at least ten days before a prospective franchise buyer writes a check or signs a document to purchase. We recommend that you ask for this valuable document well before that deadline if you're seriously interested in a particular franchise.

Don't be put off by the size of the UFOC. It contains the following valuable information, so be sure to read it cover to cover:

>> The names and addresses of the ten geographically closest franchises to the one you may buy, as well as a list of franchises that were terminated, not renewed, or bought back by the company.

Speaking with franchisees for whom things didn't work out (such as, franchises that were terminated or not renewed) may help you uncover aspects of the business that are turnoffs for you. Now isn't the time to stick your head in the sand about possible problems or drawbacks of a given franchise. After all, finding out about those downsides now is better than finding out about them after you've plunked down a chunk of your money, borrowed even more, and gone through a lot of work to buy a franchise.

>> Disclosure of pending or settled litigation, as well as a detailing of potential or actual troubles between franchisers and franchisees.

>> The employment background of the senior management of the franchiser.

>> The costs to the franchisee of purchasing a franchise, as well as required inventory, leases, and other costs.

Evaluate the franchiser's motives

A good franchising company will want to check you out as much as you should want to check it out. Successful franchisers don't want to sell a franchise to someone who is likely to crash and burn and tarnish the reputation they've worked so hard to build. These companies know that their interests are aligned with yours — they make more money from ongoing royalties if they sell franchises to solid franchisees who are determined to be successful. At the outset of your investigation, ask yourself whether the franchisers are looking for a long-term business partner or simply the fast sale of another franchise.

TIP

Closely observe how the franchising company interacts with you. Be wary if the franchiser seems more interested in selling franchises than in finding and helping the most qualified franchisees succeed. Obviously, franchising representatives will be generally enthusiastic about their company. But a fine line exists between enthusiasm and a hard sell.

Run in the opposite direction if a franchiser tells tales of great riches from just a small investment of your time and money. Run extra fast if the franchiser is pressuring you into making a quick decision to buy and is evasive about providing detailed information about the business. And if the franchiser doesn't want to give you the UFOC (see the preceding section), sprint!

Interview plenty of franchisees

INVESTIGATE

Interview as many of the company's franchisees as is practical — both current owners as well as those who quit or were terminated. Skip the list of references that the franchise company eagerly provided and go to the lists of franchisees provided in the UFOC (see the earlier section "Thoroughly review regulatory filings"). Ask the franchisees what their experiences, both good and bad, have been with the parent company. Those franchisees for whom things didn't work out are generally more forthcoming about the warts of the system, but don't take everything they say at face value. Try to identify whether some of these people were poor fits.

Conversely, active franchisees are more likely to see things through rose-colored glasses, perhaps for no other reason than to reassure themselves about their decision to buy the franchise. If active franchisees are dissatisfied, steer clear. Observe which franchisees are happiest and most successful and see whether you share their business perspectives and traits.

Understand what you're buying and examine comparables

Most reputable franchises require you to plop down a chunk of cash to get started. Home-office-based service businesses may charge a $25,000 upfront franchise fee, compared to the several hundred thousand to one million dollars required for the bricks-and-mortar locations of established franchisers, such as McDonald's. Additionally, ongoing franchise royalties can range from 3 to 10 percent of gross revenue. The UFOC should detail all the upfront costs (see the earlier section "Thoroughly review regulatory filings" for details on the UFOC).

INVESTIGATE

As you evaluate the costs involved in buying a franchise, ask yourself the following questions: What are you receiving for these payments? Are the system and brand name really worth this fee? What kind of training will you receive? What kind of assistance does corporate management provide? What programs are in place to foster communications with other franchisees?

Few franchises are unique. Compare the cost of what a franchise is offering to the cost of purchasing franchises from different companies in the same business. For example, if you're considering the purchase of a franchise from Wendy's, compare the terms and offerings to those of McDonald's and Burger King.

If you look at the "best" franchises in a particular industry and think, "Hey, I can do this as well or better and at less cost on my own," remember that you don't *have* to buy a franchise. Consider the start-up alternative. Be realistic, though, because many hidden costs — both out-of-pocket financial costs and costs in the form of time and energy — are involved in starting a business from scratch (see Part 1). And the franchise has a head start in name recognition and customer base.

Check with federal and state regulators

INVESTIGATE

Franchises are generally regulated at both the federal and state levels. The FTC regulates nationally (see https://www.ftc.gov/business-guidance/resources/consumers-guide-buying-franchise; 877-382-4357), and the state-level regulatory agency is usually called something like the Department of Corporations or the Attorney General's Office. Check with these regulators to see whether complaints about a franchiser are on file.

The UFOC should detail pending litigation against the franchising company by disgruntled franchisees (see the section "Thoroughly review regulatory filings" for details on the UFOC). For lesser-known franchises, you may also want to check with the Better Business Bureau in the city where the franchising company is headquartered to discover whether anything negative is on file.

Investigate the company's credit history

Just as you have a personal credit report on file, every business has a credit report that shows how the company has dealt with payments and debts owed to suppliers and creditors. The franchiser's credit report is a good indicator of how well it maintains its business relationships and how financially stable it is. Where the franchiser is publicly owned, obtain a copy of the company's annual report and Form 10-K. Examine the company's stock price over recent years.

Analyze and negotiate the franchise contract

If your digging has made you feel more, rather than less, comfortable with the franchise purchase, you need to get down to the nitty-gritty of the contract to move forward. Franchise contracts are usually long, tedious, and filled with legalese. Read the contract completely to get a sense of what you're getting yourself into. Also be sure to have an attorney who's experienced with franchising agreements review the contract.

In addition to the financial terms, the franchise contract should specify how disputes are to be handled, what rights you have to sell the franchise in the future, and under what conditions the parent company can terminate the franchise. Make sure that you can live with and be happy with the nonfinancial, as well as the financial, terms in the contract.

REMEMBER

Almost everything is negotiable, especially when you're dealing with a lesser-known franchiser that's in the early stages of its business growth. Although some of the more successful franchisers offer their best deal upfront and refuse to negotiate, others don't initially put their best terms and conditions on the table, hoping that you'll simply sign and accept the inferior terms and conditions.

The saying that "you name the price, I'll name the terms" applies here as well. The devil is in the details, be sure the details of the deal are negotiated in your favor.

3

Negotiating Terms and Sealing the Deal

IN THIS PART . . .

Perform due diligence to get a handle on a business's worth.

Uncover bank and nonbank sources to finance your deal.

Prepare a purchase offer with contingencies and price allocations.

Chapter **6**

Figuring Out How Much the Business is Worth

When you begin exploring businesses for sale, you don't know exactly what a given business is worth and you risk overpaying for that business if you jump into a deal too soon. However, with time and the right resources, combined with a little upfront due diligence, you can get a good handle on a particular business's worth, which may or may not align with the owner's asking price. (For more on the search process, see Chapter 4.)

TIP

You can start by taking a cue from smart home buyers and real estate investors: To find out how much a property is really worth, consider *comparable sales* — that is, the amounts that similar properties have sold for. Compared to business buyers, however, home buyers have it relatively easy. Real estate transactions are a matter of public record; small-business sales generally aren't. So you have to do some extra sleuthing to find the specific price and terms of comparable businesses that have sold.

In the end, however, after you've done the math and developed a dollar value for the business, remember one thing: Similar to buying a house, the real worth of a business is what you, or someone else, will pay for it. A business isn't a car with a factory sticker price; it's a multidimensional, complicated organization of people, assets, and systems. Its true value is in the eyes of the beholder, and the beholder is you.

The following sections walk you through the process of valuing a business. You won't have to go through every step (especially if you hire a business broker or attorney to manage the process for you), but each one is a viable option to consider.

Exploring Valuation Methods: Multiple of Earnings and Book Value

Many methods exist for valuing a business. Some are unnecessarily complicated; others won't provide you with sensible answers. For example, some advisors and business brokers advocate using a multiple of revenue to determine the value of a business — that is, if a business has $300,000 in revenues, it may be valued at $450,000 (a multiple of 1.5 times revenue).

However, revenue is a poor proxy for profitability. Two businesses in the same field can have identical revenue yet quite different profitability due to the efficiency of their operations, the pricing of their products and services, and the types of customers they attract. Also, the multiple of revenue that a business may be worth varies depending on what industry the business is in. For example, the multiple for a manufacturing business is typically higher than the multiple for a retail establishment or a restaurant.

Other measures are more exact. Here are our preferred valuation measures for small businesses:

>> **Multiple of earnings:** When you compare the sales data for comparable companies to the sales data for the one you're interested in buying, determine what multiple of earnings or EBITDA (earnings before interest, taxes, depreciation and amortization; for a detailed explanation of EBITDA, see Chapter 5) these businesses sold for. Divide the price the business sold for by its annual pre-tax earnings (profits) to arrive at the *multiple of earnings* or EBITDA (also known as the *price-earnings ratio*) of that transaction.

When the multiple is low, say 3 to 1 (for example, if the business had earnings of $50,000 and thus a selling price of $150,000), the buyer and seller don't have great expectations for the business's future earnings. However, when the multiple is high, say 12 to 1 (if the business had earnings of $50,000 and a selling price of $600,000), the buyer's and seller's expectations of future earnings are correspondingly high.

REMEMBER

Future earnings are what will provide the return on the buyer's investment; therefore, the higher the buyer expects those potential earnings to be, the more they are willing to pay for the business. (In general, a business should be able to pay for itself in three to five years. If the time period is any longer than that, you're probably paying too much for the company.)

Small, privately held businesses typically sell for lower multiples of earnings or EBITDA than larger companies in the same line of business. The reason: Small companies are less established and are riskier from an investing standpoint. Plus, your investment in their stock will be *illiquid* (that is, even in good times, the stock generally can't be converted into cash within a reasonable period of time).

>> **Book value:** In addition to looking at the sales price of other businesses relative to earnings, you can consider the value of a company's assets. The *book value* of a company is the company's assets minus its liabilities, which is the same as the net worth of the business as stated on its balance sheet. (We're assuming here that the values for

the assets and liabilities on the balance sheet are accurate; see Chapter 5 for more on balance sheets.) The figures that go into determining book value should be checked carefully to ensure that the underlying asset values and liability accounts are correct.

Of these two approaches, each of which has advantages as well as imperfections, the multiple-of-earnings approach is generally considered to be far superior to the book-value method. After all, what you're purchasing when you buy a business isn't primarily its assets but rather those assets' ability to generate profits (earnings). Some businesses, such as consulting firms, have little in the way of tangible assets — the personnel may be the firm's greatest asset, and valuing that is difficult. Because the determination of a price-earnings multiple figure is based on an income-generating formula, it's generally a better indicator than the book-value approach, which simply measures the difference between assets and liabilities.

REMEMBER

Keep in mind that the figure you come up with when using the multiple-of-earnings approach represents the goodwill portion of the business only and doesn't include the value of the business's assets. (*Goodwill* is, in essence, an estimated number that represents the value of the business's reputation and existing customer list.) Thus, you have to add the value of the assets to the goodwill number. The assets involved in a typical small-business purchase include accounts receivable (make sure that they're all collectable); inventory (make sure that what you're buying is merchantable); and equipment, furniture, and fixtures (the fair market value thereof).

Getting a Professional Appraisal

Business appraisers make a living out of estimating the value of businesses. If you want to buy a business and your initial investigation suggests that the seller is committed and serious about selling the business, consider hiring an appraiser. Although the fees professional appraisers charge varies depending on the size and complexity of the prospective business, you can usually expect to pay somewhere north of $10,000 for the typical small business.

TIP

Tax advisors, lawyers, and business consultants who specialize in working with small businesses may be able to refer you to a good business appraiser if they can't do the appraisal them-selves. The National Association of Certified Valuators and Analysts (http://www.nacva.com; 800 677-2009) can provide you with a list of association members in your area. Also, check the business-to-business Yellow Pages in your area under "Appraisers — Business."

Tracking Businesses You've Explored That Have Sold

If your search for a business to buy lasts months or perhaps years, keep track of similar businesses you've considered that eventually sell. These sales provide valuable comparables because you've seen the businesses up close and have obtained details about their financial position that give you perspective in assessing the sales.

TIP

Obtaining the final selling price of a small business can be chal-lenging. You can try asking the ex-owner, or you can speak with advisors or business brokers who are involved in such deals. For details on working with advisors, see the next section; for details on brokers, see the later section in this chapter "Enlisting the Services of a Business Broker."

Tapping the Knowledge of Advisors Who Work with Similar Companies

Business consultants, attorneys, and tax advisors you work with can assist you with pinning down sales data for companies com-parable to the one you're considering buying. The key is to find advisors who have knowledge of, and experience with, both small businesses in general and businesses similar to the one you're thinking of buying.

TIP

If you end up buying a small business, you'll benefit from having competent advisors on your team who have worked on comparable deals. But before you hire an advisor for tax, legal, or business advice, be sure to check references. Also ask the advisor for a comprehensive list of business deals (including the purchase or sale price and the industry) that they have been involved in over the past year.

Don't be deterred by the cost of such advisors, especially tax advisors and attorneys. The terms you agree to in the purchase of a business will be with you for a long, long time.

Consulting Research Firms and Publications

Finding the details on similar companies that have sold can be difficult. Wouldn't it be helpful if a service compiled such information for you? Well, you'll be happy to know that some companies do publish comparable sales information or conduct company searches for a fee.

One such company, BIZCOMPS, releases an annual publication that provides sales price, revenue, and other financial details for businesses sold. This compendium of sales information is available for different major regions and industries in the United States (Western, Eastern, Industrial, and Food Service). Visit www.bizcomps.com or call 702-454-0072 for a sample of this publication. The company also offers online access to business sales data through an annual membership fee.

Turning to Trade Publications

Trade publications can help you find out more about a particular industry, including articles on how to value companies within that industry. Most publications are willing to send you past articles on a topic, typically for a small fee. Or you may be able to access articles from the publication's website. Of course, you shouldn't take any such information as gospel, but you can use it to further your knowledge and inform the questions you ask of advisors you're working with to buy a business.

Enlisting the Services of a Business Broker

If you're already working with a *business broker* (a salesperson who lists small businesses for sale and who works with buyers as well) or looking at a business listed for sale through a business broker, the broker should be able to provide a comparable market analysis of similar businesses that the broker's office has sold.

WARNING

Don't put too much weight on a business broker's analysis. Unfortunately, a broker's "analysis" may be less analytic and more sales oriented than you want. After all, business brokers earn commissions based on a percentage of the selling price of the business that you may buy through them. (The commissions generally range from 6 to 10 percent, depending on the size and complexity of the deal.) Also, understand that business brokers generally have access to sales data only on the small number of similar businesses that their particular office has sold. Unlike real estate agents, business brokers who work for different brokerage firms in a given community don't share their sales data with one another.

REMEMBER

Before enlisting the services of a broker, be sure to check their references carefully — especially given the fact that business brokers are in a virtually unregulated industry that requires no specific credentials or educational training to enter. Be sure to involve your own attorney when the closing comes around. Having your own attorney takes the broker's bias out of the equation and helps ensure that what you get is best for you. You can generally depend on your attorney, assuming they work for a reputable firm, to represent your best interests; the same cannot be said about your business broker.

IN THIS CHAPTER

» Seeking financing from banks and
nonbanks

» Borrowing from sellers

» Paying by yourself (and maybe some
help from your friends and other
sources)

Chapter **7**

Financing Your Deal

When you buy a business, you can finance the deal yourself from your personal savings and investments or you can use outside capital from a bank or nonbank source. Some sources of capital loan you money (banks, Small Business Administration, and others); others invest their money for an equity stake in your business (family and friends, some angel investors, and the like). Many business buyers even borrow money from the sellers. All these options are described in the sections that follow.

Outsourcing Financing

Generally speaking, you'll have far more opportunity for outside financing when you're buying an established business versus when you're launching a start-up. This is because most capital providers are looking for either significant collateral and operating history (as is the case with banks and the SBA) or a business in an industry with good opportunities for return on investment (as is the case with equity investors). Angel investors are the most versatile of the outsourcing resources, but they're also the most difficult to find.

Taking advantage of seller financing

Seller financing is quite common in small-business purchases; in fact, about 90 percent of all small-business sales include some seller financing. Yes, occasionally partial financing for a business purchase can come from traditional lending sources (banks, relatives, friends, angel investors, and so on), but the seller is always your number one opportunity. Think about it: If your seller still has "skin in the game," they're that much more motivated for you to succeed, which means they'll be that much more likely to help you through the transition period.

Banking on banks

Contrary to the popular opinion that bankers enjoy turning down prospective borrowers, bankers are in business to lend money. Effects of the Great Recession may have impacted this perception, but banks are still lending, albeit with credit standards that are bit tighter, and actively looking for small-business deals to make.

Every time bankers sit down in front of a prospective borrower, they should hope that what they're about to see is a deal that will work. After all, no loans mean no lending income for the bank, and no lending income means no marble columns in the lobby — and without marble columns in the lobby, what would hold up their gold-inlaid ceilings? Make no mistake about it, banks are in business to lend money and make profits, which banks do by *playing the spread* — charging you more to use their money than they're paying somebody else (namely, depositors) to get it.

A bank's primary role in the small-business lending arena is funding growth — for example, financing the expansion of a small business that already has a track record. Most banks can offer a wide variety of creative loan packages designed to help finance existing small businesses. These loans include the following financing possibilities:

» **Asset-based financing:** The situation whereby a lender accepts the assets of a company as collateral in exchange for a loan. Most asset-based loans are collateralized against either *accounts receivable* (money owed by customers for products or services sold but not yet paid for), inventory, or equipment. Accounts receivable are the favorite of the three because they can be converted into cash more quickly (theoretically within 30 days, if you're offering these terms). Banks advance funds only on a percentage of receivables or inventory, the typical percentages being 75 percent of receivables and 50 percent, or less, of inventory.

For example, using these percentages, if your business has $30,000 in receivables due from customers and $50,000 in inventory, the bank may loan you 75 percent of $30,000 (which equals $22,500) and 50 percent of $50,000 (which equals $25,000). The total of the two ($47,500) would then be available for you to use as working capital. These percentages vary based on the industry and the quality of the receivables and inventory.

The form of asset-based lending in which the borrower's inventory is used as collateral for the loan is called *floor planning.* Car dealerships and RV dealers, for example, often use floor planning as their primary financing tool.

» **Line of credit:** The situation whereby the bank sets aside designated funds for the business to draw against the ebb and flow of cash as needs dictate. As line-of-credit funds are used, the credit line is reduced; conversely, when payments are made, the line is replenished.

An advantage of line-of-credit financing is that no interest is accrued unless the funds are actually used. Surprisingly enough, the best time to arrange for your business's line of credit is when your business is doing well and you need the money the least. Why? Because that's when getting approval from the banker for the line of credit is easiest and you can qualify for the best loan terms.

TIP

Don't make the mistake of overlooking a line of credit just because you don't presently need money. (Remember, a line of credit typically doesn't cost you if you don't draw against it.) Establish your credit line when things are going well. Sooner or later, if you're like most small businesses, you'll need the cash. (Ironically, funding the growth of a business, as opposed to its decline, is the situation that most often requires using a line of credit.)

>> **Letter of credit:** A guarantee from the bank that a specific obligation of the business will be honored. Letters of credit are most often used to buy products sight unseen from overseas vendors. The bank generates its income in these situations by charging fees for making the guarantee.

Getting money from nonbanks

Banks don't have a lock on the small-business lending market. Most nonbank lenders find their niche by specializing in a specific category of loan, such as leasing or asset-based financing. As a matter of fact, leasing companies (where you can lease your business's equipment or furniture and fixtures) are the most common nonbank financing resource; 25 percent of small businesses have some sort of leasing financing. *Leasing*, in case you've never done it, is basically the same as renting; you pay a monthly fee for the use of an item, and at the end of the lease term, you return the item to the company that leased it to you.

We explain some other important nonbank resources that small businesses can utilize in the following sections.

The Small Business Administration (SBA)

An *SBA loan* is a loan made by a local lender (bank or nonbank) that is, in turn, guaranteed by the SBA. The SBA provides its backup guarantee as an inducement for banks to make loans that otherwise may be too risky from a banker's perspective. Only in rare cases does the SBA actually provide the money itself.

SBA loans usually provide longer repayment terms and lower down-payment requirements than conventional bank loans. They're available to most for-profit small businesses that don't exceed the SBA's parameters on size (which can vary depending on the industry). SBA loans can be used for a number of reasons, including (in rare cases) start-up monies if, as with all SBA loans, you have sufficient collateral in long-term tangible assets, such as real estate, machinery, and equipment.

Getting an SBA loan isn't a sure thing; to the contrary, the agency is extremely selective about whom it approves. Consider the primary criteria the SBA looks for when considering guaranteeing a loan:

>> The owner must have invested at least 30 percent of the required capital and be willing to guarantee the balance of the loan.

>> The owner must be active in the management of the business.

>> All principals must have a clean credit history.

>> The business must be able to project adequate cash flow to pay off the loan, and the debt/net-worth ratio must fall within the SBA's approved guidelines.

TIP

To find a local bank or nonbank institution that works with the SBA, look in the Yellow Pages for SBA Approved Lending Sources (ALS) or call the SBA at 800-827-5722. On the web, go to www.sba.gov for more information about the SBA loans that may work for you.

TIP

For an inventory of the funding that the SBA makes, go to https://www.sba.gov/funding-programs, where you'll find search tools for Loans, Investment Capital, and Grants, among other categories.

Small Business Investment Companies (SBICs)

Small Business Investment Companies (SBICs) are privately owned, quasi-venture capital firms organized under the auspices of the SBA. SBICs either lend money to, or invest money in, small businesses primarily within their local area. Categorized as *Federal Licensees* (meaning that the federal government has given them its stamp of approval), SBICs either fund start-ups or provide operating funds to existing businesses that want to expand. Through their relationship with the SBA, SBICs are also able to offer particularly favorable terms and conditions to *disadvantaged businesses* (businesses owned by women and minorities).

Hundreds of SBICs operate around the country. To find out more about them, go to www.businessloans.com, call the SBA at 800-827-5722, or contact a nearby Small Business Development Center (SBDC; see Chapter 3 for the lowdown on SBDCs).

Certified Development Companies (CDCs)

Another program of the SBA, the *Certified Development Company (CDC) program* (also known as the *504 Loan Program*), provides long-term (10- and 20-year), fixed-rate loans for small businesses. This program focuses on financing fixed assets, such as real estate (land and buildings). CDCs work with a local lender; typical financing may include 50 percent from the local lender, 40 percent from the CDC, and 10 percent down from the small business being helped. The asset being purchased serves as the collateral.

Several hundred CDCs exist nationwide. To find the CDC nearest you, go to https://cdcloans.com.

Your state's Economic Development Department

Many states have an Economic Development Department (sometimes a stand-alone governmental agency; oftentimes housed within the state's Department of Commerce) that offers a variety of loan programs to statewide businesses. The programs offered are usually modeled after SBA loans but can often offer better terms and conditions than the SBA, especially for those businesses that employ many local employees.

TIP

Such state agencies also generally offer *microloan programs* that are designed to assist small-business start-ups by giving super-small businesses the opportunity to borrow money (less than $25,000) to get started. Since banks don't fund start-ups and don't like such small loans, these microloan programs are often the only available resource. Visit your state's Economic Development Department website for more information.

Angels: Investors with heart

Angel investors (often called *angels*, for short) are individuals — usually ex-entrepreneurs who are experienced enough to understand and live with the financial risks they take — with money available to lend or invest. The angels' motives may vary: Most seek to increase their net worth, some want to help aspiring entrepreneurs, and some simply crave being a part of the action.

Angels come in many forms: Some fly in flocks (that is, belong to angel organizations or investment groups), some work solo, some look for a piece of the company's ownership (equity), and others prefer lending (debt). Almost all angels demand personal involvement in your business, however, and in many cases, the know-how and potential contacts and introductions an angel can bring to the table is worth more than the capital itself.

Angels are like the highway patrol: When you need them the most, they're the most difficult to find. Fortunately, movements are afoot to make the identity of angels more accessible. For example, most large cities now have angel associations, which you can find through your favorite search engine. You can also ask your local bankers, accountants, financial advisors, or lawyers for their input on how to find a local angel-matching program. Or you can call your local Chamber of Commerce or your state's Department of Commerce.

Venture capital

Venture capital firms and their offshoot organizations offer cash in exchange for equity in start-up companies, so they are, in effect, an organized version of angel investing. As opposed to more conservative sources of capital, which look closely at a business's past performance and its collateral before handing out cash, venture capital firms focus primarily on future prospects when looking at a business plan. Thus, venture capital is useful for a few sophisticated businesses in higher-risk, higher-reward industries. Venture capital firms look for the possibility of hefty annual returns (30 percent or more) on their investments in order to offset the losses that are sure to occur within their high-risk portfolios.

REMEMBER

Few small-business start-ups are in a position to take advantage of venture capital financing. The typical venture capital firm funds only 2 percent of the deals it sees, and that 2 percent has to meet a wide range of investment criteria, such as highly attractive niches, sophisticated management, and potential for high return — criteria that the typical small-business start-up can't begin to meet. Don't be disappointed at not qualifying for venture capital funding. As this chapter details, many other, more appropriate financing resources with more attractive terms exist.

Crowdfunding

Crowdfunding is defined as the practice of funding a project or venture by raising small amounts of money from many people, typically via the Internet. There are many different forms of crowdfunding; however, typically investors do not get equity in your business, nor are you legally required to pay the money back. The crowdfunding medium is evolving and changing; if your product or service is right, there may be a crowdfunding platform that works for you. For a list of the top crowdfunding companies, check out www.crowdfunding.com.

If you plan to open such businesses as a restaurant, contracting business, or retail gift store, crowdfunding is probably not for you. Typical crowdfunding "investors" seek creative, innovative and yes, "sexy" projects, in such fields as music, technology, and consumer products. Some of the most popular crowdfunding platforms are Kickstarter, GoFundMe, Indiegogo, and Fundly.

Minority funding resources

The resources for low-income and minority funding (which in many cases includes women-owned businesses) are many. Look to the following for starters:

>> The National Bankers Association (NBA) in Washington, D.C., represents minority-owned banks that target loans to minority-owned businesses. For the nearest member bank in your area, visit www.nationalbankers.org or call 202-588-5432.

>> Most states have an agency that provides one-stop assistance on financial services for small businesses. Check your local library or search online for such an agency in your state and then ask about state-operated minority funding resources.

>> On the federal level, the SBA can help direct you to local organizations that can, in turn, help locate low-income and minority funding opportunities. Check out the SBA website at www.sba.gov or call 800-827-5722 to find the resource nearest you.

>> The U.S. Department of Commerce's Minority Business Development Agency funds Business Development Centers nationwide; one of their functions is to help minority-owned start-up businesses. Visit www.mbda.gov for more information and details.

Financing Yourself: Bootstrapping

When it comes to starting a business, financing that (largely) on your own is known as *bootstrapping*. When you think about it, the fact that bootstrapping is so pervasive and works so well for business start-ups makes sense. First, what better way to instill discipline and make things work efficiently than to have a limited supply of funds? Second, because you care deeply about risking your own money or that of family and friends, you have a powerful incentive to work hard and smart at making your business succeed. Buying a business, however, usually requires more capital than starting a business from the ground up, but "bootstrapping" a business acquisition can be done.

REMEMBER

Don't be afraid of applying for a loan. Getting a bank loan or other financing approved is much easier when you're working with an established business. Be careful, though, about risking losing your home or other assets as collateral if your business doesn't work out.

These are some of the most common places to find bootstrapping capital:

>> **Savings, investments, and salable assets:** This is always the first place to look. Theoretically, all you're doing here is transferring your assets from one investment (your savings account) to another (your new business). Okay, so you're

increasing your risk by a quantum leap, but you're also increasing your opportunity for reward.

>> **The family and friends' network:** Be sure to make your relationship loans as official as possible; always create a promissory note complete with a fixed interest rate (at least 1 percent over prime to avoid IRS scrutiny) and include cast-in-stone payback terms. Consult a lawyer when larger loans (in excess of $10,000) are required.

>> **Life insurance:** If you own life-insurance policies with a cash value, consider cashing in such policies and putting that money to far better use — your business. Besides, term life insurance is a far better deal. Remember, however, that you may owe some income tax on accumulated interest (in excess of the premiums you paid) from your life-insurance policy.

Ask yourself whether you really need life insurance at all. If you have no financial dependents, you won't need it to replace your income if you pass away. If you do need life insurance, however, secure good term life coverage before you cancel or cash in your current policy. Otherwise, your dependents will be in trouble if you pass away after you've canceled your current policy but before you've secured new coverage.

>> **Credit cards:** Credit cards provide expensive money, perhaps, but easy money as well. No personal guarantees and no bankers looking over your shoulder; just sign your name and get on with the business at hand. Given the highly competitive credit-card market, be sure to shop around instead of simply accumulating a balance on whatever platinum-hued card you currently have in your wallet or heard about in an ad. When you carry a balance from month to month, always make your credit-card payments on time unless you enjoy paying even higher interest rates — upwards of 20 percent in many cases.

WARNING

>> **Home equity:** Proceed with extreme care when borrowing against home equity. A misstep can cost you the roof over your family's head. Remember that home prices can go down and you may find yourself in a situation where you're unable to refinance and are stuck with a larger, riskier mortgage. Don't even consider this option until you've thoroughly reviewed your overall personal financial situation (see Chapter 1 for details on how to do so).

Chapter **8**

Preparing a Purchase Offer

Once you've honed in on a desirable business and done some analysis and consultation of experts to determine its approximate value (see Chapter 6), and figured your financing options (see Chapter 7), the next step is to put together a purchase offer. If you've bought a house or other real estate before or attempted to make such a purchase, then you're pretty familiar with many of the elements we're going to discuss in this chapter.

Buying a business is generally much more complicated and involved than buying a home, so the process typically starts with an expression of interest and general parameters (Indication of Interest) followed by the outlines and more details of an offer in a Letter of Intent. In addition to explaining these in detail in this chapter, we also discuss the typical contingencies your offer should include and what due diligence you should perform before closing on your deal.

Writing a Letter of Intent or an Indication of Interest (IOI)

Usually many months into the process of looking around at a number of businesses in particular industries, you may well find one that you think is "the one." Before you make an actual offer on a legal purchase contract, you will probably go through an exploratory process that many before you have used.

You will likely put something in writing that expresses your sincere interest in possibly buying the business in question. There are two generally accepted ways to do that — an Indication of Interest and a Letter of Intent. We discuss each of these in turn.

Drafting an Indication of Interest (IOI)

An Indication of Interest (IOI), usually memorialized in a written letter, of an expression of interest to buy a particular company that may or may not be formally listed for sale. Here are the key elements of an IOI:

>> It's non-binding, meaning that your expression of interest in buying the company does not obligate you to go through with a purchase. You're simply expressing a high level of interest in possibly buying the company in question.

>> It requests additional information about the business so that you can learn more about it and help further your decision to possibly purchase it.

>> The possible purchase price, if stated, is typically provided as a range. This makes sense because you need additional information in order to offer a more specific purchase price.

>> It begins the process of due diligence and may specify what initial due diligence you'd like to perform to further your decision making about possibly buying the business.

An IOI isn't mandatory and quite often is not used. Instead a prospective buyer writes a Letter of Intent, which we discuss next.

Writing a Letter of Intent (LOI)

A Letter of Intent (LOI) shows a more serious level of interest and commitment to explore buying a potential business. Here are the key elements of an LOI:

» It's non-binding with some binding elements. Overall an LOI does not obligate or force you to buy a business. There are some elements of an LOI that are binding, which are explained in the subsequent bullet points.

» Includes more specific details compared to an IOI such as a proposed price, requested seller financing, exclusivity period (during which the seller may not entertain other offers), and a proposed purchase closing date.

» Details requested due diligence, break-up fees or penalties, and confidentiality requirements.

TIP

You can view and download a sample LOI from https://esign. com/letter-of-intent/business-purchase.

Developing Purchase Offer Contingencies

When you make an offer to buy a home, you generally make your purchase offer contingent upon (dependent on) obtaining mortgage loan approval, satisfactory inspections, and proof that the property seller holds a clear title to the home. When you make an offer to buy a business, you should similarly make your purchase contingent upon important issues, including the following:

» **Inspections and due diligence:** Your purchase offer for a business should be contingent upon a thorough review of the company's financial statements and interviews of key

employees, customers, and suppliers (this overall evaluation is called *due diligence*). You should be allowed to
employ whomever you like to help you with your evaluation. The typical period of time allowed for due diligence is
30 to 60 days, more if the business is large. (For how-to
advice, see the later section "Doing Due Diligence" or turn
to Chapter 5.)

>> **Financing:** Unless you're paying cash for the full purchase
price of the business (which would be unusual), another
condition of your purchase offer may be an acceptable
seller-provided loan. Sellers can be a great financing
source, and many are willing to lend you money to
purchase their business. For more on seller financing,
see Chapter 7.

REMEMBER

Be sure to compare the terms that the seller is offering to
those of some local banks that specialize in small-business
loans. (See Chapter 7 for your best financing sources.) In
the purchase offer, specify the acceptable loan terms,
including the duration of the loan and the maximum
interest rate. If interest rates jump before your loan is
finalized, you don't want to be forced to complete your
deal at too high of an interest rate.

>> **Noncompete clause:** You don't want to buy a business
only to have the former owner set up an identical one
down the block and steal their previous customers from
you. To avoid this unpleasant possibility, be sure that your
purchase offer includes a *noncompete clause* that states
that the seller can't establish a similar business within a
certain nearby geographic area for a minimum number
of years.

TIP

You may consider asking the owner, as part of the purchase deal, to be available to consult with you, at a
specified hourly rate, for 6 to 12 months to make sure that
you tap all their valuable experience, as well as to transition
relationships with key employees, vendors, and customers.
To further align the selling owner's interests with yours,
consider having a portion of the total purchase price
dependent on the future success of the company.

If the transaction includes seller financing, most sophisticated sellers want to continue to work with you for a period

following the sale to help you get off on the right foot. Beware of those who don't want to hang around.

>> **Limited potential liabilities:** When you buy a business, you buy that business's assets and usually (but not always) its liabilities. Some potential liabilities don't show up on a company's balance sheet and can become a thorn in your side. Make sure that the seller is liable for environmental cleanup and other undisclosed existing liabilities (debts). Conduct legal searches for liens, litigation, and tax problems. (Your attorney should conduct these searches for you as a part of the closing process.)

Allocating the Purchase Price

When you pay $300,000 for a business, you're not simply paying $300,000 for the business. You're paying, for example, $60,000 for the inventory, $40,000 for the accounts receivable, $50,000 for the company equipment, $100,000 for goodwill, and so on.

REMEMBER

No matter how you determine the purchase price, you must always break down that price, or *allocate* it, among the assets of the business and other categories. This requirement applies whether you set the price of the business by determining the value of its assets (such as through the multiple-of-earnings method that we describe in Chapter 6) or by using some other method. Although the process of allocating assets may cause your eyes to glaze over, snap to attention when the subject comes up, because how you structure the purchase can save you tens of thousands of dollars in taxes.

Experienced tax advisors will tell you that you generally want to allocate much of the purchase price to specific assets of the business. Some assets are what their numbers make them out to be (such as accounts receivable), while others can be negotiable (such as equipment and goodwill). The reason for the negotiation is that different assets can be written off (or *depreciated*) over different periods of time. For instance, equipment can be depreciated over as little as 4 years, while goodwill takes 15 years to depreciate.

You must report the purchase of the business and the allocation of the purchase price among business assets on IRS Form 8594 (Asset Acquisition Statement). Make sure that you do so, because if you don't, the penalty is stiff — up to 10 percent of the amount not reported.

Doing More Due Diligence

After spending months searching for the right business to buy and finding one that fits your fancy, you may well spend weeks negotiating an acceptable deal. Just as you're about to stumble across what you think is the finish line, you realize you have plenty more work left to go.

After all, now is the time to get out the microscope and really nitpick. Before you go through with the deal and fork over the dough, you have one last chance to discover any hidden problems that exist within the business you hope to buy. Of course, all businesses have their warts, but better for you to uncover them now so that the purchase price and terms reflect those warts.

The process of thoroughly investigating your prospective business is called *due diligence*. During due diligence, you need to answer important questions like these:

>> Is the business as profitable as the financial statements indicate?

>> Will the business's customers remain after a change in ownership?

>> What lease, debt, or other obligations will you be assuming when you buy the business?

The process of performing due diligence typically takes 30 to 60 days, depending on the complexity of the company you're hoping to purchase.

TIP

The same experts you're working with to put together a good deal for your small-business purchase will form your due-diligence team. For details on how to work successfully with your outside experts, see Chapter 10.

In addition to the evaluation tips we give you in Chapter 5, we recommend that you take some additional due-diligence steps before making an offer. We go over these steps in the following sections.

Think about income statement issues

The profitability of the business is probably the single most important aspect you need to consider during due diligence. To help you deal with income statement concerns, we suggest that you take the following steps:

» **Have an experienced small-business tax advisor review the company's financial statements.** They'll know what to look out for. Just be sure to agree on a budget for the cost of the advisor's services (and, therefore, the time they will spend) up front.

» **Adjust for one-time events.** If necessary, factor out one-time impactful events from the profit analysis. For example, if the business got an unusually large order last year that is unlikely to be repeated, subtract the amount of that order from the profitability analysis.

» **Check the owner's compensation.** Examine the owner's salary to see whether it's too high or low for the industry the business is in. Owners can pump up the profitability of their company in the years before they sell by reducing or keeping their salary to a minimum or by paying family members in the business less than fair-market salaries.

» **Consider how the occupancy expense will change.** Consider whether the rent or mortgage expense will be different after you buy the business. Any large change in that cost will clearly affect the profitability of the business.

>> **Factor in financing expenses.** Be sure to calculate what will happen to profits when you factor in the financing costs from borrowing money to buy the business.

>> **Pay attention to trends.** How are the sales and the profits trending? If this year's profits were, say, $80,000 and last year's were $100,000, the trend is unfavorable. On the other hand, if this year's profits were $70,000 and last year's were $50,000, you're looking at a good trend. Knowledgeable buyers are generally willing to pay a higher multiple for favorable trends.

Consider legal and tax concerns

Before you make a deal, follow these steps to research any legal or tax issues the business may have:

>> **Look for liens.** Check to make sure that no liens are filed against assets of the business and, if you're buying real estate, that the property title is clear. A competent attorney can help with this tedious and important legal task.

>> **Get proof that all taxes are paid.** Get the seller to provide proof, certifying that federal and state employment, sales, and use taxes are all paid up.

4

Managing a Smooth Transition

Take care of pertinent business ownership tasks as soon as your deal is closed.

Handle the essential details of operating a business.

Adhere to regulatory and legal requirements.

IN THIS CHAPTER

» Notifying creditors of the transfer of ownership

» Putting together a business plan, mission statement, and financial framework

» Choosing the business entity

» Getting to know your customers and winning over employees

» Implementing small changes and asking the prior owner and a tax advisor for advice

Chapter **9**

Moving into Your Business

f you've made it through the searching, researching, negotiating, and closing phases, you're now a bona fide small-business owner. Congratulations and welcome to your new business! You've completed a lot of challenging and important work and should feel proud of yourself.

This chapter describes the tasks to take care of as soon as possible after your deal is closed.

Getting Important Things Down on Paper

As you move into your new business, take care of the following important items right away:

>> **Disclosing ownership transfer:** Notify creditors of the transfer of ownership. In the counties where the company does business, publish a transfer-of-ownership notice in a general circulation newspaper. If you omit this step, you risk having unsecured creditors come after your business for outstanding debts that the previous owner had.

>> **Writing a business plan and mission statement:** If you researched the industry and evaluated in detail the business you bought, you should be able to generate a good business plan, including an applicable mission statement, without too much hassle. Although completing your business plan will take some time and thinking, doing so early in the process will benefit you and your business in increased sales, reduced costs, and happier employees. If you ever intend to seek outside capital from a banker or investor, you'll need a good business plan.

TIP

An ideal time to begin work on this business plan is during the due-diligence phase. For full details on creating a business plan, see the latest edition of our co-authored *Small Business For Dummies* (Wiley).

>> **Planning the company's finances:** Going forward, you need to have a firm handle on the revenue, expenses, and cash flow of your business. For example, you need to set up a budget for your business and forecast future needs for capital, both of which should be included in the business plan. See Chapter 10 for more details.

Considering the Business Entity

Just because the business you bought was structured as a sole proprietorship or corporation doesn't mean that legal entity makes the most sense for you. The following sections provide the framework for you to think through this important decision, but your attorney and tax advisor should also be part of this decision.

Sole proprietorships

If you're interested in running your own business, odds are you'll do so as a so-called *sole proprietor*. About 70 percent of self-employed folks operate their businesses as sole proprietors because setting up a business this way is easier and generally less costly than other options. In this section we discuss the advantages and disadvantages of operating your business as a sole proprietorship.

Understanding the "solo" advantages

The pros of operating as a sole proprietor (going solo) may or may not outweigh the cons for a given small business owner. Each business (and owner) is unique and should weight the pros and cons. Consider the following advantages:

>> Simplest tax rules and record keeping compared with other business entity options

>> Low cost to establish or discontinue (shut down)

>> High flexibility to switch to other entity forms (corporation, LLC, and so on)

>> Good retirement plan options

So does this mean that running your small business as a sole proprietorship is the way to go for you and your company? Not necessarily — next up are the drawbacks, which you should weigh in your case.

Weighing the disadvantages of operating "solo"

WARNING

Organizing and running your small business as a sole proprietorship has its cons, and these may outweigh the pros, depending on the type of business you're running. Here are the drawbacks you should be aware of:

>> **Liability exposure:** Unlike in a corporation, where you have some shielding from liability thanks to the corporate structure, a sole proprietorship offers no such protection. However, as we discuss in the later section "Investigating liability insurance," you may be able to buy liability insurance, depending on the type of business you operate.

>> **Only one owner is permitted:** If you want to provide some small ownership stakes to key employees, you can't do that in a solo business. One exception: You can share ownership with your spouse so long as your spouse "materially participates" (that is, works) in the business. If both you and your spouse are owners, you each need to file your own Schedule C (more work), and you each need to pay Social Security tax on your share of the earnings (more tax).

>> **Estate issues:** With some business entities, the business structure survives your passing, but not so with a sole proprietorship. This may have negative consequences on the tax front and if you want your survivors to be able to easily continue with the company.

>> **You're taxed on all profits, even if you don't want to take them all out of the business:** If you have a big year or two, don't need all the money your business is generating, and want to leave some of it in the business, you still pay personal income tax on all those earnings as a solo. Not so with some other entities we discuss later in this chapter.

>> **Increased audit risks:** The IRS knows that it finds more tax mistakes and fraud with solo businesses, so on average, it tends to audit such companies at a somewhat higher rate.

Now, in enumerating these possible drawbacks to operating a business as a sole proprietorship, we're not trying to scare you off from doing so or talk you into, for example, incorporating. You need to consider which pros and cons may or may not apply to your situation and the type of business you're envisioning or operating. And you need to consider the alternative entities, like the ones later in this chapter.

C corporations

A corporation, technically speaking, is a legal entity that's separate from its founders, managers, and employees; it's owned by shareholders. Your personal assets are protected in case the corporation is sued. C corporations (the subject of this section) provide the most financial protection to shareholders, but many small businesses choose to be S corporations because they're cheaper to start and easier to maintain and have just one level of taxation compared with the two levels of taxation for C corporations. (We discuss S corporations in more detail later in this chapter.)

Before you call a lawyer or your state government offices to figure out how to incorporate, you need to know that incorporating takes time and costs money. Corporations generally involve the highest costs and most administrative hassles among the range of business entities for you to use. There are fees to incorporate, and each state levies an annual fee that you must pay, even if you have no business income that year. You also have higher legal and accounting costs thanks to the more complex tax rules and filings required of corporations.

In some instances, the decision to incorporate is complicated, but in most cases, it need not be a difficult choice. Taxes may be important to the decision but aren't the only consideration. This section presents an overview of the critical issues to consider. We discuss liability considerations, including whether you can obtain liability insurance for your chosen profession, as well as tax and other considerations.

TIP

If you weigh the following considerations of incorporating and you're still on the fence, our advice is to keep it simple: Don't incorporate. After you incorporate, un-incorporating takes time and money. Start as a sole proprietorship and then take it from there. Wait until the benefits of incorporating for your particular case clearly outweigh the costs and drawbacks of incorporating. Likewise, if the only benefits of incorporating can be better accomplished through some other means (such as purchasing insurance), save your money and time and don't incorporate.

Getting a handle on liability protection

The chief reason to consider incorporating your small business is for purposes of liability protection. Attorneys speak of the "protection of the corporate veil." Don't confuse this veil with insurance. You don't get any insurance when you incorporate. You may need or want to buy liability insurance instead of (or in addition to) incorporating (see the next section for details). Liability protection doesn't insulate your company from being sued, either.

When you incorporate, the protection of the corporate veil provides you with the separation of your business assets and liabilities from your personal finances in most situations (gross negligence and bad faith being notable counterexamples). (You must follow the ground rules, though, for being a corporation.) Why would you want to do that? Suppose that your business is doing well, and you take out a bank loan to expand. Over the next few years, however, your business ends up in trouble. Before you know it, your company is losing money, and you're forced to close up shop. If you can't repay the bank loan because of your business failure, the bank shouldn't be able to go after your personal assets if you're incorporated, right?

Unfortunately, many small business owners who need money find that bankers ask for personal guarantees, which negate part of the liability protection that comes with incorporation. Additionally, if you play financial games with your company (such as shifting money out of the company in preparation for defaulting on a loan), a bank may legally be able to go after your personal assets. So you must adhere to a host of ground rules and protocols to prove to the IRS that you're running a bona fide company. For example, you need to keep corporate records and hold an annual meeting — even if it's just with yourself!

A business can be sued if it mistreats an employee or if its product or service causes harm to a customer. But the owner's personal assets should generally be protected when the company is incorporated and meets the other protocols for being a legitimate business just discussed.

Investigating liability insurance

Before you incorporate, investigate and find out what actions can cause you to be sued. You can do this by asking others in your line of business or advisors who work with companies like yours. Then see whether you can purchase insurance to protect against these potential liabilities. Insurance is superior to incorporation because it pays claims.

TIP

If you belong to a professional group(s), especially if it has a national office, the group may be able to provide information on the percentage of members who are incorporated and on legal and insurance issues. Also, insurance agents may be able to advise on their experience with claims in your specific industry.

Suppose that you perform professional services but make a major mistake that costs someone a lot of money, or worse. Even if you're incorporated, if someone sues you and wins, your company may have to cough up the dough. This situation not only costs a great deal of money but also can sink your business. Only insurance can cover such financially destructive claims.

You can also be sued if someone slips and breaks a bone or two. To cover these types of claims, you can purchase a property or premises liability policy from an insurer.

TIP

Accountants, doctors, and a number of other professionals can buy liability insurance. A good place to start searching for liability insurance is through the associations that exist for your profession. Even if you aren't a current member, check out the associations anyway. You may be able to access any insurance they provide without membership or you can join the association long enough to get signed up. Incorporating, however, doesn't necessarily preclude insuring yourself. Both incorporating and covering yourself with liability insurance may make sense in your case.

Understanding corporate taxes

Corporations are taxed as entities separate from their individual owners. This situation can be both good and bad. Suppose that your business is doing well and making lots of money. If your business isn't incorporated, all your company's profits are taxed on your personal tax return in the year that you earn those profits.

If you intend to use the profits to reinvest in your business and expand, incorporating can appear to potentially save you some tax dollars. When your business is incorporated (as a regular or so-called *C corporation*), effective 2018, all of your profits are taxed at the 21 percent corporate tax rate, which is lower than most of the individual income tax brackets for moderate- and higher-income earners.

But, there's more to this tax rate comparison story. Unincorporated small businesses that operate as so-called pass-through entities (for example, sole proprietorships, LLCs, partnerships, and S corporations), named so because the profits of the business *pass through* to the owners and their personal income tax returns, have a new advantage. To address the fact that business owners that operated their business as a pass-through entity could face a higher personal federal income tax rate than the 21 percent rate levied on C corporations, Congress provided a 20 percent deduction for those pass-through businesses. This deduction effectively reduces the 22 percent federal income tax bracket to 17.6 percent, which is lower than the 21 corporate tax rate.

One caveat to the previous points: The 20 percent pass-through deduction gets phased out for service business owners (such as lawyers, doctors, real estate agents, consultants, and so on) at single taxpayer incomes above $191,950 (up to $241,950) and for married couples filing jointly incomes over $383,900 (up to $483,900). For other types of businesses above these income thresholds, this deduction may be limited so consult with your tax advisor.

WARNING

Resist the temptation to incorporate just so you can leave your money in the corporation, which may be taxed at a lower rate than you'd pay on your personal income. Don't be motivated by this seemingly short-term gain. If you want to pay yourself the profits in the future, you can end up paying more taxes. Why? Because you pay taxes first at the corporate tax rate in the year your company earns the money, and then you pay taxes again on these same profits (this time on your personal income tax return) when you pay yourself from the corporate till in the form of a dividend.

Another possible tax advantage for a corporation is that corporations can pay, on a tax-deductible basis, for employee benefits such as health insurance, long-term care insurance, disability insurance, and up to $50,000 of term life insurance. The owner usually is treated as an employee for benefits purposes. Sole proprietorships and other unincorporated businesses usually can take only tax deductions for these benefit expenses for employees. Benefit expenses for owners who work in the business aren't deductible, except for pension contributions and health insurance, which you can deduct on the front of IRS Form 1040.

Another reason not to incorporate, especially in the early years of a business, is that you can't claim the losses for an incorporated business on your personal tax return. On your business tax return, you have to wait to claim the losses against profits. Because most companies produce little revenue in their early years and have all sorts of start-up expenditures, losses are common.

Examining other incorporation considerations

Because corporations are legal entities distinct from their owners, corporations offer other features and benefits that a sole proprietorship or partnership doesn't. For example, corporations have shareholders who own a piece or percentage of the company. These shares can be sold or transferred to other owners, subject to any restrictions in the shareholders' agreement.

Corporations also offer *continuity of life*, which simply means that corporations can continue to exist despite the death of an owner or the owner's transfer of their share (stock) in the company.

Don't incorporate for ego purposes. If you want to incorporate to impress friends, family, or business contacts, you need to know that few people would be impressed or even know that you're incorporated. Besides, if you operate as a sole proprietor, you can choose to operate under a different business name ("doing business as" or d.b.a.) without the cost — or the headache — of incorporating.

Knowing where to get advice

If you're totally confused about whether to incorporate because your business is undergoing major financial changes, getting competent professional help is worth the money. The hard part is knowing where to turn because finding one advisor who can put all the pieces of the puzzle together can be challenging. And be aware that you may get wrong or biased advice.

SHOULD YOU INCORPORATE IN DELAWARE, NEVADA, OR WYOMING?

Some states are magnets for incorporation. The reason is simple: Select states, such as Delaware, Nevada, and Wyoming, make incorporation easier and less costly, and they tax corporations at a much lower rate than other states. Some states also allow you to do other things, such as keep the identity of your shareholders out of public view.

So should you rush out and incorporate in one of these corporate-friendly states if you live in one of the other 47 states? The answer is probably not. The reason is that the state in which you operate your company probably also requires you to register your corporation and pay the appropriate fees and taxes.

You should also consider the fact that some folks with whom you do business may be puzzled or concerned by your out-of-state incorporation. If you're considering incorporating out of state, you should definitely consult with an experienced small-business legal and tax advisor.

Attorneys who specialize in advising small businesses can help explain the legal issues. Tax advisors who do a lot of work with business owners can help explain the tax considerations. Also, a tax advisor should be able to prepare tax illustrations comparing the same business operated as a sole proprietorship, S corporation, and C corporation and the tax that the business would owe under different scenarios. If you find that you need two or more advisors to help make the decision, getting them together in one room with you for a meeting may help and ultimately save you time and money.

S corporations

Subchapter S corporations, so named for that part of the tax code that establishes them, offer some business owners the best of both worlds. You get the liability protection that comes with being incorporated as with a C corporation, and the business profit or loss passes through to the owner's personal tax returns (like in a sole proprietorship). In this section, we discuss the tax specifics of using S corporation status and the requirements for S corporations.

S corporation tax specifics

An S corporation is known as a *pass-through entity* for tax purposes. This simply means that the income that the company earns passes through to the company's owner/shareholders and is taxed at each person's individual level.

So if the business shows a loss in some years, the owners/shareholders may claim those losses in the current year of the loss on their tax returns against other income earned. This is potentially useful in the early years of a new business, a time when most companies lose money. To be able to claim losses, you must "materially participate" in the business, which generally means that you actively work in the company at least 500 hours per year, although 100 hours will suffice if that's the most among all other shareholders.

If, like most businesses, the company becomes profitable, it may actually make sense then to convert back to a regular C corporation to partake of the potential advantages of that status. That includes being able to retain earnings in the company, which you can't do with an S corporation, and being able to use tax-advantaged fringe benefits. (If you plan to take all the profits out of the company, an S corporation may make sense for you.)

Even though the corporation doesn't pay federal income tax, the company must annually complete and file IRS Form 1120S — "U.S. Income Tax Return for an S Corporation" (the form is located at www.irs.gov/pub/irs-pdf/f1120s.pdf). Also, some states levy a state income tax on S corporations, and many states require paying an annual fee.

TIP

One way an S corporation can save its owner/shareholders tax money is by paying them some of their compensation in the form of dividends. The reason this saves tax money is because dividends aren't subject to payroll or employment taxes. You must be careful, though, to ensure employee salaries are reasonable and not set artificially low and made up for by high dividend payments. Dividend payments shouldn't amount to more than 30 percent of a person's cash compensation when their salary/wages are totaled.

S corporation requirements

All corporations actually begin as so-called *C corporations*, which are the corporations discussed in the section "C corporations" earlier in this chapter. The United States has more than twice as many S corporations today as C corporations. To become an S corporation, your business must go through an additional "tax election" step. See IRS Form 2553, "Election by a Small Business Corporation."

U.S. tax laws allow most, but not all, small businesses to be S corporations. To be an S corporation in the eyes of the almighty IRS, a company must meet all the following requirements:

>> Be a U.S. company

>> Have just one class of stock

>> Have no more than 100 shareholders who are all U.S. residents or citizens and aren't partnerships, other corporations, or, with certain exceptions, trusts

TIP

Be sure to investigate limited liability companies (LLCs), discussed in the section "Limited liability companies (LLCs)" later in this chapter, before committing to forming an S corporation. LLCs offer the passing through of income that S corporations do and are generally simpler to initiate and operate.

Partnerships

A *partnership* occurs in the eyes of the tax authorities when two or more people — the *general partners* (GPs) — operate a business together and divide the profits (or losses). The division need not be done equally.

The GPs are responsible for the company's debts and liabilities. A partnership may also have *limited partners* (LPs) who generally provide financing to the business and who aren't active in the company itself. Most small business partnerships don't have LPs.

A partnership is similar to a sole proprietorship and other pass-through entities for income tax purposes. Partners pay personal income taxes on their share of the partnership's income distributed to them. This is done on IRS Form 1040 Schedule E, "Supplemental Income and Loss" (the form is available at www.irs.gov/pub/irs-pdf/f1040se.pdf). As sole proprietors do, partners pay self-employment taxes on income earned.

REMEMBER

Though the partnership itself doesn't pay any federal income tax, it has plenty of federal income tax reporting requirements. In fact, the tax rules and reporting requirements of a partnership are quite extensive and challenging. The partnership must file IRS Form 1065, "U.S. Return of Partnership Income." And the partnership must complete and annually issue IRS Schedule K-1 of Form 1065 to each partner. You'd be well advised to use the services of a tax advisor if you're going to have your business function as a partnership.

Limited liability companies (LLCs)

In the past generation, a new type of corporation has appeared. *Limited liability companies* (LLCs) offer business owners benefits similar to those of S corporations and partnerships but are even better in some cases.

Like an S corporation, an LLC offers liability protection for the owners — hence the name limited liability company. In addition to the veil of overall liability protection for the owner's personal finances, an owner's liability for business debts is limited in an LLC to their percentage ownership share in the business.

LLCs also pass the business's profits through to the owner's personal income tax returns, like a sole proprietorship or partnership. You can pass through losses as well and deduct them against your other income so long as you materially participate in the business.

LLCs are generally much simpler to set up and administer than a corporation. But, to be realistic going into it, don't expect an LLC to be as simple as a sole proprietorship. And LLCs don't give you the ability to tap into some of the tax advantages afforded specific fringe benefits that some corporations offer.

LLCs have fewer restrictions regarding shareholders than S corporations. For example, LLCs have no limits on the number of shareholders, and the shareholders can be foreigners, corporations, or partnerships.

Compared with S corporations, the only additional restriction LLCs carry is that sole proprietors and professionals can't always form LLCs (although some states allow this). All states now permit the formation of LLCs, but most state laws require you to have at least two partners for an LLC to be taxed as a partnership and not be a professional firm.

REMEMBER

Single-owner LLCs (which also include married couples in community property states) are treated as sole proprietorships and file Schedule C of Form 1040 for tax purposes, unless the owner elects to file as a corporation on Form 8832, "Entity Classification Election." A domestic entity that has more than one member will default to a partnership. An LLC with multiple owners can either accept its default classification as a partnership, or file Form 8832 to elect to be classified as an association taxable as a corporation. This form is for informational purposes only. Keep in mind that LLCs aren't taxed federally; income is passed through to the company's owners/shareholders. However, numerous states levy a tax on LLCs and require an annual tax filing. Some states like California go even further with fees. California has a fee based on gross receipts, not net income. A California LLC with $500,000 in gross receipts pays $800 tax plus a $2,500 fee for a total of $3,300, even if it reports a net loss for the year after expenses.

Gaining Insight from Others

Walk; don't run. Don't make huge changes your first day, week, or even month at the helm. Take your time to discover the culture of the business, the needs of its customers, and the idiosyncrasies of its vendors, before you attempt to make major changes. Employees, customers, and vendors don't like quick change, especially when the person behind the change is new and relatively unknown.

When you take the reins of your new business, be sure to consult the following key people for guidance and feedback:

>> **Your customers:** Get to know your best customers as soon as the ink is dry on the sales agreement. Without good customers who buy profitable products and services and who pay their bills on time, you don't have a viable long-term business. Even the best business is bound to lose customers for a variety of reasons beyond the business owner's control. So don't skimp on understanding your customers' needs, particularly what makes them buy your company's wares and what their ongoing customer service needs are. Completing your business plan can help you clarify many of these vital issues. Plus, you can get a feel for how to market your products and services to customers and how to keep your customers loyal in Chapter 13.

>> **Your employees:** Employees who liked the previous owner(s) will take time to warm up to you. Some employees may fear for their jobs or worry that a change in ownership will lead to reduced job satisfaction. Err on the side of doing more listening to your employees rather than always being

the one jabbering about all your grand plans. The employees contain a wealth of knowledge about the business from which you can learn, and the better you listen, the more the employees will grow to respect and like you.

TIP

Be sure to evaluate the employee benefits package and compensation structure (see Chapter 12). Don't make immediate and rash changes in this area, especially if you're thinking about reducing benefits and/or compensation. Early, negative changes can have ugly long-term consequences.

>> **The prior owner:** Don't expect to know everything there is to know about running your new business. No matter how much better a business manager you may think you are than your predecessor, they have certain knowledge and skills that you don't have. Don't let your ego stand in the way of asking the previous owner for advice.

>> **A good tax advisor:** You don't want to fall behind in filing your taxes or filling out the right tax forms, or you'll have a nasty surprise in the form of an unexpectedly large tax bill. The tax advisor who helped you with evaluating your business purchase may be able to recommend a tax advisor you can work with at least during your first year of business ownership. You also need to make sure you come out of the starting gates with well-organized and accurate financial statements. See Chapter 10 for more details.

Much like a first-time home buyer's excitement at moving into a newly purchased home, your euphoria at owning your business may quietly slip into anxiety when you realize that your work is just beginning. Relax, take deep breaths, and use the time-tested method of breaking a big task into many smaller manageable ones. Also, rest assured that if you take the advice we offer throughout Part 2 and you do your homework before buying your business, you should end up purchasing a company that doesn't have major problems and that you have the skills to run well.

IN THIS CHAPTER

» **Handling the details of owning a business**

» **Determining which tasks you want to outsource**

» **Establishing a bookkeeping system that works for you**

» **Managing your expenses**

» **Maintaining relationships with vendors and other people outside your business**

Chapter **10**

Business Owner Basics

Those who have started their own business know that in the beginning, you as the owner will perform all your business's chores, or at least you will personally see to it that they get done. Well, you'll personally take care of all the *important* tasks at least — those responsibilities that will, down the road, either make or break your business if they aren't done correctly.

When you buy a business, odds are that the business will have some employees and vendors that perform various functions and services for the business. The good news for you is that you shouldn't have to get down into the weeds in a way that you would with starting a business from scratch. But you should be familiar with the activities in your acquired small business so that you can manage it optimally.

In this chapter, we walk you through the many hats you must wear as you navigate these sometimes mundane, but always necessary, details.

Minding the Details of Business Ownership

When we talk about taking care of the early-stage chores of taking over and running a business, we're assuming that you've already completed the big-picture tasks, many of which we discuss earlier in this book. Now you must dive into the nitty-gritty details.

Buying insurance

One of the first things you need to do when you start a business is to purchase insurance. We're talking about liability insurance — auto, fire, theft, business interruption, and so on — as well as workers' compensation insurance.

Unfortunately, insurance is an expense that never goes away and generally increases in price every year. Making things worse is the fact that, if you're like most entrepreneurs, after you sign the original policies, you'll file them away and won't consider shopping around to get a better price for long periods of time because you're so busy running your business. In other words, unless you're the exception, the expenses related to insurance policies will be etched on your profit and loss statement as a fixed cost even though the expenses should be a variable cost — meaning that they should be reviewed every year.

WARNING

Don't even think about entrusting the creation and negotiation of your initial insurance package (and the creation of the costs related to it) to anyone else. You need to take care of this important task yourself.

Liability insurance

In most cases, insurance is a necessary expense, not unlike a host of other necessary expenses, such as rent, telephone, and salaries. In some cases, the justification for insurance is the owner's logic; in other cases, insurance is required by an outsider — a bank or a property-leasing company.

Following are the four main categories of liability insurance every small-business owner needs to consider. One of them — aptly called *liability insurance* — is a must; if you don't have liability insurance, a dissatisfied customer or even an on-premise passerby can shut your business down for good. Generally speaking, you can add the other three as your business (and its profitability) grows to the point where you can afford them.

>> **Liability insurance:** No telling what may happen on your business premises in these litigious times. *Our recommendation:* Buy enough liability insurance to protect at least twice your combined personal and business net worth.

>> **Theft insurance:** Sooner or later, someone is going to steal something of value from you. (Statistics show that this *someone* is likely to be an employee.) *Our recommendation:* If you're in the high-ticket retail or wholesale business (automobiles, appliances, and the like), you should purchase theft insurance. (You don't need to purchase enough theft insurance to cover all your inventory; just buy enough to cover what one person can reasonably steal.) Otherwise, take your chances until you're profitable.

>> **Property damage insurance:** In addition to the physical property you own, rent, or lease, property damage insurance covers your inventory. Similar to homeowner's insurance, property damage insurance is often required by the terms of a lease or bank loan. *Our recommendation:* If you're in a service business with little expensive equipment and you're leasing or renting in an office building, take your chances if your lease will allow you to do so (until you're profitable). Otherwise, buy enough property damage insurance to cover the estimated cost of replacement.

>> **Business interruption insurance:** This insurance covers the possibility of your business being halted by any number of random events, most of them being natural disasters. Business interruption insurance reimburses you for the profits you don't make during your downtime. *Our recommendation:* In your business's early stages, you probably won't have much business to interrupt. Spend your scarce money

elsewhere. However, this situation (we hope) will change. When it does, business interruption insurance is a must-buy. Your insurance agent can help you determine how much to buy. Some businesses, especially capital-intensive ones, will take a long time to open the doors after an accident or act of God. Other businesses, usually those that sell services, can get back on their feet relatively quickly.

Workers' compensation insurance

Workers' compensation is payment for insurance that provides benefits — in the form of medical expense reimbursement and replacement of lost wages — to employees injured on the job. Workers' compensation is a state-mandated, no-fault insurance system, and, when you have employees, it appears as a hefty expense on your profit and loss statement.

TIP

Shop around for a trustworthy insurance agent (use referrals from satisfied small-business customers), set up a meeting with them along with a representative of the state (your prospective insurance agent can tell you how to locate that person), and find out what you need to do to keep your experience modification factor to a minimum. The *experience modification factor* is a numerical expression of a company's accident and injury record compared with the average for the firm's industry. The higher your experience modification factor, the higher the cost for workers' compensation insurance.

In addition to the experience modification factor, job classification plays an important role in determining the cost of your workers' compensation insurance. The state assigns each job (or employee) in your small business a particular rating — and subsequently a particular premium — based on the estimated level of risk involved in the performance of that job. (The higher the job classification, the higher the cost for you. Because the classification criteria are often fuzzy, argue for the lower classification when possible.)

REMEMBER

Don't take the job classification process lightly. You can choose from a myriad of job categories, and a lot of overlap exists among various job categories. You and your business will waste a significant amount of insurance money if you don't make the effort to properly classify your employees.

Because workers' compensation insurance is a state-run program, ask your insurance agent for the telephone number and address of the applicable state agency if you have questions about the program. Or go to the National Association of Insurance Commissioners (NAIC) website (www.naic.org), click on the Map tab, and click on your state for more details.

Paying federal, state, and local taxes

Federal taxes (income, Social Security, unemployment, and excise) come in a mind-boggling array, as do state and local taxes (income, real estate, sales, and assorted other special levies, depending on your industry).

WARNING

When you're short on cash (don't kid yourself; sooner or later, it's bound to happen), make sure that you pay any taxes you owe the government first, even if you have to put off paying your private vendors. Governments, especially the federal government, have an enormous array of collection tools at their disposal, and they have the right to extract a dear price (in the form of onerous penalties and interest rates) from those who don't follow the letter of the law. So be sure to pay your taxes on time (we hope we're not the first people to tell you this). For more on the taxes that affect your small business, see the latest edition of *Small Business Taxes For Dummies*, by Eric Tyson (published by Wiley).

Negotiating leases

When you're leasing space for a start-up, aim for a two-year lease, or three years as an absolute maximum. If you think you may want the space for a longer term, consider negotiating and adding to your lease agreement an escalation clause that stipulates upfront how much the rental rate will increase should you choose to extend the lease for a subsequent year or multiyear period.

TIP

Unfortunately, reading, understanding, and creating a lease are tasks for lawyers, not laypeople. Pay the legal fees and don't get locked into any long-term leases with the lure of free rent or equipment use.

Long-term leases are a no-win situation for the small-business owner: If your business grows, it will outgrow the long-term lease and you'll pay a higher price for its cancellation; if your business doesn't grow, you'll pay an even greater price to get out of the lease. What do we mean by *long-term*? Any lease for more than two years. Many landlords offer long-term leases (three to five years) with all sorts of exotic discounts; don't be lured into taking them unless you can afford to pick up the final years out of your own pocket should the business no longer want, need, or be able to pay for the space.

Maintaining employee records

The day you hire your first employee is the same day you must create and begin maintaining your first employee-personnel folder. Be sure to maintain a written record for every employee, covering such issues as employment agreements (including salary history), performance reviews, business goals, commendations, and, of course, reprimands.

These records come in handy as you manage and motivate your employees. Such key managerial and motivational tools as goal-setting and performance reviews require that you keep detailed employee records for them to work. (For more information on these two subjects, see Chapter 12.)

Also, assuming that you employ living, breathing human beings, you can count on the fact that, sooner or later, you'll have a conflict with one or more of those living, breathing human beings — a conflict that in the worst case is likely to end up in court. When a legal battle occurs, the party who can back up their claims with the most information usually prevails. Don't be the one who's handicapped by poor record-keeping and documentation.

Some states are *at-will* employment states, which simply means the employer has the right to terminate employees "at will." In effect, you don't have to clarify the reason for termination; all you have to tell the terminated employee is that "things just aren't working out." Other states aren't so lenient or understanding. Find out where your state stands on the issue by calling your state's Employment Department; it will have a long list of rules that will determine the employee records you need to maintain.

Note: If you decide to outsource your human resource needs, as outlined later in this chapter, the human resource firm you choose will have all this information at its fingertips.

Getting licenses and permits

Almost all businesses require the filing of certain licenses and obtaining particular permits. We tell you what you need to know (and do) about permits in Chapter 11.

Signing the checks

As we're sure you already know, checks represent cash; from the day you hang out your shingle until the day you close your doors, cash will be the lifeblood of your business. The annals of small business are filled with stories of bookkeepers who helped themselves to a hardworking entrepreneur's cash.

TIP

If your spouse is your bookkeeper, you can (we hope) rest easy. But what do you do when your bookkeeper isn't your spouse? You guard your cash like it's your life because it is (well, it's your business life, anyway). Following is a list of tips on how to do exactly that:

>> Schedule an audit at the end of every year. It doesn't have to be a full-fledged, expensive, cover-every-detail audit. Simply ask your certified public accountant (CPA) to spend half a day reviewing your books. Your CPA knows the sensitive areas to focus on.

>> Make sure your bookkeeper takes a vacation every year. Most bookkeepers who are siphoning their employers' cash don't want anyone else probing their books, even for short periods of time. Thus they don't want to take vacations.

>> Review and approve every invoice yourself.

>> Balance the bank statement yourself.

>> Require two signatures on every check (or require just one signature — yours).

Outsourcing: Focus on What You Do Best

We define *outsourcing* as delegating services you don't want to do, or don't have time to do, to someone outside your company (not an employee), who can oftentimes do them better and faster. The concept of outsourcing isn't new; businesses have been outsourcing, in one form or another, for many years. We outline the basics in the sections that follow.

Surveying the most commonly outsourced tasks

The following list gives you suggestions on which small-business functions are most frequently outsourced. See the next section to determine which outsourcing options make the most sense for you.

>> **Accounting and bookkeeping:** *Accounting* (the beginning-to-end process of collecting financial data, generating financial statements, and preparing tax forms) and *bookkeeping* (the collecting-of-financial-data function only) provide the gamut of outsourcing opportunities. You can, for example, hire someone — either a person or a business — to do all your accounting and bookkeeping, or you can hire someone to do only your payroll, only your financial statements, or only your tax returns. Because the typical entrepreneur usually isn't well versed in accounting and bookkeeping skills, we suggest that these functions be among the first you consider for outsourcing.

>> **Human resources:** As your company grows, the various functions of human resources should be next in line for outsourcing consideration. Human resources includes a wide variety of nonproduct-, noncustomer-, and nonsales-related issues, such as:

- New-employee hiring procedures

- Policies and procedure manuals for employees

- Payroll and related information-gathering systems

- Employee training on human resource issues

- Employee training on a wide variety of sensitive issues, such as ethics and sexual harassment

>> **Manufacturing:** The manufacturing process for most products is expensive, time-consuming, and extremely detail oriented. For many entrepreneurs, especially the creative and/or sales types, outsourcing the manufacturing function makes a lot of sense.

Even if your core business is manufacturing, some elements of your product may lend themselves to outsourcing their manufacture to subcontractors. Even behemoth manufacturers such as General Motors and Apple subcontract a good deal of their work.

>> **Internet Technology (IT):** Most smaller small businesses, including many in the technology sector themselves, will outsource their IT needs to a local business or independent consultant. The business or consultant you choose will:

- Help you purchase and maintain your fleet of computers, servers, and related equipment

- Help you install your software systems

- Help you make important technology decisions (such as using the Cloud and/or determining which operating systems to use) that will arise in the everyday course of your business

The best way to find the right firm or consultant? Get referrals from other small business owners who are currently outsourcing their IT.

>> **Sales:** Outsourcing sales is certainly the most potentially dangerous of the outsourcing options, but some businesses, including those that employ manufacturers' reps, do it. We say "potentially dangerous" because it's difficult to impart to outside salespeople the enthusiasm and knowledge necessary to effectively sell your business's product or service. Sales is definitely the last of the responsibilities to consider outsourcing, although doing so works well for some small businesses in appropriate industries.

Figuring out what to outsource

Here's the $64,000 question: How do you determine which services to outsource and which ones to retain in-house? Each business and owner is different, of course, but answering the following questions can help you make the best decision for your situation:

>> **Can I better manage my available cash if I outsource?** The answer here primarily depends on how much cash you have. For example, by outsourcing the manufacturing process, you avoid the costs associated with maintaining an inventory of raw materials and hiring manufacturing employees. By outsourcing your sales functions, you avoid the costs associated with maintaining a sales force.

>> **What do I do best?** Because your time is finite, why spend a lot of time doing the things you don't do well (such as bookkeeping and IT) when you can farm out those duties, thereby leaving you with more time to do the things you do well? If you're sales oriented or product oriented, for example, doing your business's bookkeeping yourself simply doesn't make sense.

>> **Will the cost of the outsourcing tasks include a product (or service) whose quality is better than what you can produce at that same cost?** The answer to this question is often yes, given the fact that the best outsourcing sources are almost always specialists in their areas of expertise. Of course, you shouldn't outsource until you find a competent specialist.

>> **What do I enjoy doing the most?** We can guarantee you this: If you choose to keep your bookkeeping, human resources, or IT functions in-house, you will, over the years, end up spending no small amount of time dealing with employee-related issues related to these functions. Is this the way you want to spend your time?

In the final analysis, the decision whether to outsource should be based primarily on what you enjoy spending your time doing and where your personal skill sets lie.

Simplifying Your Accounting

If this were a perfect world, you wouldn't need an accounting system — you'd simply let your business checking account do the talking. You'd pay your bills and deposit your receipts, and whatever was left over at the end of the year would represent your profit. How simple (and inexpensive) such a procedure would be.

Alas, this isn't a perfect world, and your business checking account does the talking only when measuring one of your assets (cash). Furthermore, your checking account only measures today's cash; it doesn't give you the foggiest idea of what tomorrow's or next month's cash balance will be. Will you have enough cash in the bank to pay the month's bills, to meet next Friday's payroll, or to pay the quarterly tax payments that will be due in 30 days? Who knows? Your checking account isn't talking.

The problem is that your business's checking account can't do any of the following things:

>> Keep score (of anything but cash)

>> Give you the information you need to pay your income taxes

>> Provide you with the percentages and ratios you need to help you manage your business

>> Provide you with the trends you need to determine the direction of your business

>> Present you with the information you need to value your business

Like it or not, accounting is one of the most important functions of running your business. Whether you intend to eventually outsource your accounting or do all the work in-house, at the start-up stage, accounting demands your undivided attention. One of the most common mistakes we see entrepreneurs make is to not learn how basic accounting works or how it applies to their business. Take it from us: Learn the basics early, or you'll never take the time as your company grows.

Introducing some common systems

You have three options to consider when determining which accounting system to employ:

>> An outside accounting service

>> An in-house manual bookkeeping system

>> An in-house computer-based accounting system

If you decide to use an in-house accounting system, read on to find out more about the manual and computer-based options.

Manual bookkeeping systems

Maintaining a manual bookkeeping system is certainly the quickest and easiest of the two in-house options. All you have to do is visit your local office-supply store or its website, purchase one of the many manual bookkeeping ledger and journal systems available (the entire package should cost $25 or less), and — voilà! — before you can mutter the words *green eyeshades*, you're a bookkeeper. You won't need to buy an expensive computer or the software to go with it; the only accessories required are a #2 pencil or a pen and, depending on the complexity of your business, no small amount of your (or someone else's) time.

In addition to the low cost of a manual bookkeeping system, another advantage of using such a system is that you learn the basics of the standard double-entry accounting system from the ground up — a skill that will hold you in good stead as your business grows. (See the sidebar "A collection of accounting definitions" if you need more information about double-entry accounting.)

The downside of the manual-entry system, especially when your business has a lot of activity, is that it can be extremely time-consuming, and time is money in the small-business world. Also, the information that you collect manually won't always provide you with the depth of financial data you need for making important business decisions. Finally, manual bookkeeping is more prone to human error (intentional or unintentional) than computer-based systems. We can guarantee you this: If your business is successful and grows, you'll soon outgrow whatever manual system you adopt.

After you purchase your manual system, follow the step-by-step directions inside the ledgers and journals to perform a relatively uncomplicated, connect-the-dots, bookkeeping process. During your fiscal year, make your entries in the general journal pages (*journals* are where you make the entries; *ledgers* are where you total the journal entries). The manual system you buy will include definitions of each of the following categories, along with examples:

>> Your disbursements, according to their expense and/or capital account category

>> The receipts (income) of your business

>> Various period-ending adjusting entries designed to record such items as depreciation, accrued taxes, and accrued payroll

At the end of the year, complete your journal entries to summarize the year's activity. Then, if you prefer, you can turn over your journals to a tax advisor or CPA, wait a few weeks, and be rewarded with a professionally prepared profit and loss statement, balance sheet, and the amount due for any year-end tax payments. (See Chapter 5 for details on the different financial statements and Chapter 15 for details on small-business taxes.)

If, on the other hand, you're that special entrepreneur who actually enjoys the bookkeeping process, you can expand the manual bookkeeping process to include the year-end preparation of your profit and loss statement, as well as the balance sheet, leaving only your taxes to be computed by a tax practitioner.

Finally, in those cases where your business is a relatively uncomplicated sole proprietorship or partnership (see Chapter 5), you may decide to carry the manual process through the preparation of Schedule C of IRS Form 1040 and on into the preparation of your personal income tax return.

When it comes to how much of your own bookkeeping and taxes you perform yourself, the only limits are your time, skills, and patience. The primary issue to consider when determining how much, or how little, of your accounting you should do is how best to utilize your finite time.

In addition to the general ledger and journal functions previously described, most manual bookkeeping ledger and journal systems also include the forms you need to maintain such subsidiary records as monthly payrolls, schedule of accounts receivable, schedule of accounts payable, and inventory worksheets.

Computer-based systems

Chances are you already have a computer, either desktop or laptop; if so, using it to accomplish your bookkeeping and accounting functions almost always makes sense. (If you don't have a computer, you're going to have at least two strikes against you as you work to grow your business.) Although the least expensive computerized software package available is a tad more expensive than a comparable manual system, the computerized system (if you use it properly) should save you time, provide you with more information, and establish a base for you to grow into a more sophisticated system as your business expands.

You can consider four categories of digital systems when shopping for your first accounting package. The system you ultimately select depends on the size and complexity of your business. A description of the four categories follows, along with several basic questions and a collection of tips intended to help you make the final choice.

CATEGORY 1: QUICK AND EASY

Category 1 includes those quick-and-easy accounting systems used by many families, as well as by small businesses. The cost of these systems is usually around $50. They're basically able to categorize and cumulate expenses and generate both profit and loss statements and balance sheets. Most Category 1 systems also include the capability to pay bills electronically. The most often used example of Category 1 is Quicken.

WARNING

The primary shortcoming of Category 1 systems is that the software allows for the deletion of bookkeeping entries, so if you're interested in providing an audit trail for you or your accountant, you shouldn't purchase a Category 1 package. An *audit trail* enables you to track every dollar of income and expenses, thus making theft much more difficult. (Audit trails are required in all publicly held companies.) For this reason, most accountants don't recommend Category 1 systems to small-business owners who have prospects of future growth; these owners will eventually require the security that audit trails provide.

When your business is small and you know it's going to remain small, and you'll be the only person writing the checks, Category 1 systems may be satisfactory for you.

TIP

Category 1 systems don't include payroll systems. If you plan on eventually having employees and don't want to figure your payrolls or write your checks manually, you may as well spend another $50 to $100 and upgrade to Category 2.

A COLLECTION OF ACCOUNTING DEFINITIONS

TECHNICAL STUFF

If you're interested in mastering a manual system (or if you just want to understand the basics of accounting, no matter what system you use), here are the key accounting terms you need to know:

- **Fiscal year:** A *fiscal year* is the specific 365-day period that you have chosen to begin and end your accounting period. Most businesses must choose a calendar year as their fiscal year; in other words, their year begins January 1 and ends December 31. (All personal service businesses are required to use a calendar year, as are all partnerships and sole proprietorships.) Some corporations, LLCs, and subchapter S Corporations may decide to use a fiscal year other than the standard calendar year; for example, many retailers choose not to end their fiscal year on December 31 because they're still too busy winding up their holiday season. As a result, many retailers select a non-calendar fiscal year of February 1 through January 31 (or any such non-calendar-year 365-day period).

- **Double-entry accounting and bookkeeping:** All accounting and bookkeeping systems are *double-entry.* For each entry made on the expense side, an offsetting entry must be made

(continued)

(continued)

on the income side. Or, for every entry on the asset side, an offsetting entry must be made on the liability side. Every plus must be accompanied by an offsetting minus, or in accounting-speak, every debit to one account must be offset by a credit to another. For example, when a retail business sells goods from its inventory for cash, a credit is made to cash and a debit is made to inventory. Because of this double-entry aspect, such systems are always self-balancing. (The total debits will always add up to equal the total credits, hence the term *balance sheet.*)

- **Single-entry record-keeping:** The best example of *single-entry record-keeping* is your personal checking account — one entry and the transaction is complete. Single-entry record-keeping systems aren't self-balancing. Cash registers and the maintenance of internal ledgers are other examples of single-entry record-keeping systems.

- **Cash-basis accounting:** *Cash-basis accounting* records income at the time it's received and deducts expenses at the time they're paid. In effect, the date of the check and/or the deposit determines the date of the applicable bookkeeping entry. Most sole proprietorships and partnerships use the cash-basis accounting system because it's easier to understand and requires fewer year-end adjusting entries. However, you get much less useful information with which to manage your business.

- **Accrual-basis accounting:** *Accrual-basis accounting* records income at the time it's earned (when a sale is made as opposed to when cash changes hands) and deducts expenses at the time they're incurred (which may not necessarily be when cash changes hands). The IRS requires that businesses that have inventory use the accrual system. As a result, nearly all corporations utilize the accrual system.

If you have a choice for your business, consult with a tax advisor for advice as to which system will work best.

CATEGORY 2: PLUS PAYROLL AND INVENTORY

For about $100, *Category 2* systems provide a number of services that Category 1 systems don't. For example, Category 2 systems can perform the following functions:

>> **Compute, write, and compile employee payroll:** Some small-business owners choose to outsource this function, but for those who are watching every penny, managing your own payroll is a good place to start.

>> **Track and age *receivables* (monies your customers owe you) and *payables* (monies you owe your vendors):** *Aging* means determining the amount of time your receivables have been due to you or your payables have been due to your vendors.

>> **Establish customer receivable ledgers:** These ledgers are, in effect, a timed listing of your customers' statements.

>> **Maintain a basic inventory system:** Managing inventory is one of the small-business owner's most difficult and, thus, most unpleasant, tasks. Using an automatic system to keep track of your inventory, especially when you have many SKUs (stock keeping units), is the best way to make sure you're getting good numbers.

The primary disadvantage of Category 2 accounting software programs is that, similar to Category 1 programs, they don't provide an audit trail.

Examples of Category 2 accounting software packages include the most popular QuickBooks, as well as CashFlow Manager and Manage Your Own Business (MYOB).

CATEGORY 3: FOLLOWING THE AUDIT TRAIL

Category 3 programs provide their owners with all the benefits that Category 2 systems provide, as well as the audit trail, which is necessary for businesses in which someone other than the owners will be paying bills/writing checks and maintaining the books. Additionally, Category 3 systems allow for multiple users: the bookkeeping department, the accounts receivable department, the inventory department, and so on. Prices vary, depending on the horsepower required, but they're generally in the range of $200 to $700.

Examples of Category 3 packages include Sage BusinessWorks, Sage 50 Accounting, QuickBooks Pro (an upgraded version of QuickBooks), and BPI.

CATEGORY 4: MODULAR POWER

Unlike the software packages in Categories 1, 2, and 3, which are purchased in a single package, *Category 4* systems are purchased in *modules*, or stand-alone units. However, Category 3 and 4 programs overlap to some degree because a few of the Category 3 programs also come with modules, thus making the choice between the two a bit complicated. Because Category 4 packages have more horsepower/bandwidth, as well as more module options, they work best for larger companies (more than 200 employees). See the section "Choosing the system that's right for you," later in this chapter for details on how to select the best option for you.

Category 4 software has the following module options embedded in it:

>> Basic system manager (the module that manages all the other modules)

>> General ledger (otherwise known as the *chart of accounts* — the list of all the account titles that are tracked by every accounting system, including assets, liabilities, equity, and expenses)

>> Financial reporting (profit and loss statement, balance sheet, and so on)

>> Accounts receivable

>> Accounts payable

>> Payroll

>> Inventory

>> Job costing (a system that allows you to compute the exact cost of each of your products or services for pricing purposes)

The cost of each of these modules is approximately $500, but the total price for a complete system can begin at $2,000 and run all the way up to $10,000, depending on the bells and whistles you select. Good programs in this category are flexible and can support many types of accounting issues and business processes.

Examples of Category 4 accounting software packages include Microsoft Dynamics GP, Sage 100, Sage 300 ERP, and Quick-Books Desktop Enterprise.

Choosing the system that's right for you

We explain the pros and cons of using a manual accounting system earlier in this chapter, so we focus on computer-based systems here. The first two questions you need to ask when choosing a computer-based system are

>> How big is your business?

>> What can you afford?

Generally speaking, the smaller the business, the more likely you are to use a Category 1 or 2 system. A home-office business can easily get by with a Category 1 system, while most non-home-office businesses with 50 employees or fewer can use a Category 2 system.

You also need to consider how much inventory you'll be managing and whether or not you've decided to outsource your payroll. In other words, the more you ask of your system, the more horsepower you need.

TIP

When making your final system decision, consult with your CPA or computer professional and keep the following reminders in mind:

>> **Don't waste your time purchasing and figuring out a system that you're going to outgrow in six months or a year.** We don't want you wasting money on a system you'd get such little use out of.

>> **Don't buy a system that you think will take you three years or more to grow into.** That's too far out to accurately project. Buy a system that you think will work for you for the next two years.

>> **In addition to considering the software system itself, consider the company behind the package you're**

buying. Consider the following criteria: the support that the company provides, the history of its program updates (as a general rule, better companies provide more frequent updates), and the future of that company (will it be around to provide upgrades in future years?).

>> **In the likely event that you can't answer these questions yourself, call the company (look for a toll-free number on the package) and ask direct questions.** Your tax advisor may also be able to give you an educated opinion.

>> **Find out whether someone locally is trained to provide implementation and support services for the product you're considering.** Ask an accountant/tax advisor, or check out the manufacturer's website or call their support line.

REMEMBER

When in doubt, buy the highest category that you can afford and that you can picture yourself using within the next two years. After all, companies grow. Even if you think you want a Category 1 software package now, chances are you'll be in the market for an upgrade soon enough. The additional investment required to switch software packages isn't really the issue. The real damage comes from the time and staff retraining required to make the switch.

Controlling Your Expenses

The three ways to increase your business's profitability are:

>> Increasing sales (in which case, those increased sales may or may not have a positive impact on profitability)

>> Increasing prices (in which case, the entire amount of the increase will have a positive impact on profitability, assuming that you don't lose customers due to the price increase)

>> Decreasing — or controlling — expenses (in which case, the entire decrease will have a positive impact on profitability, assuming that you don't lose business due to the impact of the expense reduction on your product or service quality)

REMEMBER

When you increase prices or cut expenses, a one-to-one leverage factor goes to work on your bottom-line profits. This is why successful small-business owners always look to the expense and pricing categories first when they're in a profitability crunch: Results can be instantaneous, and the impact is usually dollar on dollar.

Whether you're starting a new company or running an existing one, you must remember that controlling expenses is a cultural issue, and cultural issues begin at the top. We're talking about the old practice of leading by example. If you have overstuffed chairs in your office and idle secretaries in your foyer, your employees are going to demonstrate a similar penchant for spending unnecessary money.

Whenever we walk into a business's lobby or reception area and we're greeted by the gurgle of cascading waterfalls and the sight of bronze sculptures, we're reminded again of Sam Walton and Walmart. Linoleum floors and metal desks were the order of the day for many years at Walmart's corporate offices in Bentonville, Arkansas. No wonder they could underprice and outperform such longtime competitors as Sears, Montgomery Ward, and JCPenney, whose overheads included the cost of maintaining plush corporate headquarters in the towering skyscrapers of Chicago and Dallas.

The following sections delve into the different types of expenses you need to control and explain the advantages of using zero-based budgeting.

Looking at fixed and variable expenses

As a small-business owner, you have to control two kinds of expenses:

>> **Fixed expenses:** Those expenses that don't fluctuate with sales, including such categories as insurance, rent, equipment leases, interest, and taxes. These are usually negotiated in the start-up stage and then left alone until the original negotiations lapse and you have to renegotiate them. Such periods may be anywhere from one year to five years.

>> **Variable expenses:** Those expenses that fluctuate with sales — as sales go up, variable expenses go up as well (and vice versa). These expenses include such categories as cost of goods sold, sales commissions, and outbound freight.

You can delegate the determination of the prices to be paid for variable expenses, as long as you remember that the responsibility for controlling them, in the early stages of a business anyway, should always rest with you (the owner). You need to approve all purchase orders and sign all checks that relate to variable expenses.

As the company grows, you may choose to delegate the responsibility for controlling expenses to other responsible individuals inside the company. Or you may choose to maintain control by continuing to sign the checks and questioning the invoices that support those checks (definitely our recommendation!).

TIP

A key to controlling expenses is keeping your employees cost-conscious. If your employees know that you and other key managers will question unreasonable or unnecessary expenses, they, too, will be motivated to be cost-conscious. You can also use incentives to help cut costs. If you give your employees a reason (bonus, perks, recognition) to look for unnecessary costs, they're sure to find them.

As you manage your expenses, always be aware of the *80-20 rule*, which says that you can find 80 percent of your wasted expense dollars in 20 percent of your expense categories. For businesses that have a significant number of employees, the wages and salary account is usually the largest expense category and, thus, the most often abused.

We don't mean to say that you shouldn't challenge expenses in every category. You can usually find some wasted dollars by rooting around in such expense accounts as utilities, travel, insurance, and, of course, the compost heap of expenses — the "miscellaneous" expense account.

REMEMBER

Effective expense control is not only a profitability issue but it's also an important element for controlling cash flow. Because lack of cash is usually the number one warning signal of a small business's impending troubles or failure, one of the best ways to build a solid foundation for your business is by controlling your expenses from the very beginning.

Understanding zero-based budgeting

Budgeting (also known as *forecasting*) is the periodic (usually annual) review of past financial information with the purpose of forecasting future financial conditions. If you've completed your business plan, you, in effect, prepared your first budget when you forecasted your profit and loss statement for the upcoming year. The only difference in preparing a budget for your ongoing business is that you now enjoy the advantage of having yesterday's figures to work with.

Incidentally, the process of budgeting is one that should apply not only to your business but also to your personal finances, especially if you have trouble saving money. If you aren't currently budgeting your personal revenues and expenses, start doing so now (see Chapter 1). After all, there's no better way to prepare yourself for running a business than to begin at home.

In your small business, you have two ways to budget expenses from year to year. The first — we call this *adjusted-for-inflation budgeting* — is to assume a percentage increase for each expense category, both variable and fixed. For example, say that you decide that your telephone expense (a variable expense) will increase by 5 percent next year, your rent (a fixed expense) will remain the same, and your advertising and promotion (a variable expense) will increase by 10 percent. Whoosh, a few multiplications later, and you've budgeted these expenses for the year. How much easier can budgeting get?

The other way to budget expenses is called *zero-based budgeting*. If you use this type of budgeting, you assume that last year's expenses were zero and begin the budgeting process from that point. For example, the zero-based formula assumes that your supplies' expense account begins at zero; thus, you must first determine who consumed what supplies last year, who will be consuming them this year, and how much will be consumed. Then you must determine what price you'll pay for this year's supplies. In this manner, zero-based budgeting forces you to annually manage your consumption at the same time that you review your costs.

The effect of zero-based budgeting is that you no longer include prior years' mistakes in the current year's budgets. For example, when you budget telephone expenses for the year, instead of increasing them by a flat percentage like many businesses typically do, zero-based budgeting demands that you make sure your prior year's bill was the lowest it could be. This assumption forces you to determine who's using your phones for what kind of activity and also to reprice your rates with telephone carriers. Instead of forecasting a flat 5 percent increase, you may well end up projecting a 5 percent decrease. The zero-based method also assumes that you'll check out prices with other vendors besides the ones that you're presently using.

REMEMBER

Far too many small businesses don't budget expenses at all. Furthermore, of those small-business owners who do, few use zero-based budgeting, despite its many advantages. Not budgeting is truly one of the most expensive mistakes you can make as a small-business owner. Sure, zero-based budgeting may take more time than using a percentage, but it can pay big dividends in increasing bottom-line profitability — at home or in your business.

Managing Vendor Relationships

A small business's most underrated priority is working with its vendors (suppliers). Think about it. Without a good vendor, what would happen to your business? Say you own a computer retail store. Where would you be without Apple, Hewlett-Packard, and Microsoft on your shelves? Not into computers? Say you run a restaurant. Where would you be without a reliable baker, meat supplier, and fresh vegetable resource to depend on? Every successful business owner has learned the importance of having a cadre of loyal vendors standing behind their business.

Yet few small businesses have the muscle or the clout to demand any significant degree of vendor loyalty, which means that they must build strong vendor relationships the old-fashioned way — by earning them. The following tips provide information on how to earn favored relationships with your vendors:

- **Don't nickel-and-dime your vendors.** Agree on the details of your business arrangement (price, delivery, and terms) and then try to work within those parameters for the agreed-upon time frame. (Occasional exceptions will occur.) Whatever you do, don't use the low-ball pricing of the latest vendor on the street as leverage against the longtime reliable vendor unless you're prepared to lose or greatly annoy the longtime reliable one.

- **Pay your bills on time.** Paying your bills within the designated period of time helps maintain favored-customer status. After all, isn't prompt payment what you expect of *your* customers?

- **Save your special favor requests for when you need them.** Don't cry wolf on requests for out-of-the-ordinary service; save those requests for crunch time.

- **Treat your vendor's representatives (sales or customer service employees) as you want your own employees to be treated.** The Golden Rule is alive and well when it comes to maintaining vendor relationships.

- **Remember that relationships matter.** Everyone these days is preaching "relationships, relationships, relationships" when dealing with customers, right? Well, the same thing applies with vendors. Work to build a solid relationship with yours. If your vendor is a national supplier, build a relationship with its local or regional salesperson or representative or the person at the other end of the phone line. If your vendor is a local supplier, get to know them personally, just as you would a local customer. And remember, your bankers are vendors, too (perhaps the most important ones of all)!

REMEMBER

Vendors — especially the good ones — can provide you with more than just a product or service. For instance, vendors can be a great source of new business referrals. They can also provide training to both your employees and, on some occasions, your customers — a form of assistance that typical small businesses can't get enough of. For example, in coauthor Jim's sporting-goods business, the manufacturers of many of the products the company sold (fitness products especially) offered both on-site and off-site training programs at no charge. Be sure to ask your vendors what training programs and/or sales aids they offer and make use of them.

Not every prospective vendor will measure up to your standards. Be sure to check out your new vendors carefully, especially when they don't have a reputation or a track record. You can accomplish this inspection by touring their facilities, checking out the professionalism of their website, requesting customer references, and even asking for financial statements.

The overriding point here is that creating a successful business takes a unique combination of human beings interacting together: you, your employees, your customers, your vendors, and a variety of outsiders (see the later section, "Dealing with Bankers, Lawyers, and Other Outsiders," for details). No matter which of these you consider the most important, the others all have their roles in building your successful business.

Dealing with Bankers, Lawyers, and Other Outsiders

This section is intended to help you understand the outsiders you must deal with, with the intention of helping you successfully manage the relationships that evolve with them.

Bankers

Ask the typical small-business owner what they think about bankers, and you'll usually get a reaction somewhere between a roll of the eyes and a hair-tearing tantrum. As a rule, bankers get a bad rap from the small-business community, especially since the banking community's problems that led to the 2008 financial crisis.

When bankers say no, they're only doing what they're trained to do — protecting their depositors' money. For example, we know of a banker who, as part of his spiel to would-be borrowers, would say, "I treat my bank's money as if it belonged to my parents." What this banker is really saying here is, "If there's a hint of a risk, you'll have to find your money elsewhere." After all, most of a typical bank's depositors are, in fact, *someone's* parents or grandparents.

A key part of the banker's job description is not taking big risks. Think about it: If bankers were creative and optimistic and prone to take risks, they'd be entrepreneurs, not bankers. Everyone has a role in a capitalist system. Being safe and conservative just happens to be the role of the banker.

Although bankers may not play an important role in the start-up phase of most businesses, after the business is up and running, their role can become more crucial, especially when the small business experiences rapid growth. Expansion often requires operating capital in the form of outside financing, which is where bankers come in. (On occasion, of course, the entrepreneur may go back to her original source of operating capital; more typically, however, they get their financing through bank loans.)

Here's how we recommend that you work with bankers:

>> **Help your banker do their job.** Call them more often than they call you — not just with the good news but also with the bad. Bankers don't like surprises, especially bad ones.

>> **Always ask for more money than you think you need.** A little insurance never hurt anybody, and you usually won't get everything you ask for anyway. Besides, going back to the well a second time can be difficult, as well as embarrassing.

>> **Prepare in advance for your banker's visits.** No matter what they say, your banker isn't paying social calls on you; they're kicking your tires. Include an agenda and a tour of your facilities and then review your financial results *before* they ask you for them. Finally, follow up your banker's visit with a letter outlining your discussion and thanking them for their time.

>> **Recognize that you're probably going to have to** *personally guarantee* **(legally obligate your personal assets as collateral) your business's loans.** After all, you're asking your banker to, in effect, deposit their firm's money into your business. If you were in your banker's shoes, wouldn't you ask for such a guarantee? Remember, however, that your guarantee is only one of many issues that are up for negotiation when you're borrowing money. Try to use your personal guarantee to get an offsetting concession (something in return for your benefit) in the lending agreement.

>> **Don't lose sight of the fact that a bank's interest rate, the collateral it requires, and the terms it outlines are negotiable.** What you settle on depends on the strength of your bargaining position. Don't blindly accept everything the banker offers; shop around among various banks that do small-business lending.

>> **Be prepared to answer the bank's tough questions, especially where your assets are concerned.** The banker will want to know more about such hard assets as inventory, receivables, and equipment than you ever thought possible. But remember, those assets are the bank's insurance. The better your business's assets look to the bank, the better your negotiating position will be when the time comes to work out the terms of the loan.

REMEMBER

Bankers and their conservative, close-to-the-vest ways are a fact of life. You can either learn to live with them or face life without being able to borrow their money.

TIP

Look at your local community banks first because they have historically taken the lead in small-business lending.

Lawyers

Long, long ago, lawyers used to be like FBI agents: You were aware that they existed, and sometimes you even met one, but you rarely had occasion to deal with them. They practiced their trade on someone else — never on you.

Today, lawyers are like pets. Everybody seems to have one. If you worked for General Motors, for example, lawyers would be part of the overhead — a fixed expense, similar to rent, taxes, and utilities.

But small-business owners don't work for General Motors. To you, lawyers are a large, additional expense. Lawyers' fees consume your hard-earned cash, resulting in capital expenditures that you must put on hold, new employees that you can't hire, or trade shows that you can't attend. Additionally, spending time with lawyers takes time away from work and results in lost productivity on the job.

All that said, consulting a lawyer has a time and a place. Lawyers provide protection (often against other lawyers) and force you to make plans to guard against the downsides that your entrepreneurially optimistic nature may overlook.

Yes, lawyers definitely have a time and a place. The place is always in the lawyer's office — you can't afford to pay a lawyer to travel to your office — or on the phone, and the times are:

>> When forming your corporation or LLC

>> When taking in a partner or partners

>> When creating shares of stock in your company — for you and for others

>> When signing a lease, contract, or binding agreement

>> When buying or selling a business

>> When dealing with someone else's attorney on a conflictive issue

>> When creating an employee handbook

>> When designing employee bonus programs that result in company ownership for the employees

>> When dealing with a situation that can result in expensive litigation (such as terminating a longtime or problematic/litigious employee)

>> When considering bankruptcy (we hope that never happens)

No matter how much you want to avoid the expense of consulting with a lawyer, you should definitely hire one on the preceding occasions throughout the life of your business. When these occasions present themselves, we suggest you follow these tips for how best to find and utilize your lawyer:

>> **When you absolutely, positively have to find a lawyer, don't shop just for price; shop for quality *and* price.** As with cars and quarterbacks, lawyers differ greatly in the way they perform, and that difference usually translates into winning or losing. Check references closely, just as you would when hiring a key employee.

>> **Get a quote on your prospective lawyer's hourly fees and ask for an estimate of the total tab in advance.** The estimate may not hold up, but the lawyer will know that you're watching.

>> **Always ask for itemized invoices.** A lump-sum invoice includes only time and rate, while an itemized invoice includes the date and time of each segment of work, the specific subject of each charge, and then the hourly rate. An itemized invoice also indicates work that was done by others — paralegals, for example — along with their hourly rates and charges for related materials.

>> **Don't let lawyers chitchat about anything but the business at hand if their meters are running.** Even though you enjoy talking about the latest sports or TV news as much as the next person, keep your discussions with your lawyer focused on your business. After all, we'd hate for you to pay $350 an hour to talk football!

>> **Keep in mind that lawyers are human beings, too, which means they aren't always right.** Lawyers work in a gray profession, not a black-and-white one like accountants do. The power of logic — theirs and yours — working in unison with their knowledge of the law will play a significant role in your business. You're capable of logic, too. Don't be afraid to use it in their presence. If your lawyers won't listen to you or ask for your input with important decisions, then find another lawyer.

>> **Don't be afraid to fire lawyers when they fail to perform up to your expectations.** They're no different from employees, accountants, or anyone else you hire to provide a service.

TIP

Lawyers aren't the only resource for settling disputes. Many small businesses today utilize mediation to resolve contentious issues with customers, suppliers, and employees. Mediation is significantly less expensive than litigation and can take a fraction of the time (no court dates, no judges, and no miles of red tape). Nationwide providers of mediation services include the American Arbitration Association (www.adr.org; 800-778-7879) and JAMS (www.jamsadr.com; 800-352-5267).

Tax advisors

Tax advisors, like lawyers, are professionals. The services they provide aren't rooted in conflict, but hiring and paying them can be equally discomforting and almost as expensive.

The role of tax advisors, in essence, is to provide you with the information you need to pay your taxes, make tax-wise business decisions, keep score of your progress, and manage your business.

We use the words "tax advisors" to include CPA's, accountants, enrolled agents, or whoever it is that advises you on tax-related issues.

Consultants

Hiring a consultant is akin to playing wild-card poker, meaning that fate will be a factor in determining whether you select the right one. That's not to say your success or failure is entirely in fate's hands, because the more effort you put into the hiring process, the better your chances will be to get the job done right and hire a superstar consultant.

Consultants can provide a wide array of services. Several of the areas where consultants can help the most include computer and information systems, tax issues, human resources, sales, and marketing.

You'll find more than one way to use and pay consultants. Some consultants offer their clients advice only; other consultants dive head-first into their client's business and get their hands dirty. Some consultants are paid by the hour, others by retainer (a fixed fee every month). It all depends on what you want and what you can afford.

Here are a few tips for how to get the most out of your consultant:

>> **Search for a consultant as if you were hiring a key staff employee.** Network to find the best one and always check references carefully. Avoid consultants who have had only big corporate clients, as opposed to small-business ones.

Despite what corporate consultants will tell you, most don't understand what running a small business is like. Hire only consultants with plenty of small-business experience.

>> **Whatever you do, don't hand over to your consultants the responsibility of making key decisions.** Also, never bet the house on the suggestions they make. Make your consultants prove themselves on smaller issues before you make the bigger changes they recommend. And never forget that no matter how smart or expensive they are, you're in charge.

>> **Don't offer any long-term contracts.** Build in a quick-exit option in the all-too-likely event that you don't get what you expected. And don't hesitate to show consultants the door when they aren't doing the job. Or, as the old adage goes, "Hire slowly, fire quickly."

>> **Understand that their fees are only part of the ultimate cost of engaging ineffectual consultants.** Add misdirection, upset employees, and time lost, and weak consultants can run up monumental tabs in surprisingly short periods of time.

Governments

Entrepreneurs like you need to understand that the government is often an uncontrollable, random event, like a fire or a flood or a competitor moving in next door. This is especially true of the federal government, where the small-business owner may find it quite difficult to so much as talk to those officials who are the actual decision-makers, let alone get their problems resolved.

REMEMBER

Come to terms with the fact that you'll sometimes have to comply with the government's unwieldy and often unfriendly rules and regulations. Don't antagonize government employees (especially those who work for the IRS) — they can make your life miserable. Do what needs to be done to satisfy those sometimes-disagreeable government employees (you'd probably be disagreeable, too, if you had to spend your life in their environment), treat the agreeable ones like you'd want your own employees to be treated, and don't shoot the messenger — most government employees are only trying to do their jobs. In Chapter 11, we offer helpful advice for dealing with government regulations.

Chapter **11**

Handling Regulatory and Legal Issues

O ne of the least-pleasant aspects of starting and running a small business is comprehending and adhering to the myriad government regulations that affect how and where you do business — not to mention the plethora of legal issues that can blow up in your face and culminate in a lawsuit. So we understand that you probably have a strong desire to skip this chapter. But please don't; doing so can ensnare you in government fines and legal fees that can prove disastrous to your business.

And if the thought of these penalties isn't enough, we have what we hope is an incentive for you to familiarize yourself with the issues raised in this chapter: We can save you time and headaches by showing you how to efficiently and correctly complete important legal and regulatory tasks.

Navigating Small-Business Laws

You may think that if you're starting or operating a truly *small* small business, you don't need to know much on the legal and regulatory fronts. We wish that were true, but it's not. Consider the following types of issues that most small-business owners must grapple with, both in the earlier years of their businesses and on an ongoing basis:

» **Selecting a name for your business:** You'll probably choose to keep or have to keep (with a franchise) the name of the business you acquire. If you think you can select a better name for a business you buy, keep in mind that you can't simply choose any name and start using it for your business. After all, you may select a name that another business is already using, and that owner can take legal action against you. Besides, you'll probably spend a lot of marketing money over the years to distinguish *your* business from the masses, and you don't want people (especially your customers) to confuse your business with someone else's.

» **Complying with government licensing and permit requirements:** Federal, state, and sometimes even local governments regulate and license certain types of businesses, such as restaurants, taxicabs and other transportation services, and beauty salons.

If you're operating a business that requires registration with particular government entities, the passing of certain exams, or the satisfaction of specific licensing requirements (see the later section "Complying through licensing, registrations, and permits"), you'll be breaking the law and may be put out of business if you don't comply. The possible penalties for running afoul of business laws can be steep and can include monetary fines and outright prohibition against practicing your line of work for months or even years. And if that isn't bad enough, your transgressions may become public knowledge (and permanently etched into the internet), which can hamper your ability to get your business up and running again when you're legally able to do so.

» **Protecting your ideas and work:** If you prepare a business plan and distribute it for comment or to raise money, you don't want anyone to steal your ideas, do you? If you invent or brainstorm something new and unique (often known as *intellectual property* or IP), you don't want someone else to copy your creation and profit from it, do you? Well, if you don't properly protect your ideas, work, and other creative developments through trademarks, copyrights, and patents, someone can rip you off and you'd have little, if any, legal recourse. (See the later section "Protecting ideas: Nondisclosures, patents, trademarks, and copyrights.")

>> **Establishing a retirement plan:** Perhaps you've heard of retirement plans such as profit sharing, SEP-IRAs, and so on. Over the years, these plans can slash tens, and maybe even hundreds, of thousands of dollars off your tax bill. However, if you have employees, they're entitled to certain retirement benefits that are subject to federal regulations. Your reward for violating retirement-plan rules can be the disallowance of your contributions into the plan, thereby causing you to owe the IRS taxes and penalties — ouch!

>> **Filing your taxes:** As a business owner and self-employed person, you're responsible for properly filing all federal, state, and local taxes for yourself and your business. And when you employ others, you must withhold appropriate taxes from their wages and submit the withheld taxes in a timely fashion to the various tax regulatory authorities. More than a few small businesses have failed because the owners fell behind on taxes and subsequently were buried by past-due payments. (Chapter 15 helps you stay in the good graces of the tax authorities.)

>> **Hiring and managing employees:** Employment law is a vast area. When you hire and employ workers, you must be careful about what you say to them and how you manage and behave around them. If you're not careful, you can face big legal bills and possible lawsuit damages, while your reputation as well as that of your hard-earned business are dragged through the mud during legal proceedings. (See Chapter 12 for more on finding and hiring employees.)

>> **Preparing contracts:** In many ways, contracts make the business world go 'round. When properly prepared, contracts function as legally binding, enforceable agreements that your business makes with suppliers, employees,

and others relating to the operation of your business. If you offer a contract to another person or business or seek to change the terms and conditions of an existing contract, you must first understand the legal ramifications. If you don't understand these ramifications, at a minimum, you'll have to deal with upset parties on the other end of the contract; in the worst cases, you can end up in court with soaring legal bills and potential lawsuits (see the later section "A business prenup: Contracts with customers and suppliers" for more).

Complying with Small-Business Regulations

Before you begin working with your first customer as the new owner of the business you bought, you need to invest time and money into getting your legal and regulatory ducks in a row. In this section, we assist you in saving time and money while helping you protect your business.

Complying through licensing, registrations, and permits

INVESTIGATE

To discover the various ways in which different government bodies regulate your line of business for the company you acquire, we suggest you check with the following:

>> **Trade associations for your business or profession:** Most lines of business have active trade associations, whose management and members can share war stories and information about regulations. Obviously, association members in your local area will have far more relevant experiences to share, assuming they aren't competitors. Turn to Chapter 14 for information on how to locate a trade association in your industry or check out the *Small Business Sourcebook* (a useful reference published by Gale), which you can probably find at your local library.

>> **Peers in your profession:** Those who have been there and done that can save you time by sharing their experiences. The simplest way to network with others in your line of work is to attend conferences or conventions for your industry or profession. Again, trade associations can help you locate such events, or you can network in your local area.

WARNING

A downside of the local-area strategy is that people in the same line of work in your town may view you as competition and be less than forthcoming with assistance. Also, keep in mind that others may or may not have done a thorough job of researching regulatory requirements and may have chosen not to comply with certain regulations.

TIP

If you're fortunate enough to live in a community that has a business incubator (see Chapter 14), stop in and inquire about one or more of its lessees. They are, by definition, people who recently went through the same thing you're going through now.

>> **The state agency that oversees corporations and/or small businesses:** Look online for any of the following state government agencies: Economic Development Department, Department of Commerce or Corporations, or the Office of Small Business. Hopefully, you can find the information you are looking for on their website. If you can't, then call the contact number(s) listed on their website. When you make the call, be persistent, because if the person who answers the phone is poorly trained or having a bad day, you may not get the information you need, and you may have to start over again with a different department.

>> **Other relevant local government agencies:** Many (but not all) of these agencies have information on their websites. For tax issues, look up the Tax Collector. For real estate issues, contact the Planning Department or Building Inspection Department. For health-related issues, be in touch with the Health Department. If you get stuck and can't find the correct department, most cities and towns have a city clerk or town clerk who can help you.

>> **Trade publications/websites:** You may be surprised at how many specialized occupational publications/websites

exist. (See Chapter 4 for tips on how to identify and locate them.) You can research past articles on industry regulations from such publications and websites.

>> **The local Chamber of Commerce:** Most communities have a Chamber of Commerce; the better ones have helpful information for prospective and current small-business owners (including the applicable government organizations you need to check in with and the other people you need to speak to).

>> **Small Business Development Centers (SBDCs):** Every state has an SBDC, and most SBDCs have extensive small-business libraries, as well as a wide variety of pamphlets and brochures, compliments of the applicable government organizations.

>> **Experienced small-business advisors:** Tax and legal advisors, as well as consultants experienced with businesses like yours, can help point you in the right direction. Although such advisors generally charge a hefty hourly fee, the advice can be well worth the price if you select a good advisor. An advisor may even be willing to offer free tips on general regulatory issues in order to cultivate your future business.

>> **Real estate agents and building contractors:** If your business will operate in a commercial or retail space, you can acquire knowledge by conversing with agents who sell or lease space and/or contractors who develop and renovate space similar to what your business will occupy.

In the next sections, we dig deeper into the realities of compliance and the local, state, and federal regulations you must follow.

The realities of compliance

Various government agencies — at the local, regional, state, and federal levels — impose all sorts of licensing, registration, and permit requirements on small-business owners.

If you overlook applying for one important permit or license, the government can slap you with hefty fines, and disgruntled customers can sue you, using your lack of compliance with government regulations as an indicator of slipshod business practices. And even if you're a good enough detective to ferret out and understand the government regulations with which you must comply, you may tear out your hair trying to determine the right order in which to obtain your permits and licenses.

Okay, so life can be worse — you can live in a socialist or communist country where such permits are available only to the highest bidders! Talk to as many people as you can, being a sponge, and remember that the burden for compliance falls on your shoulders. Don't toss your hands in the air, say that compliance with government regulations is too hard to figure out, and just wing it.

REMEMBER

The success or failure of a business often lies in the details — or, more specifically, in the owner's willingness to pay attention to them. Complying with all applicable regulations is an early test!

Local regulations: Taxes, zoning, and health

The town, city, and county in which you operate your business more than likely impose some requirements on businesses like yours. Even if you operate a home-based business, you can't assume that you can do what you want when and where you want to do it because home-based businesses often are even more restricted than their office-park counterparts.

Some common local regulations that affect small-business owners include the following:

>> **Taxes:** In most areas, if you're selling products through a retail store, you have to collect sales tax. In fact, even if you don't operate a retail store, you may have to collect sales tax on products or services you sell, and some cities tax all revenue from small businesses. Plus, you may be surprised to discover that some communities levy an annual property tax on certain business assets such as inventory, equipment, and furniture.

>> **Fictitious name:** Generally speaking if the name of your business is different from your own name, you need to file what's known as a *fictitious name* or *doing business as* (DBA)

form. You usually file your DBA form through the county, and you may have to publish your DBA filing in a local newspaper.

>> **Real estate:** All real estate is affected by *zoning,* which restricts the use of a given property. If you don't like the idea of local government telling you what you can and can't do on your property, consider how you'd feel if your next-door neighbors opened a chicken and pig farm on their property! Whether you're leasing or buying a property, you'll have to deal with zoning rules and regulations.

INVESTIGATE

When buying a business and you're considering different locations for it, investigate whether you can operate your business at a given location, as well as plan on dealing with the good folks in Town/City Hall if you want to do any renovations to your place of business. If those renovations raise any environmental concerns — such as disturbing or removing potentially hazardous substances like asbestos — you may need to involve your local health department as well (see the next bullet). Zoning and renovation issues often come into play when a home-office business steadily grows and the owner finally decides to add on to their house or garage in order to hire another employee or carry more products in inventory or when the business generates a level of activity that affects noise levels, traffic, and parking demands.

>> **Health and safety:** Small-business owners whose enterprises involve food are subject to all sorts of regulations from the local health department. For instance, you may need to have your water tested occasionally if you live in a less densely populated area that uses well water. And don't overlook the myriad safety regulations, such as local fire codes and elevator inspections.

State regulations: More taxes, licensing, insurance, and the environment

In addition to regulations at the local level, states impose requirements on businesses, and you need to be aware of, and comply with, these requirements. Most states have established agencies to assist business owners with doing business in the state. After all, states do have some vested interest in trying to attract and retain businesses because business tax revenues fill their coffers.

Here are the primary issues that may affect your small business due to state regulations:

>> **Licenses:** State licensing is primarily intended to reduce the consumer's likelihood of being fleeced or victimized. Although some occupations (such as doctors and lawyers) are universally required to be licensed, each state has a unique list of occupations that it regulates.

State licensing requirements vary by occupation and by state. In some states, you can get certain licenses after you complete a few forms and pay the state a fee. In most cases, however, you have to take a test or complete some form of certification in order to get a license.

>> **Taxes:** As we discuss in the local regulations section, some businesses, such as retailers, have to collect sales tax on products sold. In most states, all businesses must pay income taxes at the state level. For more information, check out the latest edition of *Small Business Taxes For Dummies,* by Eric Tyson (published by Wiley).

>> **Insurance:** To you, the small-business owner, having to pay for employee-related insurance will feel like another tax. Common state-required coverage includes workers' compensation, which compensates workers for lost wages due to job-related injuries, and unemployment insurance, which pays laid-off employees for a certain period of time or until they secure another job.

>> **Environment:** If you're a manufacturer and your plant emits unsavory smoke, particles, or odors into the air or water, you can be certain that your state (and possibly other government agencies) will regulate your activities — and for good reason. Left to their own devices, some unsavory business owners would knowingly pollute because installing control devices would add to the cost of doing business, effectively reducing profits.

Federal regulations: Still more taxes, licenses, and requirements

In addition to local and state regulations, small-business owners must comply with U.S. federal government regulations, which cover taxes and licenses as well as the health, safety, and welfare of your employees.

REMEMBER

Not all federal labor laws affect all small businesses because some issues apply only to employers with a specific number of employees. So the good news may be that your small business is small enough that you don't have to concern yourself with all the issues we cover in the following list. (Find out what issues apply to your business by consulting the resources listed in the section "Complying through licensing, registrations, and permits" earlier in this chapter.)

Here are the key federal regulations most small-business owners need to consider:

>> **Licenses:** Most businesses that require a license or permit to operate generally obtain the documentation at the state level. Some businesses, however, receive permits and licenses at the federal level. These businesses include alcohol and tobacco manufacturers, drug companies, firearm manufacturers and dealers, investment advisors, meat packing and preparation companies, radio and television stations, and trucking and other transportation companies. Some of these types of licenses may be transferable when buying a business so be sure to research that and don't take anyone's word for it.

>> **Taxes:** All incorporated businesses, or their owners if the business isn't incorporated, must file a federal income tax return. Additionally, most small-business owners — especially those who hire employees — choose to apply for and utilize a federal Employer Identification Number (EIN). The latest edition of *Small Business Taxes For Dummies,* by Eric Tyson (published by Wiley) covers these and other small-business tax issues at length.

>> **Americans with Disabilities Act (ADA):** This legislation prohibits employers with 15 or more employees from discriminating against prospective and current employees

or customers with disabilities. Such discrimination is barred in the hiring, management, and dismissal of any employee. For example, during the process of interviewing job applicants, you can get yourself into a heap of legal hot water if you exclude from consideration qualified candidates who are in some way disabled.

>> **Family and Medical Leave Act:** This legislation requires employers with 50 or more employees (within 75 miles) to provide up to 12 weeks of unpaid leave to employees who desire or need the leave for personal health issues due to a serious medical condition that affects the employee's ability to perform the regular duties of their job; to spend time with a newborn or adopted child; or to care for a family member who has a serious medical condition.

During the term of an employee's leave, the employer must continue to cover the employee under the company's group health-insurance plan under the same conditions as when the employee was working.

Eligible employees (who have been with the employer for at least one year and who have worked at least 125 hours over the previous year) who take a leave under the Family and Medical Leave Act generally can do so with the understanding that they can return to their same positions with the same pay and benefits. So-called highly paid "key" employees aren't guaranteed the same positions and compensation packages if their returns would lead to significant economic harm to the employers. (The Department of Labor defines a *key employee* as a salaried employee "... who is among the highest paid 10 percent of employees within 75 miles of the work site.")

>> **2010 federal health-insurance legislation:** Congress passed sweeping health-insurance legislation in 2010 that affects many small businesses.

Selection of a business entity

When acquiring a business, be sure to consult your attorney or tax advisor about what type of organization or business entity — for example, sole proprietorship, partnership, corporation, or limited liability company (LLC) — makes sense for your enterprise. Although the different corporate entities that you may form for your business can provide some legal protection for you and your personal assets, establishing such entities involves significant time and expense and doesn't completely insulate you and your company from lawsuits.

Given the excitement and stresses inherent in the early days of running a small business, we can understand why you may not care to spend your precious time and money on researching and consulting with legal and tax experts about what type of organization you should establish. As we discuss in Chapter 9, however, because of taxes and other issues, you should choose which entity will best serve your needs sooner rather than later.

Protecting ideas: Nondisclosures, patents, trademarks, and copyrights

The business idea and business plans behind the business you buy probably aren't 100 percent unique. Some business owners, however, have taken a different twist on something or have created a truly unique product or service. The result of this "different twist" is often referred to as intellectual property.

Even if the business you buy doesn't have intellectual property to offer, you don't want others to steal your plans and ideas. By circulating copies of your business plan, you may be giving away much of your hard work and ideas to an individual or another business that can end up being a competitor.

The following sections explain what you need to know about protecting your business and ideas in general and specifically through nondisclosures, trademarks, patents, and copyrights.

General tips for protecting your ideas

Here are some tips for how to protect your business plan and ideas:

>> **Be careful about who sees your business plan.** A friend or advisor who happens to know a lot about your type of small business, or small businesses in general, is unlikely

to have unfriendly motives in looking at your plan. On the other hand, an industry insider or a potential competitor who peruses your plans may not have your best interests at heart.

>> **Keep proprietary information out of your plan.** Don't include product designs, manufacturing specifications, unique resources, or other information unique to your company in the copies of your business plan that you distribute to others. Share such information with serious investors only if needed to gain their investments, and do so with a nondisclosure agreement attached (see the next section).

>> **Place a nondisclosure statement in the front of your business plan.** If your plan does fall into the hands of someone who may be inclined to steal your ideas, a nondisclosure statement (which we discuss in the next section) should scare them off.

>> **Get legal assistance when necessary.** If your work and ideas are proprietary and protectable, speak with an attorney who specializes in intellectual property, including copyrights, trademarks, and patents. We explain these important legal protections in the upcoming section "Patents, trademarks, and copyrights."

Nondisclosure agreements (NDAs)

Always be sure to attach a *nondisclosure agreement* (NDA) to the beginning of your business plan before you circulate it for review. The purpose of the NDA is to warn the reader that the enclosed contents are private property and are not to be spread around without your consent. (*Note:* You don't need an attorney to craft this agreement.)

REMEMBER

Simply including the NDA with your business plan isn't enough; never hand out your plan without first having the recipient sign the NDA.

Following is a sample nondisclosure agreement:

This confidential Business Plan has been prepared in order to raise financing for Wowza Widgets, Inc. This material is being delivered to a select number of potential investors, each of whom agrees to the following terms and conditions:

Each recipient of this Business Plan agrees that, by accepting this material, he or she will not copy, reproduce, distribute, or discuss with others any part of this plan without prior written consent of Wowza Widgets, Inc.

The recipient agrees to keep confidential all information contained herein and not use it for any purpose whatsoever other than to evaluate and determine interest in providing financing described herein.

This material contains proprietary and confidential information regarding Wowza Widgets, Inc., and is based upon information provided to Wowza Widgets, Inc., by sources deemed to be reliable. Although the information contained herein is believed to be accurate, Wowza Widgets, Inc., expressly disclaims all liability for any information, projections, or representations (expressed or implied) contained herein from omissions from this material or for any written or oral communication transmitted to any party in the course of its evaluation for this financing. The recipient acknowledges that this material shall remain the property of Wowza Widgets, Inc., and Wowza Widgets, Inc., reserves the right to request the return of the material at any time and in any respect, to amend or terminate solicitation procedures, to terminate discussions with any and all prospective financing sources, to reject any and all proposals, or to negotiate with any party with respect to the financing of Wowza Widgets, Inc.

The projections contained in the pro forma Financial Section are based upon numerous assumptions. Although Wowza Widgets, Inc., believes that these assumptions are reasonable, no assurance can be given as to the accuracy of these projections because they are dependent in large part upon unforeseeable factors and events. As a result, the actual results achieved may vary from the projections, and such variation can be material and adverse.

Signature (print): _____

Signature: _____

Patents, trademarks, and copyrights

When you buy a business, you may have bought in a business that created a product, service, or technology unique enough that you want to prevent others from copying it. Or maybe you simply want to restrain others from using and profiting from the name of your business or literary, musical, or artistic creations.

Welcome to the wonderful and often confusing world of patent, copyright, and trademark law. You'll be relieved to hear that this isn't a legal book, in part because your two humble authors are, happily (for us at least), not lawyers. And most small-business owners don't need to spend much time or legal expense on these issues.

If you do need to deal with patents, copyrights, or trademarks, you have to be familiar with the following very important terms. For more information, consult a lawyer who specializes in intellectual property.

>> **Patent:** If you've invented something (such as a new type of toy or computer disk) in your business, or acquired a business that has, you may want to explore patenting the invention. The reason: By filing a *patent* with the federal government, you have exclusive rights to manufacture, sell, and use the patented invention. You can, if you so choose, license usage of the patent to others.

>> **Trademark:** Companies invest significant time, effort, and money into creating brand names (for example, Coca-Cola and *For Dummies*), marketing strategies, advertising slogans (Making Everything Easier!), logos (the Dummies Man on this book's cover or the Nike swoosh, for instance), and so on. The point of the *trademark* is to protect your brands and prevent other enterprises from using and profiting from the recognition and reputation you've developed through your business's brand names, marketing/advertising images, and the words associated with your product.

Trademarked items can also include things such as the packaging, shape, character names, color, and smell associated with a product. If you think your business has identifying characteristics that you don't want copied by competitors, think about applying for trademark protection. *Note:* Patents and trademarks are handled by the U.S. Patent and Trademark Office (www.uspto.gov); copyrights are the domain of the U.S. Copyright Office (www.copyright.gov).

>> **Copyright:** *Copyright* laws cover such works as musical and sound recordings, literary works, software, graphics, and audiovisuals. The owner of the copyright of a work is solely allowed to sell the work, make copies of it, create derivations from it, and perform and display the work. The creator of the work isn't always the person or part of the organization that holds the copyright, though. For example, writers sometimes do freelance writing for publications that hold the copyright to the work that their writers create for them.

TIP

In the less complex cases, you can copyright your idea, product, or authorship yourself to save money. A two-page form is available from the U.S. Copyright Office (www.copyright.gov/forms; 202-707-3000). Follow the directions and you can register your copyright yourself. You must pay a modest filing fee for each request, but you can put similar works on one form.

TIP

When acquiring a business, inventory all the patents, trademarks, and copyrights owned by the business and be sure that those are included in the purchase of the business unless mutually agreed upon.

REMEMBER

No copyright cops are out there searching for people who are violating your patents, trademarks, or copyrights. The burden is on you to perform the detective work yourself; if you discover a violation, head immediately for an attorney.

A business prenup: Contracts with customers and suppliers

All small businesses have customers as well as suppliers (or vendors). In both relationships, small-business owners often engage in contracts, whether formally written or verbal. Here are our tips for dealing with contracts with your customers and suppliers:

>> **Get it in writing.** Otherwise, you have little or no recourse if someone (such as a supplier) doesn't deliver as promised.

>> **Don't make promises verbally that you aren't willing to put into writing.** What you say can get you into trouble, especially in terms of your customers and advertising.

>> **Get a legal perspective.** As we discuss in Chapter 10, you need to seek legal assistance for small-business operation issues at various times in the life of your business. When you're drafting contracts is one of those times.

Whether or not you should develop a contract with a vendor or a customer depends on the situation. If, for example, you're working with a local customer or vendor — especially someone you know — and you think they may be offended by your request for a formal contract, sticking with handshakes is fine. If, however, you happen to land a whale for a customer or you order products from a large vendor, neither of whom you have a personal relationship with, you should initiate a formal contract.

In fact, most large companies — whether they're customers or vendors — expect a formal contract as part of the package. If they don't get one, they may wonder about your ability to work with them on a professional level. If the professionalism issue isn't enough to convince you to develop a formal contract, let self-preservation be your motivator. After all, large businesses don't always have small businesses' best interests in mind. Why not lock in your safety with a contract?

Laboring over Employee Costs and Laws

When your business begins to hire employees, the good news is that it has probably gotten off the ground sufficiently well enough to afford the costs associated with hiring and managing them. The bad news is that, besides the salary you pay your employees, you'll encounter several significant "hidden" costs, including the following (see Chapter 12 for the lowdown on finding and hiring employees):

>> **Taxes:** On top of your employees' salaries, you're also responsible for paying Social Security taxes on their earnings, as well as other taxes, such as unemployment insurance. When hiring, you must be careful about whether you hire people as employees or independent contractors. Many small-business employers prefer to hire people as independent contractors because doing so lowers their tax bills, but the IRS has strict rules for who qualifies as an independent contractor. If you classify someone as a contractor who should be considered an employee, you can end up facing stiff penalties.

>> **Employee benefits:** Various insurance programs, paid vacation, and retirement plans help attract and retain employees. The smallest small businesses can't afford to offer many employee benefits, but you should know your options and be aware of what your competition is offering. (We cover employee benefit programs in Chapter 12.)

>> **Government regulations:** Are you surprised that a host of local, state, and federal government regulations dictate, mandate, and cajole your hiring, management, and dismissal of employees? You shouldn't be if you've read this chapter all the way through!

>> **Employee lawsuits:** Don't think that just because you're running a small business you can't and won't be sued. Although some employee suits are frivolous, others are caused by employers not exercising proper care when dealing with employees. Check out Chapter 10 for info on working with a small-business-experienced attorney.

5

Creating a Growth Trajectory

IN THIS PART . . .

Identify and retain top-performing employees.

Cultivate a loyal customer base.

Chapter **12**

Keeping and Attracting Superstar Employees

Every business has several *game-breaker* positions (key positions that will make or break your company). When you're just starting out, the game-breaker position may be yours alone because you may be the only employee. In larger, established small businesses, those game-breaker positions may include the president/CEO/Grand Poobah (that's you), the financial person, the sales manager, the marketing manager, the production manager, the office manager, the purchasing agent, the art director . . . well, you get the idea. Every success-ful, growing small business must have a team of superstars fill-ing its game-breaker positions. A *superstar* is an employee who

>> Can take on increasing responsibilities and contribute to the company's continued growth

>> Is loyal to your vision

>> Shares your ethics and principles

>> Is creative within their area of expertise

>> Adds to the synergy of the team by working effectively with other team members

>> Welcomes positive change

Assembling your team of superstars is a three-part process — hiring, training, and motivating. Unfortunately, in the process of hiring people you hope are superstars, you'll sometimes stumble and hire someone who doesn't work out. Sadly, that calls for a related process that's equally as important: firing.

In this chapter, we discuss the range of options you have when it comes to cultivating your team. From hiring and firing to encouraging superstars to stay, we show you the tools at your disposal to keep your talent in tip-top shape.

Motivating Top Performers to Stay

When you acquire a business, you'll have a better understanding of the top employees and their strengths and weaknesses once you close on the business and get far more involved. To best identify key performers and to get useful feedback and sugges-tions, you should invest the time and energy to get to know and interact with all of the business's employees.

If you really want their candid feedback on the state of the busi-ness and what should possibly be changed, you need to create a culture that encourages open communication. Assure folks that discussions are deemed private and that you won't penalize them for sharing negative comments and/or suggestions for improvement. If the company has been in business for a number of years and has had numerous employees, you may find reviews on Glassdoor that shed more light on the business and employees — just be careful of placing too much value on anonymous reviews.

People who study such things tell us that the typical employee is motivated by the following (in this particular order):

1. Recognition or appreciation

2. Interesting work

3. Wages

4. Awareness of what's going on in the company

5. Good working conditions

6. Job security

7. Feeling that management cares about the employee

Meanwhile, the typical entrepreneur is motivated by one or more of the following (in no particular order):

>> Creativity or growth

>> Money

>> Power

>> Freedom

>> Survival

Although the two lists have some overlap, the lesson here is that what motivates you, the employer/entrepreneur, is, in most cases, quite different from what motivates your typical employees. Which means, if you expect your employees to perform as you want them to, you must figure out how to motivate them differently than you motivate yourself.

To be a successful employer, you must adjust the way in which you envision the motivational process. The biblical Golden Rule needs its own special twist for employers: "Do unto your employees as they would have done unto themselves."

The following sections discuss the tools that play a primary role in the motivational process: compensation, goal-setting, performance expectations, and performance reviews. Look for the differences between you and your employees as you read.

Revisiting the Compensation Plan

Compensation (wages and/or salaries) is number three on the typical employee's list of key motivators. Although this news may be encouraging to the U.S. economic future, as well as to that of your own business, it becomes irrelevant when salary-review time comes around — Pee Wee Herman suddenly turns into Mike Tyson when his wages are on the line.

If you wonder what we mean, just try saying no to a few expected (and deserved) raises among your employees, the next time the annual salary-setting time comes around in your company. Or try cutting the salary for a few of your good employees after you've taken over the business. Number three on the list suddenly becomes number one!

REMEMBER

Nothing is more important than compensation on the day that you tell your employee whether they're getting a raise and how much it will be. Why? Because compensation is a black-and-white issue; your employees can look at it, compare it, and show it off or complain about it to their loved ones. Compensation states what a particular employee is worth, in your — the boss's — eyes, anyway. Oh yes, and compensation can also be the first foot in the door when competitors come snooping around to hire away your best employees. (A healthy salary increase is usually the opener in negotiations between an employee and a prospective new employer.)

In the following sections, we dig deeper into the types of compensation you can provide and the best plans you can create for your company and employees.

Reviewing the types of compensation

The compensation system in the business you've acquired may or may not make the most sense and you should understand what employees think of the current system. An overhaul may be in order, but a simple tweak or the current system may be working just fine.

You can compensate employees in several proven ways:

» **Hourly:** The original tool of the "paying for time" compensation method. It works for Honda and Walmart, and it can work for you, too, especially for your part-time and entry-level employees.

» **Salary:** The long-term version of "paying for time." Salaries usually come with annual cost-of-living raises and bonuses, the latter of which typically ranges anywhere from 3 percent to 25 percent of base salary. (These bonuses should be based on performance and/or achievement of goals.) As a rule, salaries represent security to their recipients, and security is number six on the employee motivation list.

» **Commission:** Always the best compensation method for the hungry, hard-charging, sales types. Security isn't important to these folks; money, accomplishment, and opportunity are.

» **Pay-for-performance:** An increasingly popular alternative to the traditional "paying for time" compensation plans. Also called *gain-sharing* or *success-sharing,* pay-for-performance usually involves a relatively small base salary — often without annual cost-of-living adjustments — with all other compensation based on either individual or team performance (or a combination of both). Specific pay-for-performance plans are as varied and creative as the small businesses that use them, and they always require an efficient measuring system to back them up.

» **Hybrids:** A mix of annual salary, pay-for-performance, annual bonuses, stock-option plans, and whatever else you can devise.

Creating a compensation plan that works for your business

The subject of compensation is one of those eye-of-the-beholder kinds of issues. If you view compensation as an expense, that's exactly what it will turn out to be — an out-of-pocket, painful expense, with all the downsides that the term implies. On the other hand, if you view your compensation plan as a motivational tool, you won't be creating and managing an expense account; you'll be developing an instrument to increase your employees' performance.

REMEMBER

The best employees are the ones who believe they're valued and treated fairly. The best *measurable* (key word here!) method of that valuation is their salary. If your employees believe their wages are consistent with the value they deliver to your business, you won't have to motivate them because they'll motivate themselves. Poof! The salary expense account suddenly becomes a salary investment account. A huge difference!

The following list outlines our advice for devising a compensation plan that will work for *your* business:

>> **Make sure that your employees thoroughly understand whatever method you use to compensate them.** Paying for performance may make all kinds of motivational sense, but it works only if the employee understands what performance formula you're using and how they can impact the results. Ditto with commission.

>> **Make sure that you can measure whatever needs measuring before you agree to pay for it.** If you can't measure it, you can't manage it.

>> **Be consistent within employee groups.** For example, with your salespeople, have one compensation method and be consistent within that group.

>> **Remember that benefits are an important part of the compensation package — important to your employees' security and to your bottom line.** Consider them carefully and be sure that you (and your employees) understand what they're really worth. For more on benefits, see the later section, "Introducing Changes to Employee Benefits."

>> **Keep the time between bonus payments as short as possible.** Rewards, financial and otherwise, lose their impact when stretched out too long. The timing on when to give bonuses varies, but for most employees, in most cases, quarterly bonuses are the most effective. For some (high-impact managers), semi-annual or annual bonuses work better, since top management's accountability is typically more long term in nature. Avoid monthly bonuses; the administration is too much of a burden.

>> **Contact your industry trade association if you're unsure of how much to pay your employees.** It may have information on what similar-sized businesses are paying employees in comparable positions.

>> **Make any period-ending bonus meaningful in size.** We suggest that you make each bonus, at the very least, 3 percent of the employee's annual salary. We also recommend that you give it to the employee personally.

WARNING

Your employee compensation plan is one area in which you don't want to be outlier. Make sure that other small businesses have successfully adopted the compensation plan you're contemplating. If you think you need to make changes, ask people who are cognizant of small-business compensation issues whether the changes you want to make can accomplish your objectives.

Bottom line: You can willingly spend a small fortune compensating your employees, but if the dollars don't help motivate the people to whom you pay them, your compensation isn't effective.

Introducing Changes to Employee Benefits

What do you think is the most valuable benefit an employee can receive from an employer? If you answered health insurance, you have plenty of company. According to the Employee Benefit Research Institute (EBRI), by a 3:1 margin, American workers view their health insurance as their most prized employee benefit in comparison to retirement benefits.

However, if you examine the long-term monetary value of all benefits that employers offer, retirement plan benefits are actually the most financially valuable in the long run.

Including insurance and other benefits

A variety of insurance and related benefits are tax deductible to corporations for all employees. If your business isn't incorporated, as the owner, you can't deduct the cost of the insurance plans discussed in this section for yourself, except for health-insurance plans, but you can deduct them for your employees.

The following sections describe some benefits to consider providing for employees — and for yourself!

Health insurance

Employees usually value their health-insurance coverage over other traditional employee benefits. Of course, not all your current and prospective employees will value health-insurance coverage the same. For example, some married employees may already be covered through their spouses' plans and may not need or want health coverage through your small business. Similarly, younger, unmarried employees, who think they're indestructible, may place a greater value on flexible/remote work schedules than they do on health insurance.

REMEMBER

One hundred percent of your health-insurance premiums are deductible for yourself and your covered family members.

Disability insurance

The purpose of disability insurance is to protect your income and that of your employees from being lost in the event of a disability. Anyone who's dependent on their own income should have disability insurance. After all, if you suffer a total disability, you probably won't be able to earn income or as much income, but you'll likely have the same or higher living expenses.

As an employer, you may be required by your state to pay into a state disability or workers' compensation program (the latter only covers injuries and disabilities suffered on the job). Additionally, through the Social Security system, you and your employees have minimal disability benefits. Although coverage through government disability programs often isn't sufficient, it's better than nothing, so you as the employer shouldn't beat yourself up for not offering disability coverage to your employees.

One good reason to offer disability coverage to your employees, however, is that your competitors offer their employees coverage and/or you can afford to pay for such coverage. As with health insurance, we strongly encourage you to share the cost of disability coverage with your employees — perhaps you can pay 50 percent.

Life insurance

We recommend that you not waste your precious compensation and benefit dollars on life insurance. Why?

>> **Few small-business employers offer life-insurance coverage.** Why waste your precious benefit dollars on something that your competitors are unlikely to provide?

>> **Many of your employees won't need it.** Those who don't have financial dependents don't need life insurance. The vast majority of your single employees, childless employees, and employees with grown children won't have the need for life insurance, either. Hence, it isn't a wise benefit to offer.

TIP

If you decide that you really want to offer the Cadillac of benefits packages, provide term life insurance, not cash-value life insurance. With *term life insurance,* you pay an annual premium for a set amount of life-insurance coverage. During the term of the policy, if you stay alive, your beneficiaries collect no death benefit and you're out the premium, but of course, you're grateful you're not deceased! With *cash-value life insurance* (also known as whole life, universal life, or variable life), you pay a much higher premium for a combination of life insurance coverage and a savings-type account. For the same amount of coverage, cash-value policies cost a whopping eight times more than comparable term policies.

Dependent care programs

A *dependent care plan* enables you and your employees to put away money from your paychecks on a pretax basis; you can then use that money to pay for child-care expenses or to care for an ill or aging parent. Dependent care plans save you federal, state, and even Social Security taxes, and they allow you to put away up to $5,000 per year in a reimbursement account to be used to pay for eligible dependent care expenses ($2,500 for those who are married and filing separately).

Dependent care spending accounts are a "use it or lose it" benefit. If you or your employees aren't able to spend the money for childcare expenses in the current tax year, at the end of the year the IRS forces you to forfeit all the money you haven't used.

Vacation

We all need downtime, and weekends just aren't enough. A full week or two off can do wonders for you and your employees.

Two weeks of paid vacation is the norm for new hires in the world of small business. For key employees and employees who have been with you for several or more years, three weeks is the norm. Many small businesses offer a graduated vacation schedule that may, for instance, offer four weeks after 10 years and five weeks after 20.

TIP

Some employees may value vacation flexibility and more time off, so if your business allows, try to accommodate such wants to keep good employees happy. For example, if an employee would rather have an extra week's vacation each year than a 2 percent pay raise, you should be indifferent financially — unless, of course, that employee is difficult or impossible to replace during that extra vacation period.

Flexible hours

A wide variety of options are available when it comes to offering flexible hours. Families with children are especially starved for time, and most employed parents greatly value flexible work hours and the ability to take additional time off, even without pay. Sensitive employers who create a family-friendly work schedule and business environment reap enormous benefits, including happier, more loyal employees.

Here are a few options that are becoming more popular for some small-business owners:

- ≫ Four 10-hour days (flex time).

- ≫ A flex-time option that allows employees to vary their working hours depending on personal requirements (for example, employees with health or childcare issues).

- ≫ A work-from-home (remote) option, which is increasingly easy to do thanks to all sorts of technology and popularized during the COVID-19 pandemic shutdowns. Also, more companies are seeking to reduce their office rental costs by leasing less space per employee and having fewer employees on site in a typical workday.

Finally, offering flexible hours in advance of or during holidays also makes a lot of sense because, by and large, worker productivity falls off drastically during these times anyway. We know of one business, for instance, that, during the week between Christmas and New Year's, works only four-hour days (from 8:00 a.m. to noon) whereas some others shutdown completely then.

Flexible benefit plans

Flexible benefit, or "cafeteria," *plans* allow employees to pick and choose the benefits on which to spend their benefit dollars. (These plans are also known as *Section 125 plans*, after the part of the IRS tax laws that sanctions such plans.) Under a flexible benefit plan, your employees can choose to receive a portion of their compensation as pay or to put those dollars toward purchasing benefits of their own choosing from a menu you offer.

The virtue of a flexible plan is that it allows employees to customize their benefit packages to suit their needs and wants. For example, a married employee with young children may prefer to spend their benefit dollars on dependent care expenses or more vacation days, whereas a single employee may prefer simply to receive more cash compensation.

Another significant advantage of a flexible benefit plan is that the associated tax benefits produce greater value for employees from their compensation dollars. Rather than receiving some of their annual pay as taxable income, employees can elect to purchase benefits with pretax dollars, thus saving on income taxes.

REMEMBER

Unless and until you offer a number of insurance benefits to your employees, offering a flexible plan won't be appropriate or worthwhile. However, if you're offering a generous number of benefits and would like to offer your employees maximum flexibility in using their benefits, a flex plan may make sense.

TIP

If you're going to go to the trouble and expense of putting a flexible benefit plan in place at your company, also invest the necessary time and cost to describe the specific benefits in the plan and explain how employees can choose among them. For many employers, small and large, too many employees don't understand the flexible plan, which hampers them from making good use of, and appreciating, the plan.

Seeing the real value in retirement plans

Retirement plans are a terrific way for small-business owners and their employees to tax-shelter a healthy portion of their earnings. Even if you don't have employees, regularly contributing to one of these plans is usually a no-brainer. With employees, the decision is a bit more complicated, but contributing is still often a great idea because it helps you attract and retain good employees.

Consider all the benefits that you and your employees can reap by saving and investing in some type of retirement account now. These benefits include the following:

>> **Contributions offer immediate tax savings.** Retirement accounts should really be called *tax-reduction accounts*. If you're a moderate-income earner, you probably pay about 30 percent in federal and state income taxes. Thus, with most of the retirement accounts described in this section, for every

$1,000 you contribute into them, you save yourself about $300 in taxes in the year that you make the contribution.

>> **Investment earnings accumulate tax-deferred.** Inside a retirement account, contributions accumulate interest, dividends, and appreciation without being taxed. You get to defer taxes on all the accumulating gains and profits until you withdraw the money, presumably in retirement. Thus, more money is working for you over a longer period of time. Even if your retirement tax rate is the same as your tax rate during your employed years, you still come out ahead by contributing money into retirement accounts. In fact, because you defer paying taxes and have more money compounding over more years, you can end up with *more* money in retirement even if your retirement tax rate is higher.

Convincing employees that retirement plans matter

Most people don't value retirement plan benefits for the simple reason that they don't understand them. So, as an employer, to get the most employee appreciation from your retirement plan, do the following:

>> **Educate your employees about the value of retirement savings plans.** For example, people, on average, need about 75 percent of their pre-retirement income throughout retirement to maintain their standard of living. See the latest edition of Eric's book *Personal Finance For Dummies* (Wiley) for helpful background information about why people should be planning ahead financially for the golden years. Get your employees to understand and appreciate your investment in their financial futures.

>> **Use your plan as an incentive to retain employees.** Many small businesses have trouble with employee turnover. A well-run retirement savings plan, especially one that includes employer contributions/matching money, can help employees feel more valued.

>> **Select the plan that best meets your business needs.** Consider offering a 401(k) or a SIMPLE plan, which allows employees to contribute money from their paychecks.

Getting the most from your contributions as an employer

Don't avoid establishing, maintaining, or upgrading a retirement savings plan for your newly acquired business just because you have employees and you don't want to make contributions on their behalf. In the long run, you build the contributions that you make for your employees into their total compensation packages, which include salary and other benefits like health insurance. Making retirement contributions doesn't have to increase your personnel costs.

The SECURE (Setting Every Community Up for Retirement Enhancement) ACT of 2019 provides for up to $5,000 in tax credits for eligible small-business owners when starting a retirement plan. This credit applies to new 401(k), profit sharing, SEP, and SIMPLE plans for small employers with up to 100 employees.

To get the most from your contributions as an employer, consider the following:

>> Educate your employees about the value of retirement savings plans. You want them to understand how to save for the future and to value and appreciate your investment.

>> If you have more than 20 or so employees, consider offering a 401(k) or SIMPLE plan, which allows employees to contribute money from their paychecks.

TIP

If you're still dreaming about owning a business, don't view your current employer's benefits package as a ball and chain tying you to your current job. As a small-business owner, you can replace the benefits provided by your former employer on your own, and you can establish a SEP-IRA, SIMPLE-IRA, or 401(k) plan to tax-shelter your self-employment earnings. In fact, some of these plans may allow you to shelter more money than corporate retirement plans do.

Deciding whether to share equity

One decision that all small-business owners must confront is whether to go it alone or take on partners. If you decide to have partners, you'll probably share ownership with some or all of those partners. Even if you go solo, over time you may benefit from sharing equity with key employees or even all your employees.

Why would you want to consider sharing equity with your employees? The answer is simple: Doing so aligns their incentives with yours. After all, one of the reasons that you may have started a small business is to benefit from the economic rewards of your work. Sharing equity allows others to benefit along with you. If your employees simply draw a standard paycheck, they have less incentive to work toward boosting the short- and long-term profitability of your business.

WARNING

Not surprisingly, sharing equity also has downsides. If you give away too much ownership to employees or outside investors, you may find yourself a *minority shareholder* (owning less than 50 percent of your business) and no longer in control of the destiny of your enterprise or your own job security.

Additionally, because of their ownership, minority shareholders have rights and, therefore, interests that may not always align with yours. (The extent of their rights depends on the state in which you live.) This disparity in interest is especially true when a minority shareholder leaves the company either on their own or with a push from you.

Stock and stock options

Shares of ownership in a company are known as *stock*. The number of shares of stock in a company is an arbitrary item. Suppose, for example, that your company is *capitalized at* (viewed to be worth) $500,000. You can have 1,000 shares of stock, 10,000 shares of stock, 100,000 shares of stock, or any number of shares of stock your heart desires. If you have 1,000 shares of stock, the price or value per share is $500, whereas if you have 100,000 shares, the price per share is $5.

When hiring a key employee, you can simply grant that person a certain number of shares of stock that they will receive after staying with you for a certain period of time. Alternatively, you can grant *stock options*, which allow the key employee to buy a specified number of shares of your company's stock at a predetermined price within a defined future period.

Continuing with the previous example, suppose you have 100,000 shares of stock in your company and the price is $5 per share, for a total value of $500,000. You've been interviewing a prospective star marketing manager, and you want to offer them some financial upside if they're able to help you expand your company. After some conversations, you decide that you'll offer them stock options to purchase up to 5,000 shares of your company's stock (5 percent of the total company stock) within the next five years at a price per share of $5. Five years from now, if your marketing manager and other key players have done their jobs, your company should be worth a whole lot more than it is now, and your stock should be worth much more than $5 per share, thus enriching the stock-option holder's compensation.

TIP

Here are some tips for offering stock and stock options to key employees:

>> **Make sure that the employee is a keeper.** Just as you should date a person before marrying, make sure that you've had ample opportunity to observe firsthand an employee's abilities and shortcomings before you offer them equity. Just because someone has an impressive resume and comes across well in a job interview doesn't mean that they'll work well in your company and is worthy of equity from day one.

>> **Make 'em earn it.** In most cases, vesting your key employee(s) in a certain portion of the stock per year makes good sense.

>> **Get expert help.** Issuing stock and granting stock options can get complicated fairly quickly and, once consummated, is irrevocable unless agreed to by both parties. Get good tax and legal advisors on your team

Employee Stock Ownership Plans (ESOP)

The Washington, D.C.–based Employee Stock Ownership Plan (ESOP) Association defines an *ESOP* as "an employee benefit plan which makes the employees the owners of stock in a company." ESOPs are most often used when the owner of a privately held small business readies for retirement, has no family successor, and wants to pass on the company to the employees. The federal government encourages small-business owners to consider ESOPs by granting tax breaks.

WARNING

ESOPs can make sense when a company has a strong balance sheet and a sustainable record of being profitable. ESOPs aren't for the start-up or for the small business that isn't performing.

ESOPs can provide an effective exit strategy for the small-business owner. Once established, an ESOP, which is, in effect, selling stock to your employees, includes a payout to the owner, the proceeds of which come from the sale of stock. (The employees don't provide the cash for that payout; a participating bank does.) As a result, ESOPs can provide a mechanism to enhance the owner's retirement as well as benefit their employees.

You can obtain more information on this unique, equity-sharing tool by contacting The ESOP Association at 202-293-2971 or www.esopassociation.org. Also, talk to your tax advisor to understand the tax and financial consequences of doing an ESOP at your company.

Buy-sell agreements

If you and a minority shareholder have a dispute (and you can bet that you'll eventually have one — especially if you have more than one minority shareholder), a buy-sell agreement is a vital legal document for your business.

Buy-sell agreements specify the terms under which owners/shareholders must sell their stock upon separation from the company. They also establish a method to determine the price of the buy-back and make provisions for the death of a shareholder.

REMEMBER

As we say earlier in this book, you should involve an attorney several times in the life of a business — and making equity decisions is certainly one of those times. Never create a minority shareholder without a lawyer!

Bringing in New Talent

Hiring is mostly science, not art. It's a methodical, repetitive, and often drawn-out process, but it's one that most small-business owners must go through eventually. The first step in the hiring process is to collect a roster of worthwhile applicants for the position, likely through one of the following methods:

>> By running ads, which increasingly is done online, including on your own website

>> By signage (at your business)

>> By encouraging referrals from employees, vendors, and customers

The best employees go to the entrepreneur who's willing to go to the most trouble to find them. Following is a list of hiring tips to help you locate and hire those elusive superstars:

>> **When posting a job opening, remember that you're selling an opportunity, not just offering a job, and write accordingly.** You want (we're assuming) to attract a career-minded employee who wants to grow with your company, so you need to paint your company, and the position, in an attractive light. Review existing postings carefully, and then use bits and pieces of the best ones.

>> **Establish a reward system to encourage your existing employees to refer qualified candidates.** The best candidates often come from inside-the-company referrals. Rewards can include anything from cash to vacation days.

>> **Always prepare a job description, which many business veterans call *performance expectations*, before you post a job opening.** Good applicants want to know exactly what the job entails and what's expected of them. As part of the posting, include the job definition, expectations of work, benefits/perks, and your business's chain-of-command, as it relates to the position being offered.

>> **Review each applicant's resume, looking for the names of businesses or people you may know who aren't listed as the candidate's official references.** The most informative references may be those that the applicant

doesn't list. Because of a variety of legal ramifications, such third-party references are usually more candid with their comments than the official references are.

» **Try to open the door to more candid conversations when you're talking to an applicant's references.** Look for areas of commonality to put the person at ease. Tune in to the little things as you listen. Ask about the applicant's weaknesses and then multiply — most references are prone to sugarcoating.

» **Have every applicant complete a job application in addition to submitting a resume.** Resumes + applications + LinkedIn = more information on candidates. Most applications ask questions about topics that don't appear on resumes, such as citizenship, green card, felony arrests, and so on. It's perfectly okay for applicants to write "see information on resume" for applicable sections of the application.

Use the U.S. government's E-Verify system, if appropriate. *E-Verify* is a free Internet-based system that compares information from an employee's Form I-9 (Employment Eligibility Verification) to data from the U.S. Department of Homeland Security and the Social Security Administration to confirm employment eligibility. You should use E-Verify when you have a reasonable doubt of an employee's legality. While participation is voluntary for some businesses, numerous states require it and more may begin doing so. About 60 percent of all jobs now are screened with E-Verify, and Congress is considering legislation that would require all U.S. employers to use E-Verify.

» **Look for the applicant's ability to listen during the interview.** If they doesn't listen well during the interview, they're unlikely to listen well after you hire them and they're on the job.

» **Find out what research the applicant has done on you and your company.** If the applicant comes to the interview unprepared and devoid of knowledge about your company and industry, you've discovered something about either their work habits or the depth of their desire for the job.

» **Remember that the hiring process usually requires you to wear two hats:**

- The detective's hat, to be donned as you interview and separate potential superstars from the rest of the pack.

- The salesperson's hat, to be donned after you confirm you're talking to a prospective superstar. Most superstars have other options, so part of your job is that of a salesperson.

Don't forget to prepare for the second role and don't incorrectly assume that your company is the only, or the best, opportunity in town. Like any good salesperson, remember to sell the benefits of the job as opposed to its features; in other words, show your prospective superstar how working for you will make their life better.

REMEMBER

Hiring right brings you an endless list of benefits. The biggest is that the better the employee you hire, the less time you must spend managing them. Instead, you can spend your time on product (or service) development; business-building activities, such as marketing and sales; hiring employees; supervising the production floor; or doing the other things you enjoy most.

CONSIDERING THE EMPLOYEE-LEASING OPTION

About 1,000 employee-leasing companies — also known as *professional employer organizations* (PEOs) — exist in the United States today, which means that at least one is probably located near you. The employee-leasing company's primary customer is the small-business owner because most large businesses develop a wide variety of human resource services in-house.

Employee leasing means that the leasing company assumes the paperwork and administrative responsibilities of dealing with employees, allowing you to concentrate on the operational activities. Thus, in effect, you're outsourcing your human resource needs. In this way, you and your PEO become *co-employers* of the employees. In return for the services the PEO provides, it charges its customers an administrative fee (its markup over costs) that's usually between 2 percent and 8 percent, depending on the dollar amount of the transaction.

We aren't advocating employee leasing for every small business; whether to lease or not is a gray area. Here's why leasing employees makes sense for some small businesses:

- PEOs do what they do best (hire and manage the administration of employees), and you do what you do best (run your business). You can focus on developing your product, selling your product, servicing your customers, and improving profitability.

- You write one check and the PEO does the rest.

- PEOs can serve as unofficial employment agencies. You can eventually hire the best of the temporary employees they send you and return the rest.

- By pooling employees, PEOs can cut costs in such areas as insurance rates.

- PEOs worry about regulatory compliance so you don't have to.

At the same time, leasing has the following disadvantages:

- When a PEO goes under, it can take your payroll cash (including tax payments) and prepaid insurance along with it. This leaves you, the employees, or both holding the bag.

- If you can provide comparable employee services at the same cost, you can, in effect, cut your expenses by hiring your own employees. Remember that every dollar saved by not paying a leasing-company fee results in an extra dollar of profit.

If you do decide to lease your employees, be extremely careful in selecting the company you use as your co-employer. Check references thoroughly and remember that everything is negotiable when signing a leasing contract. You may even want to customize the leasing agreement to meet your specific needs. Also, you may want to check with the Employer Services Assurance Corporation in Little Rock, Arkansas (www.esacorp.org), to verify that you're dealing with an accredited PEO. This self-regulating industry group has accredited PEOs in all 50 states. When in doubt as to where to look for a PEO, this is a helpful resource.

(continued)

(continued)

In the final analysis, most small-business owners make the decision to lease employees based on whether they think they can save all or part of that 2 to 8 percent administrative fee by taking care of the hiring process themselves. They also evaluate how much of their time and energy they want to spend on human resource issues. The fact that the employee-leasing industry is growing at a rapid rate indicates that increasing numbers of small-business owners have made the decision that the 2 to 8 percent charged in fees is worth the expense.

Training: An Investment, Not an Expense

Training is generally recognized as the most efficient and least expensive answer to employee improvement. Unfortunately, however, training remains close to the bottom of too many small-business owners' priority lists. Too often, small-business owners view training as an expense rather than as an investment that comes back in the form of increased productivity.

We've heard too many small-business owners complain about the cost of training, especially when that training results in the employee moving on to greener pastures — and taking their knowledge with them. Although such occurrences do take place, part of the reason that employees move on is because they don't get the opportunity to receive the training they need. Besides, as the old saying goes, "If you think training employees and watching them leave is expensive, try not training them and watching them stay!"

Training comes in many forms and from various sources. Unlike many large companies, which generate much of their training from in-house sources, small-business training usually comes from the outside. Here are your major training options:

>> **Consultants and coaches:** Although consultants and coaches have the most potential as trainers, they're also the most expensive and riskiest.

- **Vendors:** Vendors can be an excellent resource for training, and they're less costly than consultants. Many vendors provide free training on their products or services.

- **Seminars and webinars:** Seminars and webinars can be expensive in both dollars and time, and their potential value is difficult to predict. Good ones are great bargains; bad ones are outlandish scams. The seminars and webinars with the best potential (and usually the least expensive) are those put on by your trade association, which are geared to the industry you're in.

- **Continuing education:** This category includes universities, colleges, night schools, online courses (such as Coursera, Skillshare, or Udemy), and vocational training. Although continuing education is probably more dependable than seminars, the value is also difficult to predict. The benefit of the course depends largely on the quality of the instructor.

TIP

Consider offering a tuition-reimbursement program, whereby you reimburse employees' expenses for outside studies related to the business. The benefits to the company from such a program include goodwill, the development of a self-improvement culture, and the infusion of new ideas in its employees. Require a B grade (or better) for reimbursement, to be paid after the course is completed.

- **Books:** Books are a great value. In fact, a good book is the ultimate training bargain. Read it (or have your employees read it) between projects, put it down when you please, and refer to it always. Keep it forever or pass it on to a friend or another employee. If you extract and implement one good idea, the $20 or so you spent is quickly repaid, many times over. Every good idea after the first one is a bonus. (Audio and video courses fall into this same category.)

Parting Company: Firing an Employee

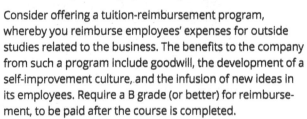

Firing an employee, as much as you'd like to avoid it, plays an integral role in the growth of a successful business (although if you hire right, train right, and motivate right, it won't happen frequently). As long as employees are people, you'll occasionally have to fire them. As a matter of fact, if you *never* fire an employee, you're bound to have a handful of nonperforming employees on your payroll — a financial burden few small businesses can afford and a condition that won't be acceptable to the rest of your employees who *are* performing.

Here's our advice to help you get through the unpleasant task of firing an employee:

>> **Explore all the alternatives before settling on dismissal.** Alternatives include demotion, grace periods, personalized retraining, and consultant contracts (hiring the employee as a consultant outside of the business to do only specific, one-time jobs). When the alternatives won't work, record the reasons why. The employee may ask.

>> **Do the firing as soon as possible after you make the decision to terminate.** The longer you wait, the more likely it is that word will leak out to the soon-to-be-fired employee. And the more stressed you and the environment will become.

>> **Know the laws of your state.** For example, do you need to provide documentation? Check with your attorney before firing a longtime employee or a member of a minority group if the reasons for the termination may appear vague to the person being terminated. You also need to involve your attorney when the firing is for an offense (sexual harassment, fighting, and other such incidents) that may wind up as a lawsuit.

>> **Prepare the firing package in the same organized and documented way you prepared the hiring package.** Include, where applicable, severance pay, continuance of health insurance, duration of benefits and perks (memberships, subscriptions, and so on), and return of company assets (keys and computers, for example).

>> **Plan the firing meeting as you would any other important business meeting.** Organize in advance, outline your presentation, and have handouts prepared if

necessary. Make the dismissal as businesslike as possible, and, above all, avoid sentimentality and reminiscing. Keep emotions subdued; they only make matters worse.

>> **Perform the termination first thing in the morning.** Doing so allows the employee to leave the company and have the rest of the day to gather their composure. At a minimum, pay the employee through the end of that day and perhaps even the rest of the week or month to help them stay on their feet financially.

>> **Don't argue.** State the reasons and the facts surrounding the termination. Show the supporting documents. Arguing will only further incense the person being fired. Let the employee rant and rave if they choose; they may feel better when they're done, and, because of your listening, you may learn how to be a better manager for the future.

>> **Arrange for outplacement services.** Small businesses can learn this lesson from watching their *Fortune* 500 cousins perfect the ritual of downsizing. You can soften the firing by helping the employee get back on their feet again.

Firing an employee plays an important role in the process of building a company, but it will never be an enjoyable part, no matter how much practice you may have at it. When you're feeling especially sorry for yourself because you have to fire an employee, keep in mind that the situation is a heck of a lot tougher on the person sitting on the other side of your desk.

USING EXIT INTERVIEWS TO GAIN FRESH PERSPECTIVE

Inevitably, your company will have employees who quit their jobs for one reason or another. These employees can be a valuable resource for you to tap into before they leave. During an *exit interview,* as the name implies, you interview the exiting employee to gain insights into the company that a current employee may be reluctant to provide.

(continued)

(continued)

Be sure to include at least the following questions in an exit interview:

- What was the main factor in your decision to quit?
- What did you like the most about our company?
- What did you like the least?
- How do you rate such issues as working conditions, cooperation and teamwork, on-the-job training, supervision, opportunity for promotion, and communication?
- If you can change one thing about this company, what would it be?

Designing Flexible Organization Charts

Some say that *organization charts* — a graphic depiction of your company's chain of command — are out of style. All you must do, these people tell us, is empower your employees and then step aside while the jobs get done. No layers, no politics, no people caught in the middle — or so the story goes. Today's empowered employees don't require management, they conclude; they simply need a flexible and lenient work environment.

We respectfully disagree. We're firm believers in organization charts and in the chain of command, but only when the person at the top of the chain is worthy of the position. We further believe that someone must manage employees, motivate them, and help them improve their performance. Someone must also promote them, demote them, and, on occasion, terminate them. Like it or not, employees, we're convinced, have to work for someone.

REMEMBER

Even so, organization charts — especially in small business — shouldn't be carved in stone. You don't want to live or die by the constrictions of your organization chart, especially when your business has relatively few employees with which to spread the work around. Rather, the org chart should serve as a structural guideline for making decisions and assigning responsibility — nothing more. So, use it administratively, but bend it and mold it to fit the skills of your employees and the ever-changing needs of your company. For instance, feel free to assemble creative and temporary secondary charts from time to time to accomplish those complicated projects and one-time jobs.

Here's how to construct your business's organization chart and use it effectively:

>> **Allow for flexibility where special projects are concerned.** For instance, if one person is particularly knowledgeable about the project-du-jour, give them the senior responsibility for that job. (This structure means that your sales manager may be working on a project headed by an IT employee — if the IT employee knows more about the project than the sales manager.)

>> **Pay by the quality of each employee's performance and their contribution to the team, not their position on the organization chart.** So, although the sales manager and the operations manager may be on the same tier of the chart, they may be compensated quite differently, based on the degree of difficulty of the position, the number of people being managed, and the relative importance of sales and operations to the overall success of the company.

>> **Determine how many employees one person can supervise.** The answer depends on the quality of the team you've assembled. One is plenty if that one is like some people we've seen over the years. On the other hand, eight employees may be a snap to manage if those eight are good ones and don't require much supervision.

Flatter organization charts (those with fewer tiers) are better, especially when you have the right employees. Flatter organization charts mean better communication — from top to bottom and from bottom to top — because the communication doesn't have to pass through intermediaries. The more tiers you have in your organization charts, the more chances you have for the message to be garbled or misconstrued.

Valuing Employee Manuals

In terms of excitement, the employee manual ranks right up there with ordering toner cartridges for your copy machine. Most entrepreneurs don't rank it in the top ten list of Things They Can Hardly Wait to Do.

However, as soon as employees are on your payroll, you need to add employee manuals to your business's preventive medicine kit. A well-prepared manual can save its user pain and suffering later on. It's possible that the small business you acquire has an employee manual already, but most don't and those that do have one often have room for improvement. The employee manual is important because of the varied and important functions it fulfills. Behold what a well-prepared employee manual can do for you:

>> **The employee manual provides the first opportunity to define your corporate missions and goals to your new employees and sets the tone for what's to come.** Imagine the message that a well-prepared employee manual sends to the recently hired employee when their questions are succinctly answered in an organized and thorough manner. (Or, imagine the message you send when those questions *aren't* answered!)

>> **The employee manual saves time — time spent on resolving problems that established policies in a manual would've prevented in the first place.** The employee manual also saves time spent by explaining the basics of the job, such as hours of work, vacation and sick days, and termination policies.

>> **The employee manual saves time, effort, and money spent on lawyers by establishing company policies for all to see.** By stating company policies publicly and in writing, you quickly and succinctly alert potential problem employees to the fact that they must either find a way to work within your policies or seek employment elsewhere.

TIP

The best way to assemble your employee manual is to use some-one else's as a template — a neighboring small business, a vendor, a trade association's template, or a small business that you've frequented over the years. AI websites like ChatGPT can provide help in writing content for employee manuals. Worthy employee manuals tend to make the rounds from small business to small business — with good reason. The manuals that have survived have already been tried and tested and can serve as a guide for constructing yours.

When compiling your employee manual (whether you prepare it yourself or you use someone else's model as a template), be sure to do the following:

>> **Include a statement of your company's mission and goals.** Keep it brief, make it specific, and put it at the beginning of the manual where you know employees will read it.

>> **Include an *employment-at-will statement* (which says that you aren't restricted to firing only for cause) if you reside in a state where it's applicable.** An attorney experienced in small-business management can advise you on the laws of your state.

>> **Declare early on that the employee manual isn't a contract and that it can, and undoubtedly will, change.** Don't overlook keeping the employee manual updated; it can quickly become out of date.

>> **Include an equal-opportunity statement.** An equal-opportunity statement is a clause that states that qualified applicants are considered for all open positions for which they apply and for advancement without regard to race, color, religion, sex, sexual orientation, national origin, age, marital status, the presence of a medical condition or disability, or genetic information.

>> **Spell out the benefits you offer, such as health insurance, maternity leave, profit sharing, company-reimbursed education, and so on.** Where applicable, include the details of the insurance plans in attachments.

- » **Define policies regarding the workday.** Also include policies regarding overtime pay, time off, and breaks, as well as those concerning performance reviews, promotions, and wage increases.

- » **Develop and define a drug and alcohol policy, including pre-employment screening and post-accident testing (if any).** Given the many negatives that result from alcohol and drug use in the workplace, you need to let your employees know exactly how your business views the subject, what the rules are, and how transgressions will be dealt with.

- » **Define standards of conduct such as dress, timeliness, and consideration of others.** Include causes for disciplinary action and termination, along with severance pay policies.

- » **Keep the employee manual current as you go and keep your employees abreast of the changes.** Post any changes on the bulletin board, at the same time you hand out or email revision attachments for your employees' manuals. You may also consider posting a copy online if you have a portion of your website that's accessible only to employees.

TIP

Before you distribute the completed manual to employees, have an attorney who's experienced in working with small businesses and employee handbooks review and edit it. That review, while probably costly, can save you grief and money down the road.

Characterizing Successful Employers

No two small businesses are alike. The reasons behind one small business's success are often greatly different from the reasons behind a second one's success. One succeeds because of its marketing efforts, another because of its product or service quality. One focuses on customers, another on employees. One has an awesome in-house sales force, another utilizes an eye-catching catalog to sell its products.

However, every successful small business (one that includes employees, anyway) has three identifiable characteristics, no matter its niche, product, or service: those three characteristics are flexibility, accountability, and follow-up.

Flexibility: The bending of rules

Consider the following examples of when flexibility should play a big role in your management decisions:

>> **Employees:** You say you have a good employee who needs additional time off to resolve a family situation? Nuts to the rules. Give them the time off and help them solve their problem. You say you have a productive employee who needs a flexible work schedule to honor their responsibilities at home? What are you waiting for? Create a flexible work schedule and help them solve their problem.

>> **Loyal, paying customers:** Rules are meant to be bent when it comes to loyal, paying customers. You say you have a good customer who needs an additional 30 days to pay an especially large invoice? Then 30 more days it is. You say you have a good customer who needs their products individually shrink-wrapped rather than bulk-wrapped? Then shrink-wrapped it is. (Yes, you may have to adjust your price to cover the additional cost.)

>> **Organization charts:** As we say earlier in this chapter, you should use organization charts only for administrative and structural purposes. If you look at your business as providing solutions rather than merely following rules, you'll be better able to meet the demands of today's ever-changing business life.

Don't get us wrong; we're not saying that you should flexibly manage everything in your business. To the contrary, a small business does need to include a number of inflexible rules and regulations among its management tools. For instance, you need inflexible rules and regulations to manage such things as

>> **Ethics and principles:** If ethics and principles are flexible, they aren't ethics and principles.

>> **Expense controls:** The best small businesses are those that are as aware of their expenses as they are of their sales. You need to control your expenses inflexibly.

>> **Quality:** Quality can't be flexible. The product or service is either fit for your most-demanding customer or it's unfit for any of your customers. There's no middle ground.

But where people enter the picture, flexibility is the order of the day, because people are different and unique and, well, flexible. One employee's reward may be another employee's punishment. Just as no two people are alike, no two responses to the way you manage them will be the same.

Accountability: Where the buck doesn't get passed

Your employees only have two options when you ask them to perform a task: Either they do it or they don't. When they don't perform the designated task, the question you must ask is "Why did they fail to do it?" The answers to that question can include the following:

>> **The employee is incapable of performing the task.** Your options are to reassign the task, reassign the employee, or replace the employee.

>> **The employee isn't properly trained.** In this case, it is your responsibility to train the employee.

>> **The task and its priority weren't clearly communicated.** Your job may be to communicate the task more clearly.

>> **The employee saw no good reason to accomplish the task and, thus, elected not to do it.** In this case, either your company doesn't include accountability as part of its culture or you have made a serious hiring mistake.

REMEMBER

Accountability — being responsible for your own actions — is a cultural issue. It begins with you, the entrepreneur, and includes making the employees who work for you accountable and then assuring that such accountability trickles down through your organization. In the process of creating an accountable culture, you must provide a system of rewards when employees perform and consequences when they don't.

To determine whether your small business has an accountable culture, answer the following four questions:

>> Are your employees motivated to achieve what you want them to achieve?

>> Does achievement make a difference in the success of the team, and do you and your employees know how to recognize that difference?

>> Can the other members of the team identify when an employee has achieved or not achieved?

>> Do your employees know that they have to achieve, or is achievement perceived as merely an option?

In the process of answering these questions, you'll recognize whether or not the following four elements of an accountable culture are in place within your business:

>> Employees have to have a reason to achieve.

>> Achievement has to be recognized and celebrated through-out the company.

>> Employees should be properly rewarded when they achieve.

>> Consequences have to be enacted when employees don't achieve.

Once these four elements are in place, an accountable culture within your business will follow.

Follow-up: The more you do it, the less you need it

Why should you have to follow up? After all, you've already gotten whatever it was off your desk the first time. Why should you have to do it all over again? After all, if *you* were an employee, you sure wouldn't need your boss following up on you. But (and this is the last time you'll hear this) you aren't an employee.

You're an entrepreneur, and if you don't remember the difference, you may not be in business for long. If you don't follow up with your employees, missions and goals won't be missions and goals anymore; they'll be hopes and wishes. And hopes and wishes don't build businesses.

The good news is that when your employees know that follow-up is coming, the need for it decreases. Translation: When you have an accountable culture firmly in place, you won't have to follow up as much anymore.

TIP

In the beginning, when your business's culture is being established, you need to follow up on every commitment your employees make, large or small. You can do so by making a simple notation on the calendar and transferring it to your to-do list on the appropriate day.

Chapter **13**

Keeping Your Customers Loyal

A huge factor in your business's long-term success is not only attracting but also satisfying and retaining customers. As a small-business owner, you may be on the front lines of dealing with your business's customers. When you have employees, they'll likely be dealing with customers, too. Therefore, the importance of providing excellent customer service must be clear to *everyone* in your organization who has any impact (direct or indirect) on customer satisfaction. This includes the receptionist, the accounts receivable clerk, the delivery truck driver, and many others.

Although the level of customer service in many businesses falls short, only a foolish business owner would assume that unhappy customers will continue to tolerate poor service or buy products that don't perform. Consumers generally have many choices, so if you and your employees don't satisfy your customers' needs, you'll likely face these unpleasant results:

» **Competitive threats:** Now more than ever, customers have many options for buying what your company has to offer. For the vast majority of businesses, competition is intense at the global, national, state, regional, and local levels. It's only a matter of time before your unhappy customers become your competitors' newest customers.

>> **Negative word-of-mouth:** Even worse than losing dissatisfied customers to the competition is *negative word-of-mouth*, whereby unhappy customers post negative reviews online and talk, telling other consumers why they wouldn't buy your products and services. Furthermore, your competitors are more than happy to recount the negative stories they've heard from your disgruntled customers. All this talk will certainly tarnish your business's reputation.

>> **Potential lawsuits:** As if losing customers and tarnishing your business's reputation aren't enough, disgruntled customers can initiate (gasp!) lawsuits. Even if those litigious customers don't prevail in court, they can cause you to face large legal bills, and your business can suffer further damage to both its profitability and its reputation.

In this chapter, we offer some helpful advice for providing excellent customer service and strategies for keeping your current customers, whether they're satisfied or dissatisfied. We also offer some tips for attracting new customers.

Retaining Your Customer Base

As the owner of a small business, you should strive to keep your customers happy. How? Well, you have an enormous impact on your customers' satisfaction through your company's products and services and the way in which you present them. This section provides you with the keys to keeping your customers satisfied. Of course, not all customers will stay satisfied and loyal to your business. So we also explain how you can learn from customer defections to minimize their happening in the future.

Getting it right the first time

As a small-business owner, if you don't get your product or service right the first time, you may not have a second chance with customers. Customers aren't stupid, and if you sell them inferior merchandise or services — especially when better merchandise or services are available from other sources — they won't come back the next time they're in the market for the products and services you offer.

What's more, some of your customers who suffered bad experiences with your company will tell others of their lousy experiences. Larger companies usually have enough cash reserves built up to weather a storm, but the typical small-business owner does not.

Continuing to offer more value

Getting your product or service right the first time isn't enough to keep customers coming back in the long run. Like life, the business world keeps changing. Because of the ever-present threat of competition, resting on your laurels is foolish. In addition to offering top-notch, quality products or services, you must regularly examine how you can offer even more value — improved products or services at the same or lower cost. If you don't, competitors who faithfully keep up with market forces will gradually eat your lunch.

Suppose that you're a dry cleaner. A new dry-cleaning technology that allows dry-cleaning establishments to get their work done 20 percent faster and 30 percent cheaper has been introduced in the marketplace. If you fail to take advantage of this improvement in your industry, you may discover the hard way, when your customers leave you for your competitors, that they want the value this new technique offers. As your competitors cut prices with faster service and reap greater numbers of customers and profits, you lose business and experience shrinking profit margins.

Remembering that company policy is meant to be bent

Flexibility is paramount in any organization, but it's especially important in a small business, where responsive and personally tailored service can set you apart from the larger companies. One place where you should be flexible is in your company policy. If a customer has a problem but you have a rule or regulation preventing you from resolving that problem, forget the rule or regulation. Bend it. Skirt it. Find a loophole in it.

To see what we mean, put yourself in the following situations:

>> You're an electrical contractor who needs material to complete a job. Your electrical wholesaler tells you that they have a problem with the order-entry system and can't process your order right now, so you'll have to come back tomorrow to place your order.

>> You're a regular customer at a dry cleaner. It's Wednesday, and you need your tuxedo dry-cleaned by Friday night. The dry cleaner informs you that it won't be ready until Saturday because of the firm's three-day turnaround.

What are the common threads here?

>> The electrical wholesaler and the dry cleaner apparently have cast-in-stone rules and regulations that dictate the way they do business, and they won't bend those rules to solve a customer's problem.

>> The two businesses are in danger of alienating a customer.

How can these business owners become more flexible to satisfy the customer? The electrical wholesaler can give the contractor the material today and run the transaction through their order-entry system tomorrow. The dry cleaner can put the customer's tuxedo in front of someone else's order, no matter what the company's operations manual dictates.

These are the moments of truth in any business — the times when what the business says it will do conflicts with what the business actually does. These times differentiate the business that *says* the customer is king from the business that *acts* as if the customer is king.

We're not saying that you should always provide extra service casually or for free. In some situations, you may want to charge more for a special service. Consider the special favor and the one-time transaction when you set your pricing strategy. Also, you don't want to tell your employees to feel free to break any rule at any time; that's the road to chaos and lack of standards, quality control, and profitability. But flexibility helps keep customers feeling happy and coming back — and recommending you to others. Let your managers and employees know that you stand behind this philosophy, and you'll empower them to always provide good customers with top-notch service.

Learning from customer defections

The costs of acquiring a new customer are often significant. After spending the marketing effort and dollars needed to secure a new customer for your business, you will want to keep that customer coming back to your business for many years. If you experience much customer turnover, your cost of doing business will rise significantly as you try to attract replacement customers, so you need to take action quickly. After all, customer turnover can indicate problems with your company's products or services and customer service.

A popular action within a business is to celebrate successes rather than examine failures. However, as a small-business owner, your business will achieve much greater success if you scrutinize your failures and make positive changes to correct them. Take the time to examine customer defections and their underlying causes. The following sections dig deeper into this topic.

Examining the value of customer loyalty

Frederick Reichheld is a management consultant who specializes in understanding, and working with corporations on, customer loyalty. He's the author of several books on customer loyalty, and his research has produced the following powerful insights and facts:

>> The average company today loses half of its customers in five years.

>> The typical *Fortune* 500 company has an average annual *real growth* (that is, growth in excess of the rate of inflation)

of 2.5 percent. If such a company retained just 5 percent more of its customers each year, its real growth would jump to 7.5 percent.

>> A 5 percent increase in customer retention in a typical company generally translates into an increase in profits of more than 25 percent. In some industries, good, long-standing customers are worth so much that reducing customer defections by 5 percent can double profits.

Clearly, retaining customers — particularly your best customers — has an enormous bottom-line impact. Given how important and valuable retaining customers is, you may think that if a business were losing many of its customers, it would seek to understand why and to correct the underlying problems. Well, if that were the case, customer loss wouldn't be as high as it is in many businesses.

Tracking customer defections

In his consulting work and research, Reichheld has also found that, not surprisingly, many businesses don't learn from their customer losses. He says,

> "Psychologically and culturally, it's difficult and sometimes threatening to look at failure too closely. Ambitious managers want to link their careers to successes; failures are usually examined for purposes of assigning blame rather than detecting and eradicating the systemic causes of poor performance."

The good news for you, the small-business owner, is that you don't have to be concerned with bosses and organizational politics when addressing the problem of customer defections. After all, you're the boss. However, it's a natural human tendency to spend more time chasing and celebrating successes than investigating and learning from failures and losses.

INVESTIGATE

Make a commitment to track the customers that you lose and ask why. (This is the customer equivalent to the exit interview that you should always perform with departing employees; see Chapter 12.) Knowing that you've lost customers isn't enough; you must find out *why* you lost them. Doing so can help keep you in business and help keep your business growing (see the upcoming section, "Expanding Your Customer Base").

Make it part of your company's culture that you don't expect employees to be perfect and that making mistakes won't necessarily lead to an employee's immediate firing. However, make it clear that you won't tolerate employees who provide sub-par service, display poor attitudes, and drive good customers away from your business. (For more employee tips, refer to Chapter 12.)

Recognizing and practicing customer service

All businesses have products or services to sell. Sometimes businesses get too focused on selling those products and services and not enough attention to the accompanying customer service that customers expect after the sale.

Maybe you can't readily define the term *customer service*, but we bet you know what it is when you get it or don't get it. For example, you surely recognize customer service in a company you do business with when:

>> Its receptionist (or at least its telephone system) connects you with your party quickly and efficiently.

>> Its bookkeeper politely answers a question you have about an invoice.

>> Its shipping clerk quickly traces your order and tells you exactly when to expect it.

>> Its salesperson gets back to you quickly with the quotes and delivery schedules you requested.

In each of these situations, the company is solving your problem or addressing your need in a manner that meets or exceeds your expectations, which is, after all, the definition of *customer service*. Customer service = solving your customers' problems or meeting their needs.

When you ask an employee for help in a business that you frequent, have you ever felt that her behavior was essentially saying to you, "That's not my department or responsibility"? In a business — large or small — that recognizes the value of customer service, the correct response to a customer question is,

"Let me find the solution for you." The solution may ultimately rest in the hands of another employee, another department, or even another business, but the employee has accepted responsibility for solving your problem.

TECHNICAL STUFF

Some larger companies have distinctly identified *customer service departments* — a person or group of people whose sole purpose is to solve customer problems. In such a company, all customer inquiries are routed through to the customer service department. In smaller companies, however, many — perhaps even all — employees are involved in customer service. In the examples from the previous bulleted list, the receptionist, the bookkeeper, the shipping clerk, and the salesperson are providing customer service. If you, the boss and Grand Poobah, get involved in solving a customer's problem, you, too, are focused on customer service. The same is true for the janitor or the night watchman.

The challenge is for your employees to understand that they're on the job to solve the business customers' problems. After all, they may believe (because this is the way their job descriptions read) that their role is simply to answer the telephone, keep the books, ship products, or sell services. Although these functions accurately describe the employees' assigned *activities*, they don't define the employees' assumed *responsibilities*.

REMEMBER

You and your employees are on the job — just as your entire company exists — for one reason and one reason only: to solve your customers' problems and satisfy their needs and wants.

Smart business owners know that customer service (and the accompanying problem solving) begins before a sale is made, continues during the sale, and continues long after the sale is complete. Remember that customers aren't just coming to your business for your products and services. The attentiveness you show toward your customers' needs — before, during, and after the sale — that comes with what you sell is an integral part of the package. Treat your customers as you would a good friend.

The following sections break down the stages of customer service so that you can see what you and your employees need to do to keep your customers coming back.

Customer service before the sale

When a customer goes to buy a product or service, part of what can close the sale or blow the deal is the quality (or lack thereof) of the customer service before the moment the customer decides to buy. When a customer schedules an appointment, they're buying not only the service provider's expertise but also the "proper care and handling" before the service is provided. And when a potential customer enters your store for a product, they want the store to be clean, well maintained, and conveniently arranged. That's all part of the customer service experience — so, too, are attentive employees who can answer questions without being pushy.

Consider the last time you bought something, whether it was a car, a bag of groceries, a medical exam, or a haircut. With each of these purchases, you interacted with the business provider before you committed to buy the product or service.

If you're like most people, you probably have some bad memories about slick salespeople who accosted you the moment you walked onto an auto dealer's lot. Some salespeople spend more time selling than they do listening and educating. The salesperson isn't trying to solve *your* problem — figuring out which car to purchase. They're trying to solve *their* problem — how to make a hefty commission to meet their next mortgage payment. Because of poor customer service at the point of sale in the car business, some people turn around and take their business elsewhere.

Customer service during the sale

After a customer commits to buying a product or service, the customer service must continue. Never halt your efforts to satisfy customers. When a customer forks over the dough for your wares and you don't meet the customer's service expectations, even if the sale is finalized, you may lose repeat business and the opportunity for referrals to other customers.

For example, after your doctor arrives in the examination room, you'll pay close attention to how well they listen to you and how they treat you. If the doctor is abrupt, bad at listening, and arrogant in asserting their opinion — instead of showing a willingness to discuss options and consider your needs — you may choose to find another physician.

Likewise, after you decide to buy a car, you won't be overjoyed if completing the transaction takes several hours. Even though you may be happy with the selection of the car, the hassle in getting on your way may make you less glowing in your recommendation to others.

Customer service after the sale

After a customer has purchased your company's products or services, your relationship with that customer, at least as it relates to that transaction, isn't over. The customer may have follow-up questions that you need to answer or problems down the road with your products or services.

SHOWING THAT YOU CARE — THE OLD-FASHIONED WAY

In the age of technology, you may be tempted to discard some of the personal touches that today's customers still appreciate. Although technology certainly answers many of your business's needs, it can never replace the following personal touches in the eyes of customers:

- **Handwriting notes:** A handwritten note is always the best way to say "thank you."

- **Thanking customers personally:** Having the owner of a company call and say "thank you" (as opposed to having an assistant or salesperson send out an email) makes a positive impression.

- **Handling mistakes honestly and quickly:** Don't waste one second trying to cover your tracks after mistakes are made. Come clean, fess up, and efficiently solve the problem. Approached correctly, mistakes can provide an opportunity to improve your business, impress your customers, and reward their loyalty.

If you or your employees treat your customers as if they're bothering you and you aren't attentive to after-sales service, you may discourage customers from making more purchases and referring others to your business. Poor after-sales service communicates to your customers that after you have their money, you don't really care what happens to them.

In addition to being attentive to all your customers' questions and concerns, be sure to solicit feedback (possibly through a formal survey) from your customers as to the quality of the customer service that your business offered them.

In some businesses, you must be careful not to give away valuable support that you can and should charge for. For example, if follow-up exams or appointments are expected, you should build the cost of those expected services into your upfront pricing or set a pricing schedule for the cost of the follow-up. Be sure that at the time customers buy from you, they know the cost of such follow-up work. Customers don't like negative surprises, especially when they affect their pocketbooks.

Dealing with Dissatisfied Customers

You can have the best products and services, offer competitive prices, and provide terrific customer service, and you'll still end up with the occasional unhappy customer. How you handle complaints — both justified and unjustified — is vital to the long-term reputation and health of your business. The following sections contain our time-tested advice for dealing with your unhappy and sometimes difficult customers.

Here's a tip to help you maintain your sanity: Keep in mind that you have your own way of doing things, that yours isn't a perfect product or service, and that you can't meet *all* your customers' needs and expectations *all* the time.

Listen, listen, listen

Most people like to believe that they're terrific listeners. The reality is that most of them aren't. And even if you *are* a good listener, you have moments when, for any number of reasons, you don't listen well. You get busy and stressed out with the competing demands on your time from work, family, friends, daily chores, and obligations. You also have days when you're tired, not feeling well, or have been on the receiving end of bad news or bad experiences.

Another impediment to good listening is that you may be convinced that an upset customer is simply being a troublemaker. As with all personal relationships, however, your preconceived notions about others can keep you from hearing legitimate and real concerns and reasons for being dissatisfied.

TIP

Before you (or one of your employees) lose your temper with a complaining customer, take a deep breath. Try to set aside all your opinions about the situation and your preconceived notions about the customer and their right to be unhappy. Stop and listen. Try to find out what the customer is unhappy about and why. Different people, not surprisingly, get upset about different things. You have no way to know and understand what's upsetting a particular customer until you take the time to ask and truly listen.

To ensure that you've really heard what your upset customer has said, paraphrase the concerns you've heard and tell the customer that you're sorry that they're unhappy. (Keep in mind that this isn't an admission of wrongdoing or guilt on your part, especially if you're worried about landing in court and being sued for product liability.) Then work on developing a solution with the customer (see the following section for how to do so).

WARNING

The absolute worst thing that you (or your employees) can do to a customer with a complaint is to interrupt and argue when they're trying to convey dissatisfaction with your products or services. And don't be defensive. We realize that this is easier said than done, but you'll do far more long-term damage to your business's reputation by further upsetting an already-unhappy customer. Even if you're 100 percent certain that the customer is the biggest buffoon you've ever dealt with and that you don't want them as a future customer, treat them with respect and try to solve their problem. Otherwise, you may end up with negative online reviews and word-of-mouth advertising, demand for a refund, and possibly a lawsuit.

Develop a solution

When a customer complains, remember that they're complaining because of dissatisfaction with the overall deal and experience that they received. The next step, after listening to the customer's complaints, is to develop a solution that addresses the complaints.

You have two ways to arrive at a solution:

>> **Ask the customer what solution they would propose and then see how it compares with what you can do.**

The advantage of asking the customer for a solution is the same as with any other form of negotiation (which, after all, is what's going on in this situation). If you let the dissatisfied customer make the opening offer, you know exactly where you stand and what you have to do to satisfy them.

Imagine the benefit you can derive when the customer's solution is less costly than what you were about to offer. In such a circumstance, the opportunity suddenly exists for you to take an unpleasant situation and turn it into an opportunity to strengthen the complaining customer's loyalty to your business.

>> **Propose a solution yourself and then wait for the customer to counter with a solution that they think is better.**

If you go this route, you don't propose a solution until the customer doesn't have, or refuses to come up with, one.

For example, suppose that you run a professional service business and you're responsible for missing a customer's appointment — either because of a scheduling mistake or because you're behind schedule and the customer simply couldn't wait any longer. You quickly determine that the customer is really angry about having been stood up after they have taken valuable time out of their workday.

Your solution to ease the customer's unhappiness can go something like this:

1. Apologize for the time they wasted.

2. Ask for their recommended solution.

3. If they don't have a solution, offer a discount (perhaps 15 or 20 percent off the appointment price when they reschedule).

4. When the customer returns for the rescheduled appointment, be absolutely certain that they're seen on time and provided with the best possible service.

TIP

The key to understanding your customers' complaints (and your employees' complaints, really) is your ability to put yourself in their shoes. After you've figured out how to view your business through the eyes of a customer, you'll find that you can solve problems the vast majority of the time.

Now suppose that your company sells products, and a customer comes in to say that a product you sold them broke and isn't worth the packaging it came in. In this case, you can offer a replacement product, fix the broken one, or offer the customer a refund. But if you're certain that the customer misused the product and that their mistake subsequently led to the breakage, you have a dilemma on your hands. You have to decide whether this person adheres to your definition of what a "good" customer should be.

REMEMBER

Even in those situations in which you determine that this person isn't what you consider to be a good customer, try to make the parting of your ways as harmonious and conflict-free as possible. It's okay if an unmanageable customer doesn't do business with you anymore. Just do everything you can to ensure that they don't go away angry and tell others that your business offers a lousy service or product.

Expanding Your Customer Base

When you acquire a business, in addition to serving and servicing well its existing customer base, you need to generate new business, which can include selling to new customers and/or selling more things to existing customers. Unless you don't care about a likely decline in revenue over time, you will inevitably lose some existing customers over time regardless of how terrific your small business and its products and services are. For example, some customers may reach a different life stage that lessens their desire for what you offer, whereas others may be lured away by an attractive competitive promotion.

INVESTIGATE

Conduct an audit or review of the marketing methods being used by the business you acquire and how effective they are. Also compare how your company's product and service offerings and pricing compare to the competition's.

Marketing is the one facet of your business that will separate your product or service from the hundreds (or however many) of competing products or services in the marketplace. Yet, marketing is typically one of the most difficult skills to master for small business owners.

Being a successful marketer requires numerous make-it-or-break-it skills that separate the mediocre (or failed) companies from the long-lived or fast-track ones. For proof of the importance of marketing as a business skill, look no further than those less-than-stellar products and services that are quite successful thanks to first-class marketing efforts (for example, Subway's sandwiches aren't among the best and neither are Taco Bell's tacos and burritos). On the other hand, rarely are first-rate products successful through inadequate marketing efforts.

Marketing defined

You aren't alone if you can't readily identify the difference between marketing, sales, and distribution. The definitions of these key terms (ones you'll hear over and over in the business world) are as follows:

>> **Marketing:** The manner in which product development, sales, promotion, distribution, and pricing are bundled together to create an overall plan designed to communicate and deliver your company's products or services to the marketplace and, hence, to the ultimate customer.

>> **Sales:** The way your company either directly or indirectly connects with, convinces, and contracts with customers to purchase your products or services. Take note: Sales represents only one component of the marketing process.

>> **Distribution:** The channels (such as retailers, wholesalers, e-commerce, and catalogs) that you use to deliver your product or service to your customers.

In large corporations, the senior executive in charge of marketing carries the burden of broadcasting and selling the product or service; the work they do is pivotal to the success or failure of the business. In a small business, however, the marketing function usually rests on the shoulders of the owner.

Mastering the key elements of marketing

The following are the key tasks in making your marketing top notch:

>> Refining and developing products or services

>> Evaluating pricing strategy

>> Reviewing your distribution system

>> Promoting your products or services and creating buzz with publicity

>> Understanding and harnessing the role of online marketing

>> Realizing the importance of sales and customer relationships

We encourage you to pick up a copy of the latest edition of our *Small Business For Dummies* (Wiley).

The Part
of Tens

IN THIS CHAPTER

» **Connecting with mentors and peers who can help and assembling a board of advisors**

» **Finding a partner and tapping into trade associations and business incubators**

» **Surveying other small-business resource options**

Chapter **14**

Ten (or So) Ways to Learn from the Experiences of Others

A lack of capital, a poor location, and inadequate marketing and distribution aren't causes of small-business failure; they're just symptoms — symptoms of the dreaded disease Owner's Isolation Syndrome. The symptoms of this syndrome affect every small-business owner at one time or another, but if you commit yourself to preventing the disease, you can avoid many of the symptoms.

Considering our status as charter members of the Never-Bring-Up-a-Problem-without-an-Accompanying-Solution Club, we use this chapter to present a collection of options that will help you minimize the trial-and-error method of small-business management and maximize learning from the experiences of others.

Utilize Mentors

Effective *mentors* are basically consultants — who usually work for free. What they have to offer is the ability to draw upon their extensive experience, always one of the best teachers of them all. You can go to a mentor to deal with strategic issues — you know, the long-term, fundamental, and always-critical issues, like strategy, vision, and financing. (Note that most mentors prefer to focus primarily on your business's strategic concerns, as opposed to your operational issues.)

To find an effective mentor, begin by compiling a list of prospective mentors. Ask your banker, your accountant, your lawyer, and folks around town who are wired into the small-business community (people at the Chamber of Commerce, Service Corps of Retired Executives, and Small Business Development Centers) for the names of veteran small-business owners who may be interested in helping you succeed. Then contact the person that your research and intuition indicate may be the best mentor for you.

TIP

The best mentor is typically someone who has current or previous experience within your chosen industry, although this isn't a prerequisite. (General business experience/knowledge, however, *is* a prerequisite.) Oftentimes, a good mentor is retired and, thus, may be motivated to help others to stay involved in business while also giving back.

Network with Peers

Imagine the power of putting a dozen or so current small-business owners in the same room. Imagine the wealth of solutions that may appear when one of the members presents a nagging problem or a thorny issue and asks for help. Do you have a problem with an employee who can't seem to get to work on time? Surely, another business owner has had the same problem before; don't be afraid to discover from your peers what has worked for them. (See Chapter 12 for our two cents on the employee issue.)

Peer networking works because, as we say throughout this book, a small business's problems are mostly generic — that is, they're usually not unique to your industry or niche. Thus, the solutions are often generic, too.

TIP

Some cities already have for-profit or nonprofit peer-networking programs up and running, and they're spreading the word of the value of the concept. You can ask at your local Chamber of Commerce, Small Business Development Center, or your city's or state's small-business magazine or newspaper to find out what and where these programs are in your area. Here are just a few of the peer-networking organizations that you may find helpful:

>> **Vistage International, Inc. (formerly The Executive Committee):** www.vistage.com

>> **American Business Women's Association:** www.abwa.org

>> **The Alternative Board (TAB):** www.thealternativeboard.com

>> **President's Resource Organization (PRO):** www.propres.com

>> **Opportunity Knocks (OK):** www.opp-knocks.org (founded in 1996 by coauthor Jim)

One or more of these organizations (or another with a similar agenda) may surface in your city. Keep your eyes peeled.

Form a Board of Advisors

Boards of advisors are like breath mints: Almost everybody can benefit from one, but too few people partake.

Like a mentor, a board of advisors provides you with an afford-able, outside perspective. Boards replace trial and error with experience and knowledge. They act as sounding boards, rebound boards, and boards of inquiry. They open needed doors and close unnecessary ones, while giving you an inside look at the outside business world.

Incidentally, we're not talking about a board of *directors* here; we're talking about a board of *advisors*. Directors are responsible for directing the company; advisors are responsible only for advising the president or chief executive officer (CEO) — that's you! (Note: Boards of directors generally require D&O insurance. Boards of advisors don't.)

Find a Partner

Here's a fact that not everyone knows: Partnerships outperform sole proprietorships by a wide margin. This statement is nothing more than simple math at work: One plus one equals at least two. Sometimes, one plus one equals significantly more than two if the partners can blend their skills and talents. (Google, Ben & Jerry's, Apple, Procter & Gamble, and Hewlett-Packard are examples of companies that began as small-business partnerships.)

Why might a partnership make sense for you? Here are just a few reasons:

>> **Complementary skills:** Although you're probably aware of your own strengths, you may overlook your weaknesses. Ask those who know you well — family, friends, and current or previous coworkers — what complementary skills you should seek in a business partner.

>> **Additional capital:** Two savings accounts are better than one.

>> **Greater problem solving capacity:** Two heads are (usually) better than one.

>> **More flexibility:** One partner goes on vacation or gets sick; the other one minds the business.

>> **Ease of formation:** Partnerships are easier and less expensive to form than corporations (but not as easy or inexpensive as sole proprietorships; see Chapter 5).

>> **Less risk:** Profits aren't the only thing partnerships share. They share problems and losses, too.

For sure, you may have plenty of reasons not to want to take a partner (or multiple partners) into your business. Everyone has heard juicy horror stories about business partnerships that turned sour and even ended up in court, destroying the business in the process (assuming anything was left to destroy). After all, warring partners seldom go down alone.

REMEMBER

The number one rule of a partnership is this: Don't enter into one without first consulting an experienced small-business lawyer. Have the attorney advise you and your prospective partner about the many obstacles that lie in the path of a successful partnership. Then ask the lawyer to assist you in drawing up an ironclad, airtight, cast-in-stone, buy-sell partnership agreement to overcome those obstacles. That Partnership Agreement, by the way, will be tested many times throughout the life of your business. (For more on partnerships and Partnership Agreements, see the latest edition of our *Small Business For Dummies* [Wiley].)

Join a Trade Association

Thousands of trade associations exist in the United States, and we wholeheartedly recommend that you join one. No matter who you are or what industry you're in, a trade association is probably available for you. The best trade associations offer a wide range of potential benefits — everything from business contacts to skill-building workshops to industry-specific information to group insurance programs. In addition, most trade associations host industry-wide trade shows at least once a year, during which you can mingle with suppliers and peers.

The two kinds of trade associations are industry-specific trade associations and small-business-specific trade associations. The following list breaks down these options:

>> **Industry-specific trade associations:** Consult your local library to find the trade association or organization that caters to your industry. Flip through the *National Trade and Professional Associations of the United States* (Columbia Books), which lists more than 7,500 associations in the United States today. Your local library should have a copy of this $149 publication. Or you can search the web by opening a search engine and keying in the name of the specific industry you're in, followed by the word *association* — as in *sporting-goods association* or *restaurant association.*

>> **Small-business-specific trade associations:** These trade associations include the following:

- **National Small Business Association (NSBA):** This association watches congressional actions and reports on issues affecting small businesses. Visit the NSBA website at www.nsba.biz or call 800-345-6728 for details.

- **National Association for the Self-Employed (NASE):** NASE offers resource materials and a monthly magazine. Visit its website at www.nase.org or call 800-649-6273 for details.

- **National Association of Women Business Owners (NAWBO):** This association brings together women entrepreneurs for support and assistance. Surf its website at www.nawbo.org or call 800-55-NAWBO for more information.

- **National Federation of Independent Business (NFIB):** The NFIB is the largest lobbying organization for small businesses in the country. Visit its website at www.nfib.com or call 800-634-2669 for details.

WARNING

Trade associations aren't without their warts. First, don't assume that products and services marketed to the association's members are necessarily the best of what's out there. Many associations, for example, offer insurance programs to their members — programs that the members can purchase at (assumedly) a lower cost elsewhere. *Remember:* The programs a trade association offers are only as good as the people who determine what that association will and won't offer its members.

Locate a Small Business Development Center

Small Business Development Centers (SBDCs) are cooperative programs designed to provide current (and potential) business owners with advice and information on running their businesses. SBDCs are sponsored by a partnership between the Small Business Administration (SBA), a local college or university, and often your state's Economic Development Department. Every state has a central SBDC, and the United States has nearly 1,000 of such service centers, most of which are located on college or community college campuses.

WARNING

As with any type of consultant, the quality of SBDC counseling varies widely from one SBDC office to another. Tread carefully and don't bet the farm on their advice.

To locate the SBDC nearest you, visit www.sba.gov/sbdc or call 800-8-ASK-SBA.

Give SCORE a Try

The *Service Corps of Retired Executives* (SCORE) is affiliated with the SBA and offers one-on-one counseling through its 10,000-plus experienced counselors across the country. SCORE is a wonderful concept, but its offerings sometimes fall short of its potential. The quality of SCORE's advice varies widely and depends on the individual counselor. Similar to the SBDCs, proceed cautiously when accepting advice from SCORE volunteers. Once a SCORE counselor has proven their worth, however, the relationship can be hugely beneficial to the small-business owner.

TIP

SCORE volunteers (usually *Fortune* 500 graduates) will probably be most helpful to you if you're trying to determine whether to leave your day job and make the risky leap to business ownership.

SCORE offices are easy to locate. Log on to www.score.org to find the chapter nearest you.

Tap into Small-Business Information

Talk about information overload! Well, to be honest, a lot of what is out there in the small business realm is advertising dressed up as something else. So, please be careful and skeptical.

Magazines and books (and associated videos, podcasts, and CDs) that focus on helping the small-business owner are everywhere. Where small business is concerned, you name it and a book has been written about it — including this one! We love books, and the best ones offer a crash course on various small business topics and issues.

Read your industry trade publications (which you can often find through your industry's trade associations, a resource we discuss earlier in this chapter). Also, we suggest that you check out the *Small Business Sourcebook* (Gale), a huge reference that you can find in most public libraries.

The number of websites and small-business blogs available online have grown to a near-infinite number. We suggest that you put the online medium to work to keep up to speed on new trends and offerings under the small-business category. (Check out Chapter 3 for helpful government resources, such as the Small Business Administration.)

Chapter **15**

Ten Ongoing Tax Jobs

Running your own business means hard work and long hours.

One of the ways that you keep score is to track your business revenue and expenses; the difference between the two is the profit or loss for your company. We strongly recommend that you utilize a system for accounting for your business inflows and outflows. This helps you stay on top of what's going on in your business and to ease the pains of completing the never-ending stream of tax forms required by state and federal government tax authorities quarterly and annually.

In this chapter, we describe the basics of developing a business accounting process for your small business. We also discuss how to fulfill the myriad filing requirements of the tax authorities by keeping proper records.

Keeping Track of Your Small Business Revenues and Costs

If you're thinking about starting a business or you're already in the thick of one, make sure you keep a proper accounting of your income and expenses. If you don't, you'll have a lot more stress and headaches when it comes time to complete and submit the necessary tax forms for your business.

Besides helping you over the annual tax-filing hurdle and fulfilling quarterly requirements, accurate records allow you to track your company's financial health and performance during the year. How are your profits running compared with last year? Can you afford to hire new employees? Analyzing your monthly or quarterly business financial statements (profit and loss statement, balance sheet, and so on) can help you answer these and other important questions.

WARNING

Here's another reason to keep good records: The IRS may audit you, and if that happens, you'll be asked to substantiate particular items on your return. Small business owners who file IRS Form 1040 Schedule C, "Profit or Loss From Business," with their tax returns are audited at a much higher rate than other. Although that dubious honor may seem like an unfair burden to business owners, the IRS targets small businesses because more than a few small business owners break the tax rules, and many areas exist where small business owners can mess up.

REMEMBER

If your small business is audited, well-prepared and organized financial records will help. Being organized in and of itself helps establish you in the auditor's eyes as a responsible business person.

Separating Business from Personal Finances

One of the IRS's biggest concerns is that, as a small business owner, you'll try to minimize your company's profits (and therefore taxes) by hiding business income and inflating business expenses. Uncle Sam thus looks suspiciously at business owners who use personal checking and personal credit card accounts for company transactions. You may be tempted to use your personal accounts this way because opening separate accounts is a hassle — not because you're dishonest.

TIP

Take the time to open separate accounts (such as bank accounts and credit card accounts) for your business and your personal use. Doing so not only makes the tax authorities happy but also makes your accounting easier. And don't make the mistake of thinking that paying for an expense through your business account proves to the IRS that it was a legitimate business expense. If the IRS finds that the expense was truly for personal purposes, it will likely dig deeper into your company's financial records to see what other shenanigans are going on.

Documenting Expenses and Income in the Event of an Audit

It doesn't matter whether you use file folders, software, apps, or a good old-fashioned shoe box to collate receipts and other important financial information. What does matter is that you keep complete and accurate records of both expenses and income, and here are some tips for doing so:

>> **Expenses:** You'll probably lose or misplace some of those little pieces of paper that you need to document your expenses. Thus, one advantage of charging expenses on a credit card or paying by check is that these transactions leave a trail, which makes it easier to total your expenses come tax time and prove your expenses if you're audited.

WARNING

Just be careful when you use a credit card because you may buy more things than you can really afford. Then you're stuck with a lot of debt to pay off. I generally recommend only charging on a credit card what you can pay off in full by the time your statement payment due date rolls around.

On the other hand (as many small business owners know), finding lenders when you need money is difficult. Borrowing on a low-interest-rate credit card can be an easy and quick way for you to borrow money without groveling to bankers for a loan. (See the latest edition of my book *Personal Finance For Dummies,* published by John Wiley & Sons, Inc., for details.)

>> **Income:** Likewise, leave a trail with your revenue. Depositing all your receipts in one account helps you when tax time comes or if you're ever audited. Be sure to use a dedicated account for your business; don't be tempted to deposit business income into a personal account. (See the next section for details.)

Keeping Current on Income, Employment/Payroll and Sales Taxes

When you're self-employed, you're responsible for the accurate and timely filing of all your income taxes. Without an employer and a payroll department to handle the paperwork for withholding taxes on a regular schedule, you need to make estimated tax payments on a quarterly basis.

If you have employees, you need to withhold taxes from each paycheck they receive, and you must make timely payments to the IRS and the appropriate state and local authorities. In addition to federal and state income taxes, you must withhold and send in Social Security and any other state or locally mandated employment (payroll) taxes and sales taxes, and you need to issue W-2s annually for each employee and 1099-MISCs for each independent contractor paid $600 or more. Got a headache yet?

For paying taxes on your own self-employment income, you can obtain Form 1040-ES, "Estimated Tax for Individuals." This form comes complete with an estimated tax worksheet and four payment coupons to send in with your quarterly tax payments. It's amazing how user-friendly government people can be when they want your money!

To discover all the amazing rules and regulations of withholding and submitting taxes from employees' paychecks, ask the IRS for Form 941, "Employer's Quarterly Federal Tax Return." Once a year, you also need to complete Form 940, "Employer's Annual Federal Unemployment (FUTA) Tax Return," for unemployment insurance payments to the feds.

TIP

If your business has a part-time or seasonal employee and the additional burden of filing Form 941 quarterly, the IRS has made the paperwork a tad easier. You may be able to file Form 944, "Employer's Annual Federal Tax Return," if your tax withholding on behalf of employees doesn't exceed $1,000 for the year (which translates to about $4,000 in wages). If you qualify, you need to file only once each year. To see whether you qualify, call the IRS at 800-829-0115 or visit its website at www.irs.gov. If you do qualify, the IRS will send you something in writing.

Also check to see whether your state has its own annual or quarterly unemployment insurance reporting requirements. Look for your state's department of labor or use the links on the U.S. Department of Labor website at www.dol.gov/whd/contacts/state_of.htm. And unless you're lucky enough to live in one of those rare states with no state income taxes, don't forget to get your state's estimated income tax package.

TIP

Falling behind in paying taxes ruins some small businesses. When you hire employees, for example, you're particularly vulnerable to tax land mines. If you aren't going to keep current on taxes for yourself and your employees, hire a payroll company or tax advisor who can help you jump through the necessary tax hoops. (For info on finding a good tax advisor, see Chapter 9.) Payroll companies and tax advisors are there for a reason, so use them selectively. They take care of all the tax filings for you, and if they mess up, they pay the penalties. Check with a tax advisor you trust for the names of reputable payroll companies in your area. Generally, using a payroll service for form preparation and tax deposits is money well spent. The cost is much less than the potential penalties (and time) if you prepare yourself.

Reducing Your Taxes by Legally Shifting Income and Expenses

Many small business owners elect to keep their business accounting on what's called a *cash basis*. This choice doesn't imply that all business customers literally pay in cash for goods and services or that the company owners pay for all expenses with cash. Cash-basis accounting simply means that, for tax purposes, you recognize and report income in the year you received it and expenses in the year you paid them.

By operating on a cash basis, you can exert more control over the amount of profit (revenue minus expenses) that your business reports for tax purposes from year to year. If your income fluctuates from year to year, you can lower your tax burden by doing some legal shifting of income and expenses.

Suppose that you recently started a business. Assume that you have little, but growing, revenue and somewhat high startup expenses. Looking ahead to the next tax year, you can already tell that you'll be making more money and will likely be in a much higher tax bracket. Thus you can likely reduce your tax bill by paying more of your expenses in the next year. Of course, you don't want to upset any of your company's suppliers. However, you can pay some of your bills after the start of the next tax year (January 1) rather than in late December of the preceding year (presuming that your business's tax year is on a regular January 1 through December 31 calendar-year basis). *Note:* Credit card expenses are recognized as of the date you charge them, not when you pay the bill.

Likewise, you can exert some control over when your customers pay you. If you expect to make less money next year, don't invoice customers in December of this year. Wait until January so that you receive more of your income next year.

WARNING

Be careful with this revenue-shifting game. You don't want to run short of cash and miss a payroll! Similarly, if a customer mails you a check in December, IRS laws don't allow you to hold the check until January and count the revenue then. For tax purposes, you're supposed to recognize the payment as revenue when you receive it.

Note: One final point about who can and who can't do this revenue and expense two-step. Sole proprietorships, partnerships (including limited liability companies, also known as LLCs), S corporations, and personal-service corporations generally can shift revenue and expenses. On the other hand, C corporations and partnerships that have C corporations as partners may not use the cash-accounting method if they have annual receipts of more than $5 million per year. Chapter 2 has details on all these business entities.

Ensuring a Complete and Accurate Tax Return

In case you don't feel like flipping through countless pages of government instructions on what constitutes a "complete and accurate" return, here are some common tax situations at a glance and the types of records normally required:

>> **Business expenses:** As I mention in the earlier section "Separating Business from Personal Finances," the IRS is especially watchful in this area, so be sure to keep detailed proof of any expenses that you claim. This proof can consist of many items, such as receipts of income, expense account documentation and statements, and so on. Keep in mind that the IRS doesn't always accept canceled checks as the only method of substantiation, so make sure that you hang on to the bill or receipt for every expense you incur.

>> **Car expenses:** If, for the business use of your car, you choose to deduct the actual expenses rather than the standard mileage rate (which is 67 cents per mile for tax year 2024), you need to show the cost of the car and when you started using it for business. You also must record your business miles, your total miles, and your expenses, such as insurance, gas, and maintenance. You need a combination of a log and written receipts, of course! Stationery and office supply stores carry inexpensive logbooks that you can buy for your vehicle usage and expense tracking. You can also obtain smartphone apps to serve the same purpose.

>> **Home office expenses:** If you run a business from you house, you need your utility bills, general repair bills, and housecleaning and lawn-mowing costs to calculate your home office expense.

Tracking Tax Information on Your Computer or Smartphone

A number of financial software packages and smartphone apps enable you to keep track of your spending for tax purposes. Just don't expect to reap the benefits without a fair amount of upfront and continuing work. You need to figure out how to use the software, and you must enter a great deal of data for the software to be useful to you. Don't forget, though, that you still need your receipts to back up your claims; in an audit, the IRS may not accept your computer records without verifying them against your receipts.

If you're interested in software, consider a business-oriented program, such as QuickBooks, for your small-business accounting. Check out their smartphone apps as well. For really simple businesses, consider Quicken. You can merge data into QuickBooks at a later date if you desire. Whichever software you choose, keep in mind that the package tabulates only what you enter or download into it. So if you use the software to write your monthly checks but neglect to enter data for things you pay for with cash, for example, you won't have the whole picture.

Deciding When to Stash and When to Trash

REMEMBER

One of the most frequently asked questions is how long a tax-payer needs to keep tax records. The answer is easy — a minimum of three years. That's because the statute of limitations for tax audits and assessments is three years. If the IRS doesn't adjust or audit your 2024 tax return by April 15, 2028 (the three years start running on April 15, 2025), it missed its chance.

On April 15, 2028, feel free to celebrate another audit-less year with a "Shredding the 2024 Tax Return" party. (If you filed after April 15 because you obtained an extension, you must wait until three years after the extension due date rather than the April 15 tax date. The same is true when you file late — the three-year period doesn't start until you actually file your return.)

TIP

Save all records for the assets your business owns. Keep these records in a safe deposit box in case you suffer a (deductible casualty) loss, such as a fire. Some business owners take the practical step of videotaping their place of business and its contents, but if you do, be sure to keep that record in a secure offsite location.

WARNING

In situations where the IRS suspects that income wasn't reported, IRS agents can go back as far as six years. And if possible, tax fraud is involved, forget all time limitations!

WARNING

Watch out for state differences. Although the IRS requires that you keep your records for only three years, your state may have a longer statute of limitations with regard to state income tax audits. If you're curious what your state's rules are, check with your state's income tax collecting authority. Hang on to records that may be important for longer than three years — especially if a dispute is possible. Check with a legal advisor whenever you have a concern because statutes of limitations vary from state to state.

Replacing Lost Business Records

If your business records have been lost or destroyed, you can often obtain duplicate bills from major vendors. You shouldn't have a great deal of trouble getting copies of the original telephone, utility, rent, credit card, oil company, and other bills. Reconstructing a typical month of automobile use can help you make a reasonable determination of the business use of your car.

If that month's use approximates an average month's business use of an auto, the IRS usually accepts such reconstructed records as adequate substantiation.

If you deposited all your business income in a checking or savings account, you can reconstruct that income from duplicate bank statements. Although banks usually don't charge for copies of bank statements, they do charge for copies of canceled checks if you can't obtain them online. These charges can be quite expensive, so do some legwork before ordering copies of all your checks. For example, obtain a copy of your lease and a statement from your landlord saying that all rent was paid on time before you request duplicate copies of rent checks.

By ordering copies of past returns with Form 4506, "Request for Copy of Transcript of Tax Form," you can have a point of reference for determining whether you accounted for typical business expenses. Past returns reveal not only gross profit percentages or margins of profit but also the amounts of recurring expenses. (You can find this form at www.irs.gov/pub/irs-pdf/f4506.pdf.)

Index

I

J

L

About the Authors

Eric Tyson, MBA, has been a personal financial writer, lecturer, and counselor for the past 25+ years. As his own boss, Eric has worked with and taught people from a myriad of income levels and backgrounds, so he knows the small-business ownership concerns and questions of real folks just like you.

After toiling away for too many years as a management consultant to behemoth financial-service firms, Eric decided to take his knowledge of the industry and commit himself to making personal financial management accessible to everyone. Despite being handicapped by a joint BS in Economics and Biology from Yale and an MBA from Stanford, Eric remains a master at "keeping it simple."

An accomplished freelance personal-finance writer, Eric is the author or coauthor of numerous other For Dummies national bestsellers on personal finance, investing, for seniors, and home buying, and is a syndicated columnist. His *Personal Finance For Dummies* won the Benjamin Franklin Award for Best Business Book.

Eric's work has been critically acclaimed in hundreds of publications and programs, including *Newsweek*, *The Los Angeles Times*, *The Chicago Tribune*, *Kiplinger's Personal Finance Magazine*, *The Wall Street Journal*, *Bottom Line Personal*, as well as NBC's *Today* show, ABC, CNBC, PBS's *Nightly Business Report*, CNN, FOX-TV, CBS national radio, Bloomberg Business Radio, and Business Radio Network. His website is www.erictyson.com.

Jim Schell has not always been a grizzled veteran of the small-business wars, contrary to what some people may think. Raised in Des Moines, Iowa, and earning a BA in Economics at the University of Colorado, Jim served in the U.S. Air Force in Klamath Falls, Oregon. Jim's entrepreneurial genes eventually surfaced when he and three Minneapolis friends started The Kings Court, at the time the nation's first racquetball club. Two years later, Jim bought General Sports, Inc., a struggling sporting-goods retailer and wholesaler. After another two years, he started National Screenprint, and, finally, he partnered with an ex-employee in Fitness and Weight Training Corp. Each of the start-ups was bootstrapped, and each was privately held. For a period of exhausting years, Jim involved himself in the management of all four businesses at the same time. His third business, National Screenprint, ultimately grew to $25 million in sales and 200 employees.

Relocating to San Diego, Jim began a long-simmering writing career, authoring four books (*The Brass Tacks Entrepreneur, Small Business Management Guide, The Small Business Answer Book*, and *Understanding Your Financial Statements*) and numerous columns for business and trade magazines.

Publisher's Acknowledgments

Executive Editor: Steve Hayes

Compilation Editor:
Colleen Diamond

Project Editor: Colleen Diamond

Copy Editor: Jennifer Connolly

Senior Managing Editor:
Kristie Pyles

Production Editor: Pradesh Kumar

Cover Image: © Jonathan Storey/
Getty Images